nicht alles tun

cannot do everything

Impressum / Colophon

Herausgegeben von/edited by Jens Kastner & Elisabeth Bettina Spörr
nicht alles tun. Ziviler und sozialer Ungehorsam an den Schnittstellen von Kunst, radikaler Politik und Technologie / cannot do everything. Civil and social disobedience at the interfaces between art, radical politics, and technology

Diese Publikation erscheint im Rahmen der Ausstellungen „nicht alles tun. Ziviler und Sozialer Ungehorsam an den Schnittstellen von Kunst, radikaler Politik und Technologie" in der Galerie IG Bildende Kunst, Wien (12. Juni bis 18. Juli 2008) und „nicht alles tun. Ziviler und Sozialer Ungehorsam in Kunst und Aktivismus" im Kunstraum :emyt in Berlin (14. Juni bis 26. Juli 2008).

The present book ispublished in connection with the exhibitions „cannot do everything. Civil and Social Disobedience at the Interfaces between Art, Radical Politics, and Technology" at Galerie IG Bildende Kunst, Vienna (June 12 through July 18, 2008) and „cannot do everything. Civil and Social Disobedience in Art and Activism" at Kunstraum :emyt in Berlin (June 14 through July 26, 2008).

Bibliografische Information der Deutschen Bibliothek: Die Deutsche Bibliothek verzeichnet diese Publikation in der Deutschen Nationalbiografie; detaillierte biografische Daten sind im Internet über http://dnb.dbb.de abrufbar. / Bibliographic Information published by Die Deutsche Bibliothek. Die Deutsche Bibliothek lists this publication in the Deutschen Nationalbiografie; detailed bibliographic data are available in the internet at http://dnb.dbb.de.

bm:uk Dieses Buch wurde gefördert durch das österreichische Bundesministerium für Unterricht, Kunst und Kultur / This book was supported by the Federal Ministry for Education, the Arts and Culture.

© UNRAST-Verlag, Münster
Postfach 8020 48043 Münster
Tel. 0251.666293 info@unrast.de
Mitglied in der Assoziation Linker Verlage aLIVe

1. Auflage Juli 2008
ISBN-13: 978-3-89771-481-6

Umschlaggestaltung / cover design, Layout: Susi Klocker / LIga
Druck: Interpress Budapest

Danksagung / Acknowledgments
Wir danken sehr herzlich allen AutorInnen dieser Publikation, den KünstlerInnen der Ausstellungen in Wien und Berlin, Susi Klocker für das Konzept und die grafische Gestaltung der Publikation, Dietmar Ebenhofer für seine unermüdliche Unterstützung bei der Realisation der audiovisuellen Arbeiten, Thomas Ehringer für die Hilfe bei der Gestaltung der Ausstellung in Wien, anschläge. Das feministische Magazin (Mujeres Creando), el projecto in New York (Coco Fusco) sowie der Generali Foundation, Wien für das Bildmaterial zu Allan Sekula. Außerdem danken wir dem Team der IG Bildende Kunst, insbesondere Dagmar Höss und Regina Wuzella, sowie Lilian Engelmann vom Kunstraum :emyt für ihre Unterstützung.

We would like to cordially thank all the contributors to the present book, the artists in the exhibitions in Vienna and Berlin, Susi Klocker for the concept and the graphic design of the book, Dietmar Ebenhofer for his support in realizing the audiovisual works, Thomas Ehringer for his advice regarding the exhibion design in Vienna, anschläge. Das feministische Magazin (Mujeres Creando), el projecto in New York (Coco Fusco), and the Generali Foundation, Vienna for providing the Allan Sekula images. We would also like to thank the team of IG Bildende Kunst, especially Dagmar Höss and Regina Wuzella as well as Lilian Engelmann of Kunstraum :emyt for their support.

Bildnachweis / Photo credits
© Fotos, Grafiken wenn nicht anders angegeben / Photos, graphics unless noted otherwise: KünstlerInnen / Artists
Dietmar Ebenhofer, Videostills: 168-171, 180-183, 186-187, 190-191
Generali Foundation: 184-185

Textnachweis / Text credits
© Texte / Texts: AutorInnen / The authors
Übersetzung Kurztexte KünstlerInnen / Translation short texts artists: Gerrit Jackson

17 **cannot do everything**
Civil/social disobedience and art
Jens Kastner and Elisabeth Bettina Spörr

35 **On Poetry and Revolution**
John Holloway

61 **One Century of Revolutionary Civil Disobedience**
A brief sketch of activist civil disobedience
from a nonviolent-anarchist perspective
Lou Marin

87 **Civil and social Disobedience =
Refusal plus Utopia?**
Ulrike Laubenthal

107 **From Civil to Social Disobedience and Back Again**
On the Conceptual Politics of Alter-Globalization Protest
Andrea Pabst

131 **The Serpent's Coils**
Minoritarian Tactics in the Age of Transparency
Inke Arns

151 **Offensive Flight instead of Breaking the Law**
On Civil Disobedience in View of the Thoreauvian Imperative
Jens Kastner and Gerald Raunig

9 **nicht alles tun**
Ziviler/sozialer Ungehorsam und Kunst
Jens Kastner und Elisabeth Bettina Spörr

25 **Über Poesie und Revolution**
John Holloway

43 **Ein Jahrhundert des Revolutionären Zivilen Ungehorsams**
Kurzer Abriss des aktivistischen Zivilen Ungehorsams
aus gewaltfrei-anarchistischer Sicht
Lou Marin

77 **Ziviler und Sozialer Ungehorsam gleich Verweigerung plus Utopie?**
Ulrike Laubenthal

97 **Vom zivilen zum sozialen Ungehorsam und zurück**
Zur Begriffspolitik globalisierungskritischer Proteste
Andrea Pabst

117 **Die Windungen der Schlange**
Minoritäre Taktiken im Zeitalter der Transparenz
Inke Arns

143 **Offensive Flucht statt Gesetzesbruch**
Zum Ungehorsam angesichts des Thoreau'schen Imperativs
Jens Kastner und Gerald Raunig

KünstlerInnen/Artists

- 160 Zanny Begg
- 162 Heath Bunting
- 164 Bureau of Inverse Technology
- 166 Büro Bildwechsel
  (Sandy Kaltenborn/Pierre Maite)
- 168 Critical Art Ensemble
- 170 Coco Fusco
- 172 Andrea Geyer/Sharon Hayes
- 174 h.arta
- 176 Christopher LaMarca
- 178 fran meana
- 180 Mujeres Creando
- 182 Oliver Ressler/Dario Azzellini
- 184 Allan Sekula
- 186 Surveillance Camera Players NYC
- 188 Nasan Tur
- 190 Videogruppe Bürgerinitiative
  Umweltschutz Lüchow Dannenberg
- 192 Christoph Wachter/Mathias Jud

nicht alles tun

Ziviler/sozialer Ungehorsam und Kunst

Jens Kastner und Elisabeth Bettina Spörr

Die kurze Schrift „Über die Pflicht zum Ungehorsam gegen den Staat" (1849) von Henry David Thoreau (1817-1862) gehört zu den einflussreichsten Texten in den sozialen Bewegungen des 20. Jahrhunderts. Thoreau entwickelte den Gedanken des Ungehorsams als eine individuelle Reaktion auf strukturelles Unrecht.[1] Sein Ausgangspunkt war dabei ganz konkret: Die seinerzeit in den USA legale Sklaverei einerseits und die US-Intervention in Mexiko (1846-1848) andererseits veranlassten ihn, die Zahlung der Steuern zu verweigern, um diese Politik nicht weiter mit zu tragen. Verschiedene Bewegungen entwickelten aus der von Thoreau als individuelle Gewissensfrage formulierten moralischen Pflicht zum Ungehorsam bei einmal erkanntem Unrecht politische Konzepte. Diese waren auf verschiedene Arten kollektiven Handelns zugeschnitten und dem jeweiligen Kontext angepasst. Die zentrale Formulierung in Thoreaus Text ist die Aufforderung zum Gesetzesbruch, der in der Folge zum Kern zivilen Ungehorsams wurde: „...wenn aber das Gesetz so beschaffen ist, dass es notwendigerweise aus dir den Arm des Unrechts an einem anderen macht, dann, sage ich, brich das Gesetz." (Thoreau 1973: 18)

Dieser Imperativ enthält bereits sowohl die passive Dimension der Verweigerung gegenüber ungerechten Gesetzen als auch die aktive Ebene des tätigen Bruchs mit ihnen. Beide Stränge wurden innerhalb der sozialen Bewegungen des 20. Jahrhunderts in unterschiedlicher Intensität verfolgt. Leo Tolstoi, der die

Schrift Thoreaus kannte und seine Übersetzung ins Russische unterstütze, knüpfte mit seinem Konzept des „passiven Widerstands" eher an die Verweigerungsdimension an, die auch in der Bewegung M. K. Gandhis für die Unabhängigkeit Indiens von Großbritannien eine große Rolle spielte. Aktive, eingreifende Praktiken entwickelten sich systematisch und massenhaft dann vor allem innerhalb der schwarzen Bürgerrechtsbewegung in den USA der 1950er und 1960er Jahre (vgl. Carson 2004). Mehr als dreißig Jahre später sollten sich die ProtagonistInnen des in den 1990er Jahren in Theorie und Praxis entwickelten elektronischen zivilen Ungehorsam explizit auf die schwarze Bürgerrechtsbewegung berufen.²

Thoreaus Betonung des Gesetzesbruchs geht vom einzelnen Individuum aus, das sich im Konflikt mit der Regierung des Staates sieht. Die politische Ausdehnung des Konzepts hat nicht nur dazu geführt, dass Gruppen oder größere Bevölkerungsteile gegen bestimmte Regierungsentscheidungen oder gegen Regierungen als solche vorgingen. Auch kollektives Handeln in Übereinstimmung mit der Regierung ist innerhalb des zivilen Ungehorsams vorstellbar: So kam es 1923 während der französisch-belgischen Besetzung des Ruhrgebietes zu massenhaften zivilem Ungehorsam gegen die Besatzer, nachdem der deutsche Kanzler Wilhelm Cuno die Bevölkerung zum „passiven Widerstand" aufgerufen hatte. (Vgl. Müller 1995) Gegen eine feindliche Besatzungsmacht kamen Praktiken zivilen Ungehorsams auch im Zweiten Weltkrieg zum Einsatz. Im Zuge der Résistance gegen die nationalsozialistischen deutschen Truppen in Frankreich wurden diverse koordinierte Aktionen organisiert.

Im Anschluss an die US-amerikanische Bürgerrechtsbewegung kam es im Kontext der „68er Jahre" an vielen Orten der Welt zu massenhaften und vielfältigen Praktiken zivilen Ungehorsams. Werden mit „1968" im Allgemeinen eher die Barrikadenkämpfe des Pariser Mai assoziiert und die militanten Proteste nicht selten als direkte Vorstufen der bewaffneten Stadtguerillas der 1970er Jahre konzipiert, muss demgegenüber die große Bandbreite zivilen Ungehorsams hervorgehoben werden.³ Ohne auf den – möglicherweise vermeintlichen – Gegensatz gewaltfreier und militanter Politikformen an dieser Stelle näher einzugehen, muss doch angemerkt werden, dass Methoden kollektiv angewandten Ungehorsams von Sit-Ins über Blockaden bis zur gemeinsamen Kriegsdienstverweigerung nicht nur wesentlich weiter verbreitet waren als spätere Guerilla-Aktionen, sondern häufig auch größere politische Wirksamkeit entfalteten; und das selbst, obwohl brennende Autoreifen, eingeschlagene Fensterscheiben oder schwarze AktivistInnen, die mit geschulterten Gewehren durch Vororte patrouillieren, hinsichtlich der Aufmerksamkeit der Medien immer im Vorteil gegenüber gemeinsam Rumsitzenden sind.

In den Neuen Sozialen Bewegungen spielte der zivile Ungehorsam ebenfalls eine große Rolle: von den Blockaden gegen die Stationierung von Pershing-Raketen in der bundesdeutschen Friedensbewegung der frühen 1980er Jahre und den sich angesichts der AIDS-Krise formierenden Aktionsgruppen ACT UP in den USA,⁴ über „Ernteaktionen" auf gentechnischen Versuchsfeldern in der Anti-Gen-Technik-Bewegung, bis hin zu in die Gegenwart reichenden, verschiedensten Aktionen in der Anti-AKW-Bewegung.

Die Debatte allerdings scheint, zumindest im deutschsprachigen Raum, mit dem Abflauen der sozialen Bewegungen der 1980er Jahre abzureißen. Nicht, dass es seit den 1990er Jahren keine Aktionen zivilen Ungehorsams mehr gegeben hätte, aber die wesentlichen deutschsprachigen Publikationen stammen doch aus den 1980er Jahren (vgl. Ebert 1984, Jochheim 1984, graswurzelrevolution 1985, Redaktionsgruppe 1986), der aktuellste Sammelband, der sich dezidiert dem Thema widmet, wurde kurz nach dem Fall der Berliner Mauer konzipiert (Komitee für Grundrechte und Demokratie 1992).

Dabei ist es mit dem Aufkommen der globalisierungskritischen Bewegungen im Anschluss an den zapatistischen Aufstand in Chiapas/Mexiko (1994ff.) zu einer erneuten Ausweitung zivilen Ungehorsams gekommen:

Zum einen wurde im Kontext des zapatistisch inspirierten Ya-Basta!-Netzwerkes der zivile zum sozialen Ungehorsam ausgeweitet. Die 2001 aus den italienischen Tute Bianche entstandenen Disobbedienti (Die Ungehorsamen) formulierten dieses Konzept, blieben allerdings hinsichtlich konkreter Praktiken relativ unbestimmt (vgl. Azzellini 2002). Die 2005 als landesweiter Zusammenhang aufgelösten Disobbedienti bezogen sich allerdings weniger auf eine pazifistische Tradition im Sinne Gandhis oder Martin Luther Kings. Hier stammten Ideen und Praktiken des Ungehorsams aus der Geschichte der autonomen ArbeiterInnenbewegung, dem Operaismus. Die so genannte Arbeiterautonomie zählte Arbeitsverweigerung und Sabotage in den 1960er und 1970er Jahren zu ihren bevorzugten, massenhaft diskutierten – und angewandten – Praktiken. (Vgl. Birkner/Foltin 2006)

Zum anderen wurden die Orte zivilen Ungehorsams ausgeweitet auf den virtuellen Raum. Erste Tendenzen, sowohl aktivistische als auch künstlerische Praktiken auf den elektronischen Raum auszudehnen, zeichneten sich bereits Mitte der 1990er Jahre ab.

Die Computer-Revolution in den frühen 1980er Jahren sowie die darauf folgende Entwicklung des Internet und dessen rasche Verbreitung in den 1990er Jahren haben im künstlerischen und politisch-aktivistischen Feld einerseits zu Euphorie und der Proklamation eines „elektronischen Utopia" geführt und andererseits große Skepsis ausgelöst. Die Verfügbarkeit von Informationen sowie deren schnelle und weltweite Verbreitung begründete die Hoffnung auf „kulturelle Grenzen überschreitende künstlerische und kritische Kollaborationen" (Critical Art Ensemble 2007: 27). Gleichzeitig gab sich niemand der Illusion hin, dass mit dem Internet ein genuin demokratisches, anti-rassistisches, anti-sexistisches und herrschaftsfreies Medium entstanden war. Zu oft waren in der Vergangenheit bereits derartige, in neue Medien gesetzte Hoffnungen enttäuscht bzw. zunichte gemacht worden. Solche Hoffnungen kamen beispielsweise in der Radiotheorie Bert Brechts zum Ausdruck, der in den 1920er und 1930er Jahren die Demokratisierung des Mediums und dessen Transformierung von einem Distributions- in einen Kommunikationsapparat propagierte. Auch das Aufkommen der Video-Technologie in den 1970er Jahren, von der sich KünstlerInnen durch den einfachen und billigen Zugang zu Produktionsmitteln ebenfalls eine Demokratisierung der Kunst versprochen hatten, blieb in seinen Effekten hinter den Erwartungen zurück.[5]

Eine Reihe unterschiedlicher, subversiver Taktiken entstand in der Folge, zu der unter anderem Persiflage und Appropriation kommerzieller Nutzungsformen des Internet zählen, wie sie zum Beispiel vom Institute for Applied Autonomy, dem Bureau of Inverse Technology oder den Yes Men eingesetzt werden. Gleichzeitig wurde eine grundsätzlich neue Protestform entwickelt: der elektronische zivile Ungehorsam. Propagiert wurde diese Form des Widerstandes vor allem von einer Reihe von Kollektiven, die an der Schnittstelle von politischem Aktivismus und aktivistischer Kunst angesiedelt sind. Neben dem Critical Art Ensemble zählen die italienische Anonymous Digital Coalition und das aus dem Critical Art Ensemble hervorgegangene Electronic Disturbance Theater zu den PionierInnen des elektronischen zivilen Ungehorsams, die neben wesentlichen Beiträgen zur Theoriebildung auch grundlegend zur Entwicklung von funktionierenden Aktionsformen im Netz beigetragen haben.

Elektronischer ziviler Ungehorsam versteht sich in der Tradition des zivilen Ungehorsams als gewaltlose partizipatorische Massenaktion und schließt ebenso die Bereitschaft ein, Regeln und Gesetze zu verletzen bzw. zu brechen, um damit einem höheren Zweck Geltung zu verschaffen. Gleichzeitig bedeutet dies das uneingeschränkte Bekenntnis zu Gewaltfreiheit, Transparenz und Bekanntmachung der Gründe und Ziele der Aktionen. Der Begriff des elektronischen zivilen Ungehorsams geht ursprünglich auf das Critical Art Ensemble zurück, das mit seinen Büchern „The Electronic Disturbance" (1994) und „Electronic Civil Disobedience and Other Unpopular Ideas" (1996) die theoretischen Grundlagen für elektronischen zivilen Ungehorsam als Protestform im Cyberspace geschaffen hat.

Aktionsformen und Taktiken des elektronischen zivilen Ungehorsams wurden im Umfeld des pro-zapatistischen Solidaritätsnetzwerks und der globalisierungskritischen Bewegungen entwickelt. Der 1994 begonnene Befreiungskampf der Zapatistas gilt als wesentlicher Impulsgeber für westliche soziale Bewegungen und steht am Beginn der globalisierungskritischen Bewegung, die spätestens nach den Protesten und Ausschreitungen im Rahmen des WTO-Treffens in Seattle[6] 1999 zur „Bewegung der Bewegungen" avancierte.[7] „Angriffsziele" elektronischer Sit-Ins sind neben Regierungseinrichtungen transnationale Konzerne und internationale Organisationen wie die WTO.

Der Aufstand der Zapatistas in Chiapas/Mexiko und der von der EZLN (Ejército Zapatista de Liberación Nacional) geführte Kampf um Selbstbestimmung nehmen in der Geschichte des elektronischen zivilen Ungehorsams eine zentrale Rolle ein: Obwohl es das erste dokumentierte virtuelle Sit-In[8] bereits 1995 gab (vgl. Initiative Libertad 2006: 22), fanden die ersten massenhaften Aktionen elektronischen zivilen Ungehorsams 1998 als Solidaritätsaktionen mit den Zapatistas statt. Die italienische Gruppe Anonymous Digital Coalition und das Electronic Disturbance Theater riefen 1998 nach dem Massaker von Acteal/Chiapas, bei dem 45 Menschen getötet wurden, zu einem virtuellen Sit-In[9] auf. Die eigens dafür programmierte Protest-Software „Flood Net" war für die weitere Verbreitung dieser Protestform wegweisend. Im September desselben Jahres rief das Electronic Disturbance Theater im Rahmen ihrer Teilnahme am Ars Electronica Festival in Linz wieder zu einer Solidaritätsaktion mit der zapatistischen Guerillabewegung auf, an der sich etwa 20.000 Menschen aus 23 Ländern und fünf Kontinenten beteiligten (vgl. Nadir-Netzkritik 1999).

Im von den elektronischen Sit-Ins ausgelösten Medieninteresse sehen viele einen Grund für die globale Verbreitung der Anliegen der Zapatistas einerseits und ihr Überleben andererseits.[10] Digitaler Zapatismus, d.h. der erfolgreiche Aufbau eines Gegeninformation-Netzwerks mittels Email-Kommunikation und Webseiten durch die Zapatistas und zapatistische Solidaritätsgruppen, zählt bis heute zu den erfolgreichsten politischen Verwendungen des Internet.

Eine in mehrfacher Hinsicht spektakuläre Aktion elektronischen zivilen Ungehorsams fand im Frühjahr 2001 in Deutschland statt. AktivistInnen des Netzwerks kein mensch ist illegal und der Initiative Libertad! riefen dazu auf, die Internetseite der deutschen Fluggesellschaft Lufthansa zu blockieren. Das Unternehmen war bereits zuvor in die Kritik geraten, weil es sich an aus Deutschland vorgenommenen Abschiebungen illegalisierter Flüchtlinge beteiligt und daran verdient. Die Blockade der Seite war ausdrücklich keine Sabotage, es wurde also nichts zerstört, sondern sie wurde als Demonstration ordnungsgemäß angemeldet mit der schönen Angabe: „Versammlungsort: www.lufthansa.com" (vgl. Initiative Libertad 2006: 16). Damit wurde nicht nur gegen einen Konzern agiert, sondern auch der virtuelle als sozialer und politischer öffentlicher Raum reklamiert. Brisant war die Aktion gegen die Lufthansa vor allem durch das Gerichtsverfahren, dass sie nach sich zog. Die Fluggesellschaft zeigte den Betreiber der Domain libertad.de wegen Nötigung an. Vier Jahre später wurde er in erster Instanz verurteilt, erst in zweiter Instanz erfolgte der Freispruch. Die Begründung des Erstgerichts, dass durch den Aufruf zur Teilnahme am Sit-In andere zur Ausübung von Gewalt (durch den Mausklick) aufgefordert wurden, konnte sich in der Revision nicht durchsetzen. Dieser Prozess war weltweit die erste juristische Konsequenz eines virtuellen Sit-Ins und hat einen Präzedenzfall geschaffen: Onlinedemos sind keine Gewalt und Nötigung, sondern zielen auf die Meinungsbildung der Öffentlichkeit ab.

Die vielfältigen Formen zivilen und sozialen Ungehorsams innerhalb gegenwärtiger sozialer Bewegungen sind allerdings kaum aufgearbeitet. Noch schlechter bestellt ist es um das Thema im Zusammenhang mit zeitgenössischer Kunst. Zwar hat die beschriebene Aktion des Electronic Disturbance Theater auch im Kunstfeld Wellen geschlagen und es sogar in eine auflagenstarke Anthologie zu New Media Art geschafft (vgl. Tribe/Jana 2006: 40). Aber obwohl sich auch andere renommierte und weniger bekannte KünstlerInnen in den letzten Jahren theoretisch wie praktisch den Fragen gewidmet haben, ob und wie Kunstpraktiken zivilen und sozialen Ungehorsam abbilden, reflektieren, diskutieren und selbst Teil dessen werden können, existieren dazu kaum systematische Abhandlungen. Die produktiven

Aspekte der Überlappungen und Verkettungen des künstlerischen und des politischen Feldes werden sogar noch negiert, wenn, wie im Buch des Kunstsammlers Harald Falckenberg (2002: 10), unter dem Titel „Ziviler Ungehorsam" unter Absehung von jeglicher begrifflichen wie historischen Bezugnahme auf die Praxis sozialer Bewegungen für die „Autonomie der Kunst und die Subjektivität des Künstlers" plädiert wird.

Mit dem hier vorliegenden Buch wird eine gänzlich andere Richtung eingeschlagen und damit versucht, die beschriebene Lücke zu schließen.

Allerdings haben gegenwärtige Aktivismen es mit anderen Bedingungen zu tun als jene der 1960er oder auch der 1980er Jahre. Die gemeinhin als Neoliberalismus bezeichneten Umstrukturierungen der westlich-kapitalistischen Gegenwartsgesellschaften – ökonomisch als Privatisierung, Deregulierung und Liberalisierung durchgesetzt und in vielfältiger Form auch in sozialpolitische Programme gegossen – haben einer Machttechnik zu besonderer Relevanz bei der Sicherung von Herrschaft verholfen, die Michel Foucault (2000: 64) als „gouvernementale Führung" beschrieben hat. In einer Verknüpfung der Vokabeln gouverner, regieren und mentalité, Denkweise, setzt die Gouvernementalität auf Aktivierung des Subjekts, seine selbstständige Führung. Die Gouvernementalität löst andere Machttechniken im Verständnis Foucaults nicht ab, sondern ergänzt sie, kann aber durchaus zur vorherrschenden einer bestimmten konkret-historischen Situation werden. Herrschaft zeichnet sich demnach heute also weniger durch repressive Regime und klassische Untertanenverhältnisse und in geringerem Maße als früher durch normierte und regulierte Lebensbedingungen aus. Während Antonio Gramsci schon die individuelle (Selbst)Führung als Bestandteil der Sicherung gesellschaftlicher Machtverhältnisse ausgemacht hatte, beschreibt Foucault die im Zuge der neoliberalen Ökonomisierung des Sozialen installierte gouvernementale Führung zudem als eine Form der Selbstführung, in der sich die Subjekte als UnternehmerInnen ihrer Selbst formieren.[11] Herrschaft scheint dabei mehr und mehr aus den Staatsapparaten in die Subjekte und ihre zivilgesellschaftliche Formierung und Umgebung zu diffundieren.

Der moderne Staat als langjähriger und monopolartiger Adressat zivilen Ungehorsams hat zwar immer schon als gesellschaftliches Kräfteverhältnis und nie allein als repressives Subjekt oder Instrument einer Klasse fungiert. In den Jahren der neoliberalen Hegemonie aber hat sich offenbar nicht nur die Angriffsfläche zivilen Ungehorsams erneut verändert, sondern dabei gleich das ungehorsame Verhalten als solches und folglich auch als Politikform in Frage gestellt: Denn was ist noch ungehorsam, wenn es keine auf Gewalt basierende Autorität als Gegenüber mehr gibt, die den Gehorsam einfordert?

Zwar hat sich der Staat verändert, gesellschaftliche Machtverhältnisse und Herrschaft aber haben sich dabei nicht aufgelöst. Dementsprechend wurde auch in den vergangenen Jahren, in Zeiten also, in denen der Staat weniger in Form eines repressiven Gegenübers denn als strukturierend zivilgesellschaftliche Diffusität auftritt, eine Vielzahl unterschiedlichster Formen und Praktiken zivilen (oder sozialen) Ungehorsams entwickelt – von illegalen Grenzübertritten bis zum Netzaktivismus. Viele dieser Prozesse werden aus dem Kunstfeld heraus reflektiert, in einige sind KünstlerInnen aktiv involviert.

Entscheidender als die berühmte, eingangs zitierte Thoreau-Stelle vom Gesetzesbruch, der neben einem klar abgrenzbaren Gegner auch eigene Stärke und eine fast heroische Entschlossenheit zur Tat voraussetzt, ist dabei vielleicht ein anderer Satz Thoreaus. In „Über die Pflicht zum Ungehorsam…" heißt es, nur ein paar Zeilen weiter, wesentlich bescheidener: „Ein Mensch soll nicht alles tun, sondern etwas; und weil er nicht alles tun kann, soll er nicht ausgerechnet etwas Unrechtes tun." (Thoreau 1973: 18) „Nicht alles tun" heißt dabei einerseits, nicht mitzumachen, sich zu verweigern, zu blockieren, zu sabotieren und bedeutet andererseits, sich nicht dumm und passiv machen zu lassen, also wenigstens etwas zu tun – was und was nicht, unter welchen Umständen und wie, genau das steht zur Debatte. In solche Diskussionen greifen nicht nur aktivistische Zirkel und globalisierungskritische Organisationen, sondern auch künstlerische Arbeiten ein. Das Buch versteht sich als Beitrag zu diesen Debatten und zugleich als Untersuchung der Schnittstellen und Überlappungen zwischen künstlerischer Produktion und sozialen Bewegungen hinsichtlich Formen zivilen und sozialen Ungehorsams.

Literatur:

Azzellini, Dario (2002): Genua. Italien – Geschichte – Perspektiven, Berlin/Hamburg/Göttingen (Assoziation A).
Birkner, Martin und Robert Foltin (2006): (Post-)Operaismus. Von der Arbeiterautonomie zur Multitude. Geschichte und Gegenwart, Theorie und Praxis. Eine Einführung, Stuttgart (Schmetterling Verlag).
Boltanski, Luc und Ève Chiapello (2003): Der neue Geist des Kapitalismus, Konstanz (UVK Verlagsgesellschaft).
Bradley, Will und Charles Esche (Hg.) (2007): Art And Social Change. A Critical Reader, London (Tate Publishing).
Carson, Clayborne (2004): Zeiten des Kampfes. Das Student Nonviolent Coordinating Committee (SNCC) und das Erwachen des afro-amerikanischen Widerstands in den sechziger Jahren, Nettersheim (Verlag Graswurzelrevolution).
Critical Art Ensemble (2007): Elektronischer Widerstand, Wien (Passagen Verlag).
Daniels, Dieter (2002): Kunst als Sendung. Von der Telegrafie zum Internet, München (Verlag C.H.Beck).
Ebert, Theodor (1984): Ziviler Ungehorsam. Von der APO zur Friedensbewegung, Waldkirch (Waldkircher Verlagsgesellschaft).
Falckenberg, Harald (2002): Ziviler Ungehorsam. Kunst im Klartext, Regensburg (Verlag Lindinger + Schmid).
Foucault, Michel (2000): Die „Gouvernementalität", in: Bröckling, Ulrich, Susanne Krasmann und Thomas Lemke (Hg.): Gouvernementalität der Gegenwart. Studien zur Ökonomisierung des Sozialen, Frankfurt a. M. (Suhrkamp Verlag), S. 41-67.
graswurzelrevolution (1985): Sonderheft „Soziale Verteidigung", Nr. 98/99, Hamburg, November 1985, 3. Aufl.
Horn, Gerd-Rainer (2007): The Spirit of ´68. Rebellion in Western Europe and North America, 1956-1976, Oxford (Oxford University Press).
Initiative Libertad (2006): Netzaktivismus gegen Abschiebung. Erfolg einer Imageverschmutzungskampagne, in: dies. (Hg.): go.to/onlinedemo. Handbuch Online Aktivismus, Frankfurt a. M. (Verlag edition libertad), S. 11-18.
Jochheim, Gernot (1984): Die gewaltfreie Aktion. Ideen und Methoden, Vorbilder und Wirkungen, Hamburg (Verlag Rasch und Röhrig).
Kastner, Jens (2004): Zapatismus und Transnationalisierung. Anmerkungen zur Relevanz zapatistischer Politik für die Bewegungsforschung, in: Kaltmeier, Olaf, Jens Kastner und Elisabeth Tuider (Hg.): Neoliberalismus – Autonomie – Widerstand. Soziale Bewegungen in Lateinamerika, Münster (Verlag Westfälisches Dampfboot), S. 251-275.
Kerkeling, Luz (2006): La Lucha Sigue! Der Kampf geht weiter! EZLN – Ursachen und Entwicklungen des zapatistischen Aufstands, Münster (Unrast Verlag), 2. überarb. und erw. Aufl.

Komitee für Grundrechte und Demokratie (Hg.) (1992): Ziviler Ungehorsam. Traditionen, Konzepte, Erfahrungen, Perspektiven, Sensbachtal (Komitee für Grundrechte und Demokratie e. V.).
Lorey, Isabell (2007): Vom immanenten Widerspruch zur hegemonialen Funktion. Biopolitische Gouvernmentalität und Selbst-Prekarisierung von KulturproduzentInnen, in: Raunig, Gerald und Ulf Wuggenig (Hg.): Kritik der Kreativität, Wien (Verlag Turia + Kant), S. 121-136.
Mellon, Christian (1992): Die Geschichte eines Begriffes von Thoreau bis in unsere Tage, in: Komitee für Grundrechte und Demokratie (Hg.): Ziviler Ungehorsam. Traditionen, Konzepte, Erfahrungen, Perspektiven, Sensbachtal (Komitee für Grundrechte und Demokratie e. V.), S. 47-56.
Müller, Barabara (1995): Passiver Widerstand im Ruhrkampf, Münster/Wien (LIT Verlag).
Nadir-Netzkritik (1999): Digital Zapatismo, in: Arranca!, Berlin, Nr.17, Mai 1999, S. 46-51.
Redaktionsgruppe (Hg.) (1986): Wege des Ungehorsams. Jahrbuch II für gewaltfreie & libertäre gewaltfreie Aktion, Politik & Kultur 1986, Kassel (Verlag Weber, Zucht & Co.).
Thoreau, Henry David (1973): Über die Pflicht zum Ungehorsam gegen den Staat, in: ders.: Über die Pflicht zum Ungehorsam gegen den Staat und andere Essays, Zürich (Diogenes Verlag), S. 7-35.
Tribe, Mark und Reena Jana (2006): New Media Art, Köln/London/Los Angeles/Madrid/Paris/Tokyo (Taschen Verlag).

1 Christian Mellon (1992: 47) macht darauf aufmerksam, dass Thoreau, obwohl er als Begründer des zivilen Ungehorsams gilt, den Begriff selber wahrscheinlich nie verwendet hat. Unter dem bekannten Titel war die Schrift erst 1866, also nach seinem Tod, erschienen. Zu Thoreaus Lebzeiten war sie als „Resistance to Civil Government" (1849) publiziert worden, im Text taucht der Begriff „ziviler Ungehorsam" nicht auf.
2 Vgl. http://www.thing.net/~rdom/ecd/oecd.html (04.06.2008)
3 Theodor Ebert (1984) beschreibt einige der Aktionen zivilen Ungehorsams und die Debatten darum innerhalb der westdeutschen 68er-Bewegung und stellt sie als direkte Vorläufer der später in der Friedensbewegung praktizierten Aktionsformen dar.
4 Vgl. http://www.actupny.org/ (24.01.2008).
5 In der gemeinsamen Geschichte von Kunst und neuen Medien spielen laut Dieter Daniels (2002: 12) gerade jene „uneingelösten Utopien der Medienentwicklung" immer wieder eine bedeutende Rolle für die Neuentwicklung künstlerischer Entwürfe.
6 1999 riefen die Elektrohippies zu einer Aktion gegen das WTO-Treffen in Seattle auf, an der sich weltweit rund eine halbe Million Menschen beteiligt haben soll (vgl. Initiative Libertad 2006: 24).
7 Zum Zapatismus allgemein vgl. Kerkeling 2006, zum Transnationalismus der Zapatistas vgl. Kastner 2004.
8 Virtuelle Sit-Ins – auch als Internet-Blockaden, elektronische Abstimmungen sowie direkte Aktionen im Internet bezeichnet – zielen durch Überlastung der „attackierten" Webseite(n) auf einen temporären Ausfall derselben ab, ohne – und damit rekurriert der elektronische zivile Ungehorsam explizit auf die von der „analogen" Vorgängerbewegung propagierte Gewaltfreiheit und richtet sich gleichzeitig gegen Hackerpraktiken – Daten oder Computersysteme zu zerstören.
9 Am 18.1.1998 hat die italienische Gruppe Anonymous Digital Coalition zum virtuellen Sit-in am 29.01.1998 von 16:00 bis 17:00 GMT aufgerufen. Der Protest richtete sich gegen fünf mexikanische Finanzinstitutionen als Symbole des mexikanischen Neoliberalismus. Vgl. http://www.thing.net/~rdom/ecd/anondigcoal.html (05.06.2008)
10 Vgl. z.B. Critical Art Ensemble 2007: 37 und http://gothamist.com/2004/11/29/ricardo_dominguez_artist _and_electronic_civil_disobedience_pioneer.php (05.06.2008)
11 In den aktuellen Debatten um neue Arbeitsverhältnisse wird immer wieder vor allem auf die Rolle abgehoben, die künstlerische Lebensentwürfe bei der Durchsetzung dieser auf Selbsteffizienz basierenden Machttechnik gespielt haben und spielen (vgl. u. a. Boltanski/Chiapello 2003). Im Anschluss an Foucault stellt beispielsweise Isabell Lorey (2007) heraus, dass es gerade die dissidenten Lebensformen und die künstlerischen und sozialbewegten alternativen Praktiken der Vergangenheit waren, die zur Um- und Durchsetzung der gouvernementalen Führung beigetragen haben. Dass ehemals ermächtigende und emanzipatorisch gedachte Begriffe und Konzepte wie Autonomie, Selbstverwaltung, Eigeninitiative und Kreativität zu wesentlichen Merkmalen neoliberaler Herrschaft geworden sind, macht selbstverständlich auch die Antworten auf die Frage nach Formen zivilen Ungehorsams komplizierter. Eine gesonderte Diskussion wäre dann darüber zu führen, ob und falls ja, inwiefern auch einstmaliger ziviler Ungehorsam zur kapitalistischen Modernisierung beigetragen hat, ob also tatsächlich der „Spirit of '68" (Horn 2007) ungebrochen „Der neue Geist des Kapitalismus" (Boltanski/Chiapello 2003) ist.

cannot do everything

Civil/social disobedience and art

Jens Kastner and Elisabeth Bettina Spörr

Henry David Thoreau's (1817-1862) short essay "On the Duty of Civil Disobedience" (1849) is one of the most influential sources for the social movements of the 20th century. Thoreau developed the idea of civil disobedience as an individual reaction to structural injustice.[1] His point of departure was a very specific one: slavery, then legal in the United States, on the one hand and the U.S. intervention in Mexico (1846-1848) on the other hand prompted him to refuse to pay his taxes in order to withhold his support from these policies. Various movements derived political concepts from the moral duty, framed by Thoreau as a matter of the individual conscience, to engage in civil disobedience once an injustice has been identified. These concepts were designed to apply to a variety of forms of collective action and adapted to the respective contexts. At the center of Thoreau's essay stands the instigation to break the law, which was to become the core of civil disobedience: "… but if [the injustice] is of such a nature that it requires you to be the agent of injustice to another, then I say, break the law" (Thoreau 1849: 198).

    This imperative already contains both the dimension of the passive refusal to comply with unjust laws and the active one of a deliberate break with them. The social movements of the 20th century pursued these two strains with varying intensities. For his concept of "passive resistance," Leo Tolstoy, who knew Thoreau's essay and supported its translation into the Russian, drew mostly on the dimension of refusal, which was also to play an important role in Mahatma Gandhi's movement demanding India's independence from Great Britain. Active and interventionist practices were then developed systematically and on a mass scale primarily in the African-American Civil Rights Movement in the U.S. during the 1950s and 1960s (cf. Carson 2004). More than thirty years later, the protagonists of electronic civil disobedience, a form of action whose theory and practice developed in the 1990s, would explicitly invoke the authority of the African-American Civil Rights Movement.[2]

The emphasis Thoreau places on breaking the law results from his focus on the isolated individual who finds himself or herself in conflict with the government of the state. The political expansion of the concept not only led groups or larger sections of a population to take action against specific government decisions or against governments as such. Collective action in agreement with the government is equally conceivable within the concept of civil disobedience: for instance, in 1923, mass civil disobedience arose against the French and Belgian occupiers of the Ruhr area after the German Chancellor Wilhelm Cuno had called on the populace to offer "passive resistance" (cf. Müller 1995). Practices of civil disobedience were similarly employed against a hostile occupying force during World War II. Various coordinated actions were organized as part of the Résistance against the Nazi German troops in France.

Subsequent to the American Civil Rights Movement, a great variety of practices of mass civil disobedience emerged in many places across the globe in the context of the "years of 1968." If "1968" generally associates the May battles on the barricades of Paris, and if these militant protests are not infrequently conceptualized as immediate precursors to the armed urban guerilla movements of the 1970s, it is necessary to emphasize by contrast the great bandwidth of civil disobedience.[3] Without discussing the antithesis—which may be illusory—between nonviolent and militant forms of politics in detail, we should like to note that methods of collective disobedience, from sit-ins and blockades to coordinated conscientious objection, were not only much more widespread than later guerilla actions, they also often had greater political effect; the fact notwithstanding that burning car tires, shattered window and black activists patrolling through suburbs with guns over their shoulders will always enjoy an advantage over sit-in participants when it comes to media attention.

Civil disobedience also played a large role in the new social movements: from blockades against the deployment of Pershing missiles organized by the German peace movement of the early 1980s and the action groups called ACT UP which formed in the U.S. in the face of the AIDS crisis[4] across "harvest actions" directed against trial cultivations of genetically altered crops held by the anti-genetic-engineering movement to a great variety of actions organized by the ongoing anti-nuclear movement.

At least in the German-speaking world, however, the debate seems to have come to an abrupt end with the wane of the social movements in the late 1980s.

Not that there haven't been any actions of civil disobedience since the 1990s: but the most important theoretical contributions in German were published in the 1980s (cf. Ebert 1984, Jochheim 1984, graswurzelrevolution 1985, Redaktionsgruppe 1986); the most recent collection of essays to address the issue explicitly was conceived shortly after the Fall of the Berlin Wall (Komitee für Grundrechte und Demokratie 1992).

By contrast, the practice of civil disobedience has seen a renewed expansion with the rise of the anti-globalization movements subsequent to the Zapatista uprising in Chiapas (Mexico) since 1994:

On the one hand, civil disobedience was expanded to create social disobedience in the context of the Zapatista-inspired Ya Basta! Network. The Disobbedienti (the disobedient ones), a group that emerged from the Italian Tute Bianche in 2001, framed this concept but remained relatively vague with respect to concrete practices (cf. Azzellini 2002). However, the Disobbedienti, whose nationwide organization was dissolved in 2005, made comparatively little reference to a pacifist tradition in Gandhi's or Martin Luther King's sense. Their ideas and practices of disobedience came from the history of the autonomous labor movement, or Operaism. In the 1960s and 1970s, the so-called labor autonomy counted the refusal to work and sabotage among its preferred practices, which were discussed—and applied—on a mass scale (cf. Birkner/Foltin 2006).

On the other hand, the purview of civil disobedience was expanded to include virtual space. The tendency to expand both activist and artistic practices to electronic space emerged as early as the mid-1990s.

On the one hand, the electronic revolution of the early 1980s and the subsequent development of the Internet and its rapid expansion in the 1990s evoked euphoria in the fields of art and political activism, leading to the proclamation of an "electronic utopia"; on the other hand, they met with much skepticism. The availability of information and its rapid worldwide dissemination gave rise to the hope for "artistic and critical collaborations" that would "transcend cultural borders" (Critical Art Ensemble 2007: 27). At the same time, nobody was so deluded as to believe that a medium had come into being with the Internet that would be genuinely democratic, anti-racist, anti-sexist, and free of domination. Such sanguine expectations regarding new media had too often been disappointed or dashed in the past. Such hopes had been expressed, for instance, in the radio theory of Bert Brecht, who advocated, in the 1920s and 1930s, the democratization of the medium and its transformation from an apparatus of distribution into one of communication. Similarly, the rise of video technology in the 1970s and the consequent easy and cheap access to the means of production, which, thus artists had hoped, would lead to a democratization of art, fell short of such expectations.[5]

Subsequent years saw the emergence of a number of different subversive tactics, among them the persiflage and appropriation of commercial uses of the Internet such as deployed, for instance, by the Institute for Applied Autonomy, the Bureau of Inverse Technology, and the Yes Men. At the same time, a fundamentally new form of protest developed: electronic civil disobedience. This form of resistance was advocated primarily by a number of collectives located at the interface between political activism and activist art. Besides the Critical Art Ensemble, these pioneers of electronic civil disobedience, who made seminal contributions not only to its theory but also to the development of functioning forms of net action, include the Italian Anonymous Digital Coalition and the Electronic Disturbance Theater, a formation that emerged from the Critical Art Ensemble.

In the tradition of civil disobedience, electronic civil disobedience aims at non-violent participatory mass action; like its traditional counterpart, it includes the willingness to infringe against rules and break laws in order to assert a higher purpose. At the same time, it is committed without qualification to non-violence, transparency, and the public announcement of the reasons for and aims behind an action. The concept of electronic civil disobedience was originally coined by the Critical Art Ensemble, whose books "The Electronic Disturbance" (1994) and "Electronic Civil Disobedience and Other Unpopular Ideas" (1996) laid the theoretical foundations for electronic civil disobedience as a form of protest in cyberspace.

The forms of action and tactics of electronic civil disobedience were developed in the context of the pro-Zapatista solidarity network and the anti-globalization movements. The Zapatista struggle for liberation, which began in 1994, is regarded as a central source of impulses for the social movements of the West and marks the beginning of an anti-globalization movement which, at the latest with the protests and riots surrounding the WTO meeting in Seattle in 1999,[6] rose to become the "movement of movements."[7] "Targets" of electronic sit-ins include, besides government facilities, transnational corporations and international organizations such as the WTO.

The Zapatista uprising in Chiapas (Mexico) and the battle for self-determination led by the EZLN (Ejército Zapatista de Liberación Nacional) play a central role in the history of electronic civil disobedience: although the first documented virtual sit-in took[8] place as early as 1994 (cf. Initiative Libertad 2006: 22), the first mass actions of electronic civil disobedience, which took place in 1998, were demonstrations of solidarity with the Zapatistas. In 1998, after the massacre at Acteal (Chiapas), during which 45 people were killed, the Italian group Anonymous Digital Coalition and the Electronic Disturbance Theater called for a virtual sit-in.[9] A software specifically created on this occasion, "Flood Net," was seminal to the later proliferation of this form of protest. In September of the same year, the Electronic Disturbance Theater, as part of its contribution to the Arts Electronica Festival, Linz (Austria), called for a second demonstration of solidarity with the Zapatista guerilla movement, in which ca. 20,000 people in 23 countries and five continents participated (cf. Nadir-Netzkritik 1999).

Many observers believe that the media interest awakened by the electronic sit-ins contributed to the global dissemination of the Zapatistas' demands as well as their survival.[10] To this day, digital Zapatism, i.e. the successful creation of a network of e-mail communication and web sites through which Zapatistas and groups of Zapatista sympathizers spread their message, constitutes one of the most successful political uses of the Internet.

An action of electronic civil disobedience that was spectacular in more than one way took place in Germany in the spring of 2001. Activists of the network kein mensch ist illegal [no human being is illegal] and Initiative Libertad! called for a blockade of the German airline company Lufthansa's web site. The company had already been criticized because it participates in, and profits from, the deportation of illegalized refugees from Germany. The blockade of the web site was explicitly not an act of sabotage, since there was no permanent damage; in fact, it was duly announced to the authorities as a demonstration, neatly listing as its "meeting place: www.lufthansa.com" (cf. Initiative Libertad 2006: 16). The demonstrators thus not only acted against a corporation but also reclaimed virtual space as a social and political public space. The action directed against Lufthansa was especially explosive because of the lawsuit that followed. The airline company filed coercion charges against the owner of the domain libertad.de. Four years later, the latter was convicted; an appellate court later vacated the conviction, unconvinced by the first court's opinion that the call for participation in the sit-in amounted to an incitement to violence (in the form of a mouse click). The trial was the first time a virtual sit-in led to legal consequences, and set a precedent: online demonstrations do not constitute violence or coercion but rather aim to contribute to the education of public opinion.

Yet there has been virtually no critical appraisal of the great variety of forms of civil and social disobedience within contemporary social movements. Things look even worse with respect to the nexus between civil disobedience and contemporary art. The abovementioned action performed by the Electronic Disturbance Theater drew attention also from within the art field, and even made it into a high-circulation anthology on New Media Art (cf. Tribe/Jana 2006:40). But even though other renowned as well as lesser-known artists have in recent years addressed in their theory and practice the question as to whether and how artistic practices can depict, reflect, discuss, and indeed become part of civil and social disobedience, there is almost no systematic academic work on the issue. The productive aspects of moments of overlap and concatenation between the artistic and political fields are even explicitly negated when, as in a book by the art collector Harald Falckenberg (2002: 10), a discussion entitled "Civil Disobedience" forgoes any conceptual or historical reference to the praxis of social movements and instead makes a case for the "autonomy of art and the subjectivity of the artist."

The present book embarks in an entirely different direction, seeking to close this gap.

Contemporary activisms, however, are facing conditions different from those confronted by the activisms of the 1960s or even the 1980s. The processes of restructuring generally called neo-liberalism that are at work in the Western-capitalist societies of the present—pushed through on the economic level as privatization, deregulation, and liberalization, as well as cast into a variety of social policies—have rendered a technique of power Michel Foucault (1991: 100-101) called "governmental control" especially relevant to the stabilization of domination. In fusing the words gouverner, to govern, and mentalité, way of thinking, governmentality is predicated on an activation of the subject, on its self-governing control. Governmentality, thus Foucault's view, does not supplant other techniques of power but complements them; nonetheless, in specific concrete-historical situations, it can indeed become the prevalent one. Today's domination, then, is characterized less by repressive regimes and classical sovereign-subject-relations, and less by normalized and regulated conditions of life, than in the past. Whereas Antonio Gramsci had already identified individual (self)control as a component of the stabilization of social power relations, Foucault goes further in describing the governmental control installed with the neo-liberal marketization of the social as a form of self-control in which the subject takes shape as an entrepreneur of itself.11 Domination thus seems to become more diffuse, progressively seeping from the apparatuses of the state into the subjects and into their formation and environments in civil society.

The modern state, as a lasting and monopolistic addressee of civil disobedience, has indeed always already functioned as a relation of social forces and never as a purely repressive subject or as the instrument of one class. In the age of neo-liberal hegemony, however, the areas vulnerable to civil disobedience have shifted once again; and what is more, disobedient behavior as such and, hence, as a form of politics has been called into question: for what would even constitute disobedience when there is no single antagonist, no single authority based on the use of force that demands obedience?

The state has indeed changed, but social power relations and social domination have not simply dissolved. Accordingly, recent years—an era, that is, in which the state appears less as a repressive antagonist than as a diffusely structuring element of civil society—have seen the development of a great variety of forms and practices of civil (or social) disobedience—from illegal border-crossings to net activism. Many of these processes are reflected in the field of art; in some, artists are actively involved.

In this context, another sentence in Thoreau's "On the Duty of Civil Disobedience" may be more important than the famous passage quoted in the beginning about breaking the law, which presupposes not only a clearly delineated antagonist but also strength and an almost heroic determination on the part of the disobedient. Just a few lines down, Thoreau writes much more modestly: "A man has not everything thing to do, but something; and because he cannot do every thing, it is not necessary that he should do something wrong." (Thoreau 1849: 198) "Not to do every thing" means here, on the one hand, not to join in, to refuse, to blockade, to sabotage; it means, on the other hand, to refuse to be rendered stupid and passive, that is, to do at least something—what and what not, under which circumstances and how, that is precisely what is under debate. It is a debate in which, besides activist circles and anti-globalization organizations, works of art also intervene. The present book intends to be a contribution to these debates as well as an examination of the interfaces and overlaps between artistic production and social movements with a view to forms of civil and social disobedience.

Translated from the German by Gerrit Jackson

Literature:

Azzellini, Dario (2002): Genua. Italien – Geschichte – Perspektiven, Berlin/Hamburg/Göttingen (Assoziation A).
Birkner, Martin und Robert Foltin (2006): (Post-)Operaismus. Von der Arbeiterautonomie zur Multitude. Geschichte und Gegenwart, Theorie und Praxis. Eine Einführung, Stuttgart (Schmetterling Verlag).
Boltanski, Luc and Ève Chiapello (2005): The New Spirit of Capitalism, London/New York (Verso).
Bradley, Will and Charles Esche (eds.) (2007): Art And Social Change. A Critical Reader, London (Tate Publishing).
Carson, Clayborne (2004): In Struggle. SNCC and the Black Awakening of the 1960s, Cambridge, Mass. (Harvard University Press).
Critical Art Ensemble (2007): Elektronischer Widerstand, Wien (Passagen Verlag).
Daniels, Dieter (2002): Kunst als Sendung. Von der Telegrafie zum Internet, München (Verlag C.H.Beck).
Ebert, Theodor (1984): Ziviler Ungehorsam. Von der APO zur Friedensbewegung, Waldkirch (Waldkircher Verlagsgesellschaft).
Falckenberg, Harald (2002): Ziviler Ungehorsam. Kunst im Klartext, Regensburg (Verlag Lindinger + Schmid).
Foucault, Michel (1991): Governmentality, in: Burchell, Graham, Colin Gordon and Peter Miller (eds.): The Foucault Effect. Studies in Governmentality, Chicago, IL (University of Chicago Press), pp. 87-104.
graswurzelrevolution (1985): Sonderheft „Soziale Verteidigung", Nr. 98/99, Hamburg, November 1985, 3. Aufl.
Horn, Gerd-Rainer (2007): The Spirit of '68. Rebellion in Western Europe and North America, 1956-1976, Oxford (Oxford University Press).
Initiative Libertad (2006): Netzaktivismus gegen Abschiebung. Erfolg einer Imageverschmutzungskampagne, in: Initiative Libertad (ed.): go.to/onlinedemo. Handbuch Online Aktivismus, Frankfurt a. M. (Verlag edition libertad), pp. 11-18.
Jochheim, Gernot (1984): Die gewaltfreie Aktion. Ideen und Methoden, Vorbilder und Wirkungen, Hamburg (Verlag Rasch und Röhrig).
Kastner, Jens (2004): Zapatismus und Transnationalisierung. Anmerkungen zur Relevanz zapatistischer Politik für die Bewegungsforschung, in: Kaltmeier, Olaf, Jens Kastner und Elisabeth Tuider (Hg.): Neoliberalismus – Autonomie – Widerstand. Soziale Bewegungen in Lateinamerika, Münster (Verlag Westfälisches Dampfboot), pp. 251-275.
Kerkeling, Luz (2006): La Lucha Sigue! Der Kampf geht weiter! EZLN – Ursachen und Entwicklungen des zapatistischen Aufstands, Münster (Unrast Verlag), 2. überarb. und erw. Aufl.
Komitee für Grundrechte und Demokratie (ed.) (1992): Ziviler Ungehorsam. Traditionen, Konzepte, Erfahrungen, Perspektiven, Sensbachtal (Komitee für Grundrechte und Demokratie e. V.).
Lorey, Isabell (2007): Vom immanenten Widerspruch zur hegemonialen Funktion. Biopolitische Gouvernmentalität und Selbst-Prekarisierung von KulturproduzentInnen, in: Raunig, Gerald und Ulf Wuggenig (eds.): Kritik der Kreativität, Wien (Verlag Turia + Kant), pp. 121-136.
Mellon, Christian (1992): Die Geschichte eines Begriffes von Thoreau bis in unsere Tage, in: Komitee für Grundrechte und Demokratie (ed.) 1992: Ziviler Ungehorsam. Traditionen, Konzepte, Erfahrungen, Perspektiven, Sensbachtal (Komitee für Grundrechte und Demokratie e. V.), pp. 47-56.
Müller, Barabara (1995): Passiver Widerstand im Ruhrkampf, Münster/Wien (LIT Verlag).
Nadir-Netzkritik (1999): Digital Zapatismo, in: Arranca!, Berlin, No. 17, May 1999, pp. 46-51.
Redaktionsgruppe (Hg.) (1986): Wege des Ungehorsams. Jahrbuch II für gewaltfreie & libertäre gewaltfreie Aktion, Politik & Kultur 1986, Kassel (Verlag Weber, Zucht & Co.).
Thoreau, Henry David (1849): Resistance to Civil Government [Civil Disobedience], in: Elizabeth Peabody (ed.): Aesthetic Papers, Boston and New York (Peabody and Putnam), pp. 189-211.
Tribe, Mark und Reena Jana (2006): New Media Art, Köln/London/Los Angeles/Madrid/Paris/Tokyo (Taschen Verlag).

1   As Christian Mellon (1992: 47) points out, Thoreau, even though he is regarded as the founder of civil disobedience, probably never used the term himself. The famous essay was not published under this title until 1866, that is, after Thoreau's death. During his lifetime, it had been published as "Resistance to Civil Government" (1849); the term "civil disobedience" does not appear in the text.
2   Cf. http://www.thing.net/~rdom/ecd/oecd.html (06/04/2008).
3   Theodor Ebert (1984) describes some actions of civil disobedience and the debates over them within the

West German student movement of '68; he presents them as immediate precursors of the forms of action later practiced by the peace movement.
4   Cf. http://www.actupny.org/ (01/24/2008).
5   In the shared history of art and new media, thus Dieter Daniels (2002: 12), such "unfulfilled utopias of media development" have time and again played an important role in the development of new artistic conceptions.
6   In 1999, the Elektrohippies called for an action against the WTO meeting in Seattle in which ca. half a million people worldwide are said to have participated (cf. Initiative Libertad 2006: 24).
7   On Zapatism in general, cf. Kerkeling 2006; on the Zapatistas' transnationalism, cf. Kastner 2004.
8   Virtual sit-ins—also called Internet blockades, electronic ballots, and direct actions on the Internet—aim at temporary shutdowns of the web sites they "attack" by overburdening their systems without—and in this respect, electronic civil disobedience takes explicit recourse to the non-violence preached by its "analogue" precursor movements and simultaneously opposes hackers' practices—destroying data or computer systems.
9   On January 18, 1998, the Italian group Anonymous Digital Coalition called for a virtual sit-in on January 29, 1998 between 4 and 5pm GMT. The protest was directed against five Mexican financial institutions as symbols of Mexican neo-liberalism. Cf. http://www.thing.net/~rdom/ecd/anondigcoal.html (06/05/2008).
    Cf. e.g. Critical Art Ensemble 2007: 37 and
    http://gothamist.com/2004/11/29/ricardo_dominguez_artist_and_electronic_civil_disobedience_pioneer.php (06/05/2008).
10 Contributions to the current debates over new labor relations frequently discuss the role artistic lifestyles have played and continue to play in establishing the prevalence of this technique of power based on the efficient use of the self (cf., among others, Boltanski/Chiapello 2005). For instance, Isabell Lorey (2007) emphasizes, drawing on Foucault, that yesterday's dissident visions of life and alternative practices developed by artists and participants in social movements precisely contributed to the implementation and prevalence of governmental control. That ideas and conceptions such as autonomy, self-government, initiative, and creativity, once associated with self-empowerment and emancipation, have become central characteristics of neo-liberal domination, obviously also complicates answers to the question regarding forms of civil disobedience. Whether and to which extent the civil disobedience of the past has contributed to capitalist modernization—whether, that is, the "Spirit of '68" (Horn 2007) is indeed "The New Spirit of Capitalism" (Boltanski/Chiapello 2005)—: that is a separate discussion.

Über Poesie und Revolution*

John Holloway

Es ist aufregend und eine Ehre, in einer anderen Welt zu sein, einer merkwürdigen Welt der KünstlerInnen. Als ich darüber nachgedacht habe, was ich möglicherweise über Kunst zu KünstlerInnen sagen könnte, erinnerte ich mich daran, dass mich jemand einige Monate zuvor den Poeten der globalisierungskritischen Bewegung genannt hatte. Ich weiß nicht, warum er das sagte, aber ich fühlte mich sehr geschmeichelt, auch wenn mir bewusst war, dass die Person, die es gesagt hatte, es als Beleidigung oder zumindest als Abqualifizierung gemeint hatte. Er meinte es als Beleidigung, weil er sagte, revolutionäre Theorie solle nicht mit Poesie vermischt werden. Poesie ist gefährlich, denn sie hat mit einer schönen, aber irrealen Welt zu tun, während revolutionäre Theorie von der realen Welt harter Kämpfe handelt. In dieser realen Welt des Kampfes, spielen Poesie und Kunst und Schönheit keine wichtige Rolle: Revolutionärer Kampf konfrontiert Hässlichkeit mit Hässlichkeit, Gewehre mit Gewehren, Brutalität mit Brutalität. Für Poesie und Schönheit und Kunst wird es nach der Revolution Zeit geben.

Ich bin nicht einverstanden mit diesem Argument. Im Gegenteil, ich möchte argumentieren, dass revolutionäre Theorie und Praxis künstlerisch sein muss, da sie ansonsten nicht revolutionär wären, und dass auch die Kunst revolutionär sein muss oder sonst keine Kunst wäre.

(Verzeihen Sie, dass ich von Revolution spreche. Ich weiß, dass dieses Wort aus der Mode gekommen ist. Ich nehme bloß zum Ausgangspunkt, was wir alle wissen, dass der Kapitalismus eine Katastrophe für die Menschheit ist, und dass, wenn es uns nicht gelingt, ihn los zu werden, wenn es uns nicht gelingt, die Welt radikal zu verändern, dass es dann sehr gut möglich ist, dass wir Menschen nicht mehr sehr lange überleben werden. Das ist der Grund, warum ich von Revolution spreche.)

Bekanntermaßen sagte Adorno, dass es nach Auschwitz unmöglich wäre, noch Gedichte zu schreiben. Wir müssen nicht die sechzig Jahre bis nach Auschwitz zurückdenken, um zu verstehen, was er meinte. Gräuel kennen wir zur Genüge, vielleicht gerade in Kolumbien, gerade in Lateinamerika, gerade in der heutigen Welt (Abu Ghraib, Guantánamo). Der Gedanke an die Erschaffung von etwas Schönem, erscheint in dieser Welt wie eine furchtbare Gefühllosigkeit, fast wie eine Verhöhnung jener, die genau in diesem Moment gefoltert, misshandelt, vergewaltigt, getötet werden. Wie können wir Gedichte schreiben oder Bilder malen oder Vorträge halten, wenn wir wissen, was um uns herum geschieht?

Aber was dann? Hässlichkeit gegen Hässlichkeit, Gewalt gegen Gewalt, Macht gegen Macht ist keine Revolution. Revolution, die radikale Umwälzung der Welt kann nicht symmetrisch sein: Wenn sie es ist, ist es keine Umwälzung, sondern bloß die Reproduktion desselben Gegenstands mit anderem Aussehen. Asymmetrie ist der Schlüssel zu revolutionärem Denken und Handeln. Wenn wir kämpfen, um etwas anderes zu schaffen, dann muss unser Kampf ebenfalls etwas Anderes sein.

Die Asymmetrie ist von äußerster Bedeutung, denn wir kämpfen nicht nur gegen eine Gruppe von Menschen, sondern gegen eine Art und Weise, Dinge zu tun, gegen eine Form, die Welt zu organisieren. Das Kapital ist ein gesellschaftliches Verhältnis, eine Weise, in der Menschen mit anderen in Beziehung treten. Das Kapital ist der Feind, aber das bedeutet, dass der Feind eine bestimmte Form der gesellschaftlichen Verhältnisse ist, eine Form gesellschaftlicher Organisation, die auf der Unterdrückung unserer Selbstbestimmung über unser eigenes Tun, auf der Objektivierung des Subjektes, auf Ausbeutung basiert. Unser Kampf für eine andere Welt muss bedeuten, den gesellschaftlichen Verhältnissen, die wir bekämpfen, andere entgegenzusetzen. Wenn wir symmetrisch kämpfen, wenn wir die Methoden und Formen der Organisierung des Feindes in unserem Kampf akzeptieren, dann reproduzieren wir ausschließlich das Kapital innerhalb unserer Gegnerschaft zu ihm . Wenn wir auf dem Terrain des Kapitals kämpfen, verlieren wir, selbst wenn wir gewinnen.

Aber worin besteht diese Asymmetrie, diese Andersheit, die wir dem Kapital entgegensetzen?

Zuallererst bedeutet Asymmetrie Ablehnung, die Ablehnung des Kapitals und seiner Formen. Nein, wir akzeptieren nicht. Nein, wir akzeptieren nicht, dass die Welt vom Profit geleitet werden sollte. Nein, wir lehnen es ab, unser Leben dem Geld unterzuordnen. Nein, wir werden nicht auf deinem Terrain kämpfen, wir werden nicht tun, was du von uns erwartest. Nein!

Unser Nein ist eine Schwelle. Dahinter eröffnet sich eine neue Welt, eine Welt anderen Tuns. Nein, wir werden unser Leben nicht nach den Erfordernissen des Kapitals gestalten, wir werden tun, was wir für notwendig oder wünschenswert halten. Wir werden nicht unter dem Kommando des Kapitals arbeiten, wir werden etwas anderes tun. Einer Form von Aktivität setzen wir eine ganz andere Form von Aktivität entgegen. Marx bezog sich auf den Unterschied zwischen diesen beiden Formen von Aktivität als den „Doppelcharakter der Arbeit" und er insistierte, dass dieser Doppelcharakter der Arbeit „der Springpunkt ist, um den sich das Verständnis der politischen Ökonomie dreht" (Marx 1989: 56) – und dadurch der des Kapitalismus. Er bezog sich auf die zwei Seiten der Arbeit als „abstrakte Arbeit" auf der einen und der „konkreten oder nützlichen Arbeit" auf der anderen Seite. Abstrakte Arbeit verweist auf die Abstraktion, die der Markt dem Akt des Schaffens auferlegt: Sie ist jeder Konkretion entleert, ihrer besonderen Merkmalen beraubt, sodass eine Arbeit der anderen gleicht. Es ist entfremdete Arbeit, von den Menschen, die sie leisten, entfremdete oder abstrahierte oder abgespaltene Arbeit. (Das Konzept der abstrakten Arbeit hat nichts mit dem materiellen oder immateriellen Charakter der Arbeit zu tun.) Konkrete oder nützliche Arbeit geht auf die kreative Aktivität zurück, die in jeder Gesellschaft existiert und die potenziell nicht-entfremdet, frei von Fremdbestimmung ist. Um die Unterscheidung noch etwas klarer zu machen, werden wir von abstrakter Arbeit auf der einen und nützlich-kreativem Tun auf der anderen Seite sprechen.

Unser Nein öffnet die Tür zu einem nützlich-kreativen Tun, zu einer auf dem Gebrauchswert und nicht dem Tauschwert basierenden Welt, einer Welt des Tuns, das in Richtung Selbstbestimmung drängt. Wo ist diese Welt? Die orthodoxe marxistische Theorie sagt uns, dass sie in der Zukunft existiert, nach der Revolution, aber das ist nicht wahr. Sie existiert hier und jetzt, aber sie existiert in den Rissen, in den Schatten, immer auf der Schwelle zur Unmöglichkeit. Ihr Kern ist das nützlich-kreative Tun, das Drängen in Richtung Selbstbestimmung, das in der, gegen die und jenseits der abstrakten Arbeit existiert. Sie existiert innerhalb der abstrakten Arbeit in der alltäglichen Aktivität von uns allen, die wir unsere Arbeitskraft verkaufen, um zu überleben; sie existiert gegen die abstrakte Arbeit in der andauernden Revolte gegen diese selbst, sowohl von innerhalb der Beschäftigungsverhältnisse als auch in der Verweigerung, in sie einzutreten; und sie existiert jenseits der abstrakten Arbeit in den Versuchen von Millionen von Menschen überall auf der Welt, ihr Leben – individuell oder kollektiv – dem zu widmen, was sie für notwendig oder wünschenswert halten.

Wenn der Kapitalismus als Kommandosystem verstanden wird, dann können diese Versuche, dieses Tun, das sich gegen die abstrakte Arbeit und darüber hinaus (aus)richtet, als Risse im System verstanden werden. Es sind die Leute, die individuell oder kollektiv, manchmal in aller Deutlichkeit sagen „Nein, wir machen nicht, was uns das Geld befiehlt, wir, an diesem Ort, in diesem Moment, werden tun, was wir für notwendig und wünschenswert halten und wir werden jene gesellschaftlichen Verhältnisse schaffen, die wir haben wollen." Diese Risse mögen so klein sein, dass niemand sie sieht (die Entscheidung einer Malerin, ihr Leben der Malerei zu widmen, was auch immer die Konsequenzen sein mögen), oder sie mögen größer sein (die Gründung einer alternativen Schule, oder die Ausrichtung einer Konferenz, zum Beispiel), oder sie mögen riesig sein (die Revolte der Zapatistas, oder die der Piqueter@s oder jene der Indigenen in Bolivien). Diese Risse sind immer widersprüchlich (es kann niemals rein antikapitalistische Orte innerhalb der kapitalistischen Welt geben) und sie existieren immer am Rande der Unmöglichkeit, weil sie gegen den herrschenden Fluss der Welt hervortreten. Besser als irgendjemand sonst wissen KünstlerInnen vielleicht , dass es schwierig ist, alleine von Leidenschaft zu leben. Und dennoch ist es das, was viele KünstlerInnen tun: Trotz der Schwierigkeiten, stellen sie ihr kreatives Tun vor die abstrakte Arbeit, stellen sie den Gebrauchswert vor den Tauschwert, lehnen sie es ab, die Logik des Geldes zu akzeptieren und versuchen, zu leben. Nicht alle, aber viele.

Trotz der Tatsache, dass sie der Logik der Welt entgegenstehen, existieren diese Risse überall, und je mehr wir uns auf sie konzentrieren, desto mehr erkennen wir, dass die Welt voll von Rissen ist, voll von Leuten, die sich weigern, sich anzupassen und die es ablehnen, ihr Leben unterzuordnen. Von Rissen zu sprechen hat nichts mit Marginalität zu tun: Es gibt nichts Gewöhnlicheres als antikapitalistisch zu sein. Die Revolution ist ganz einfach die Anerkennung, Schaffung, Ausweitung und Multiplikation dieser Risse. (Ich rede von Rissen statt von Autonomien, um drei Punkte zu betonen: Erstens, dass sie Brüche sind, die in der Negation wurzeln, und dass sie sich gegen das herrschende Fließen richten. Zweitens, dass sie Brüche in Bewegung sind – Risse laufen, weiten sich aus oder werden gekittet. Und drittens, dass eine Welt von Rissen eine fragmentierte Welt ist, eine Welt der Besonderheiten, in der die Risse dazu tendieren, sich zu verbinden, aber nicht notwendigerweise zur Einheit.)

Unsere Vision der Welt ändert sich, sobald wir in eine andere Welt eintreten, eine nicht auf abstrakter Arbeit sondern auf nützlich-kreativem Tun, eine nicht auf Tauschwert sondern Gebrauchswert basierende Welt. Das ist die Welt des Kommunismus, aber sie ist nicht (oder nicht nur) in der Zukunft, sondern eine Welt, die bereits hier und jetzt existiert, in den Rissen, als Bewegung. Die Welt des Kapitalismus erscheint eindimensional, aber sie ist es nicht. Nie werden alle Alternativen vollständig eingeebnet. Es gibt immer eine andere Dimension, eine Dimension des Widerstands, der Andersheit – die Welt des Kommunismus, die in den Rissen existiert, in den Schatten, eine unterirdische Welt.

Diese halb unsichtbare Welt ist eine Welt des Schmerzes, aber nicht des Leidens. Es ist eine Welt des Schmerzes, weil die andere Welt, die Welt der abstrakten Arbeit, auf ihr sitzt und sie unterdrückt. Die Welt abstrakter Arbeit ist eine Welt des Geldes, der Dinge, eine Welt fetischisierter gesellschaftlicher Verhältnisse, der Objektivierung menschlicher Subjekte, der Objektivierung bis zum Mord, zur Vergewaltigung und zur Folter. Der Schmerz, aber nicht das Leiden befindet sich im Zentrum unserer Welt. Das Leiden bedeutet die Objektivierung zu akzeptieren. Aber unsere Welt ist die Welt des Subjektes, das gegen ihre Objektivierung kämpft, es ist die Welt der Schaffenden, die gegen die Negation ihrer Kreativität kämpft. Unser Schmerz ist nicht der Schmerz des Leidens, sondern der Schmerz des gequälten Schreis, der Schmerz von Verletzung und Wut, der Schmerz, der uns zum Handeln bewegt.

Unser Schmerz ist der Schmerz der Würde.
In unserem Herzen war so viel Schmerz, so viel Tod und Verletzung, dass es nicht länger passte, Brüder, in diese Welt, die unsere Großeltern uns gaben, um weiter darin zu leben und zu kämpfen. So groß war der Schmerz, dass er nicht länger in die Herzen einiger weniger Menschen passte, und er lief über und füllte andere Herzen mit Kummer und Schmerz, und die Herzen der Ältesten und Weisesten unserer Völker füllten sich, und die Herzen der jungen Männer und Frauen sie alle gewappnet, füllten sich, und die Herzen der Kinder, selbst der kleinsten, füllten sich, und die Herzen der Tiere und der Pflanzen füllten sich mit Schmerz und Kummer, und das Herz der Steine, und unsere ganze Welt war erfüllt von Schmerz und Leid, und der Wind und die Sonne fühlten den Kummer und den Schmerz, und die Erde fühlte den Kummer und den Schmerz. Alles war Schmerz und Kummer, alles war Stille.

Dann brachte uns das Leiden, das uns verband, zum Sprechen, und wir erkannten, dass in unseren Worten die Wahrheit lag, wir wussten, dass nicht nur Schmerz und Leiden in unserer Zunge lebte, wir erkannten, dass es immer noch Hoffnung gibt in unseren Herzen. Wir sprachen mit uns selbst, wir sahen in uns hinein und sahen in unsere Geschichte: Wir sahen die meisten unserer Vorfahren leiden und kämpfen, wir sahen unsere Großväter kämpfen, wir sahen unsere Väter mit Wut handeln, wir sahen, dass uns nicht alles weggenommen worden war, dass wir das Wertvollste hatten, das, was uns am Leben erhält, das, was unseren Schritt über die Pflanzen und Tiere erhob, das, was den Stein neben unsere Füße legte, und wir sahen, Brüder, dass alles, was wir hatten, die WÜRDE war. Und wir sahen, dass die Scham groß darüber war, dass wir das vergessen hatten, und wir sahen, dass WÜRDE gut für Menschen war, um wieder Mensch zu werden und so begann die Würde wieder in unseren Herzen zu leben und wir waren wieder neu, und die Toten, unsere Toten, sahen, dass wir neu waren und sie riefen uns wieder, zur Würde, zum Kampf. (Brief des Geheimen Revolutionären Indigenen Rates [CCRI] der EZLN vom Januar 1994)

Unsere Welt ist nicht nur eine Welt des Schmerzes, sondern eine Welt der Würde. Würde ist die Weigerung in uns, die Weigerung, sich zu unterwerfen, die Verweigerung, ein Objekt zu sein und deshalb ist es mehr als eine einfache Verweigerung. Wenn ich es ablehne, ein Objekt zu sein, dann behaupte ich mich immer noch als Subjekt gegenüber allem, was mich auf den Status des Objekts reduziert, und ich gestalte, ich gestalte anders. Würde ist die Affirmation nützlichkreativen Tuns gegen die Abstraktion der Arbeit, hier und jetzt und nicht in der Zukunft. Würde ist die Affirmation dessen, dass wir keine Opfer sind. Wir werden ausgebeutet, erniedrigt, unterdrückt, gefoltert: Aber wir sind keine Opfer. Warum? Weil wir trotz allem über das verfügen, was uns über Pflanzen und Tiere erhebt: Wir haben immer noch etwas, das jenseits davon existiert, etwas, das unsere Erniedrigung und unsere Objektivierung überflutet. Es liegt eine Welt der Differenz zwischen einer Politik der Würde und einer Politik des armen Opfers. Opfer sind die unterdrückten Massen, sie brauchen Anführer, hierarchische Strukturen. Die Welt der Opfer ist die Welt der Macht, eine Welt, die sich bestens in die Strukturen des Staates, die Welt der Partei, die Welt des Monologes eingliedert. Aber wenn wir von der Würde ausgehen, wenn wir von dem Subjekt ausgehen, die gegen ihre und jenseits ihrer Objektivierung existierten, führt uns dies zu einer vollkommen anderen Politik, einer Politik des Dialoges statt des Monologes, des Zuhörens statt des Redens. Es führt uns nicht zu einer Politik der Parteien und der hierarchischen Strukturen, sondern zu einer Politik der Versammlungen oder der Räte, zu Formen der Organisierung, die darauf abzielen, die Stimmen der Würde zu artikulieren, eine Politik, die nicht darauf abzielt, die vom Staat symbolisierte instrumentelle Macht (power over) zu erringen, sondern die kreative Macht (power to do), die von unten kommt, zu stärken. Auch eine Politik des Tuns, nicht des Beklagens. Opfer beklagen sich, Würde tut.

Würde bedeutet die Anerkennung dessen, dass wir in uns selbst gespalten (self-devided) sind, jede/r und alle von uns. Würde ist ein Antagonismus in uns selbst, ein Selbst-Antagonismus, der vom Leben in einer selbst-antagonistischen Gesellschaft nicht zu trennen ist, ein Sich-Wenden nicht nur gegen den Kapitalismus sondern auch gegen uns selbst. Wir unterwerfen uns, aber wir tun es nicht. Wir erlauben uns selbst, als Objekte behandelt zu werden, aber dann heben wir unsere Köpfe und sagen Nein, wir sind kreative Subjekte. Während wir das Kapital zerschlagen, brechen wir uns selbst. Würde ist eine Ek-stase in uns selbst, ein aus uns heraus- und gegen uns vor- und über uns hinausgehen. Wir wären Opfer, hätten wir nicht diese ek-statische Würde in uns, die uns die Steine unter den Füßen hält. Die Steine sind unter unseren Füßen, weil sie keine Würde haben. Wenn wir auf sie treten, bleiben sie als Betretene zurück. Steine sind Identitäten: Sie sind. Unsere ek-statische Würde ist unsere Nicht-Identität, oder besser, unsere Anti-Identität, unsere Verweigerung einfach zu sein. Das Kapital erzwingt eine Identität und sagt uns, dass wir sind. Unsere Würde erwidert, dass wir nicht sind: Wir sind nicht, weil wir tun, wir (er)schaffen und indem wir es tun, negieren und erschaffen wir uns selbst. Wir übersprudeln alle Identitäten, all die Rollen und Personifizierungen und Charaktermasken, die das Kapital uns aufdrückt. Wir überquellen alle Klassifizierungen. Das Kapital bürdet uns Klassifizierungen auf, teilt uns in Klassen (ein). Unser Kampf ist ein Klassenkampf, aber nicht, um unsere Klassenidentität zu stärken, sondern um damit zu brechen, um Klassen aufzulösen, um uns von allen Klassifizierungen zu befreien. Das ist wichtig, denn, unter anderem macht es Sektierertum unmöglich. Sektierertum basiert auf identitärem (d. h. kapitalistischem) Denken: Es bezeichnet, und begreift Menschen als klar in eine Klassifizierung passend. Wenn unser Ausgangspunkt die Würde ist, heißt das zu akzeptieren, dass wir und andere widersprüchlich, selbst-antagonistisch, übersprudelnd, unklassifizierbar sind.

Indem wir die Identität überfluten, übersprudeln wir die Zeit selbst. Die identitäre Zeit, die Zeit der Uhren. Unsere Welt des Schmerzes und der Würde, unsere schattenhafte Welt des Tuns gegen-die-und-über-die-Arbeit hinaus ist eine Welt der noch-nicht-gestorbenen-Toten, eine Welt der noch nicht geborenen Neugeborenen. Unsere Toten sind nicht tot, sie warten. Wie sowohl die ZapatistInnen als auch Walter Benjamin deutlich gemacht haben, erwarten die Toten ihre Erlösung. Wir sahen unsere Väter mit Wut handeln und nun ist es an uns, sie zu erlösen. Sie haben es während ihrer Lebzeiten nicht geschafft, eine Welt der Würde zu schaffen und jetzt ist es an uns, sie zu erlösen. Diese Welt der Würde, für die unsere Vorfahren gekämpft haben, ist eine Welt, die noch nicht existiert, aber das bedeutet, dass sie als Noch-Nicht existiert, wie Ernst Bloch uns gelehrt hat. Wenn die Kämpfe der Vergangenheit in der Gegenwart unserer Welt existieren, so gilt das auch für die mögliche Zukunft. Sie existiert tatsächlich als Noch-Nicht, in den Rissen, in unseren Träumen, in unseren Kämpfen, in unseren Brüchen mit der herrschenden Welt, in unseren Kreationen, die eine andere Welt ankündigen, in der immer fragilen Existenz der möglichen Zukunft in der Gegenwart.

Fragil, schattenhaft, halb unsichtbar, auf der Schwelle zum Unmöglichen schwankend: Das ist die Welt, in der wir leben, arme verrückte Rebellinnen und Rebellen, die über keine Gewissheiten verfügen außer über diese eine: unseren Schrei des Nein gegen den Kapitalismus, gegen diese Welt, die uns und die Menschheit zerstört. Manchmal erscheint alles hoffnungslos. Unsere Würde existiert zwar die ganze Zeit über, aber manchmal scheint sie zu schlafen, betäubt von Geld, Arbeit oder Angst. Unsere Ek-stase existiert immer, aber manchmal scheint sie erdrückt unter dem Gewicht der Routine. Unsere Nicht-Identität existiert, aber manchmal scheint sie vollkommen gefangen im eisernen Käfig der Identität. Das Noch-Nicht existiert, aber manchmal scheint es fest an die Zeiger der Uhr und ihr Tick-Tack gebunden, Tick-Tack, Keine-Hoffnung, Tick-Tack, Keine-Hoffnung.

Wie erwacht unsere Würde? Wie kommt sie mit anderen Würden in Berührung? Wie sprechen unsere Würden miteinander? Wir sind „sin voz" (ohne Stimme), wie die Zapatistas gesagt haben. Das hat nicht nur damit zu tun, dass wir keinen Zugang zu Radio- und Fernsehsendern haben, sondern auch mit einem tieferen Grund. Unser Kampf, der nicht-identitär in dem Sinne ist, dass er sich gegen Identitäten und über sie hinaus richtet, ist in dem gleichen Sinne auch ein antibegrifflicher Kampf, ein Kampf, der Konzepte durchbricht und über sie hinausreicht, der sich gegen die Sprache der Konzeptualität richtet. Das Konzept identifiziert, schließt ein und ist deshalb unbrauchbar um das zu fassen, was mit Identitäten bricht. Die Sprache der Würde muss sich in Begriffen ausdrücken (um zu verstehen und zu kritisieren, was wir tun), aber sie muss auch über das Begriffliche hinausgehen, muss nach anderen Formen des Ausdrucks Ausschau halten. Revolutionäre Theorie muss folglich beides sein, rigoros und poetisch.

Unsere Welt ist eine Welt auf der Suche nach einer Sprache, nicht nur jetzt sondern permanent, zum Teil weil die andere Welt, die der abstrakten Arbeit, uns die ganze Zeit über die Sprache stiehlt, aber auch weil wir immer neue Formen des Tuns und neue Formen des Kampfers erfinden. Gesellschaftstheorie, Kunst und Poesie sind alle Teil dieser permanenten Suche.

Wahrscheinlich haben die Zapatistas diese Suche und die Einheit von Ästhetik und Revolution besser verstanden als alle anderen Gruppen. Ich beziehe mich dabei nicht nur auf die Sprache der Kommuniqués, sondern auch auf ihren tiefgründigen Sinn für Theater und Symbolik. Als sie am 1. Januar 1994 ihren Aufstand begannen, brachten sie nicht nur ihre eigene Würde zum Ausdruck, sondern erweckten unsere Würden zum Leben. „Als mehr und mehr Kommuniqués der Aufständischen veröffentlicht wurden, realisierten wir, dass die Revolte in Wirklichkeit aus den Tiefen unserer Selbst kam", merkte Antonio García de León an. Die Würde der Zapatistas in Chiapas schuf eine Resonanz mit unseren schlummernden Würden und weckte sie auf.

Eine Politik der Würde ist eine Politik der Resonanz. Wir erkennen die Würde in den Menschen um uns herum, im Sitz neben uns, auf der Straße, im Supermarkt, und versuchen, eine Verbindung dazu herzustellen. Es handelt sich nicht um die Frage der Bildung der Massen oder darum, ihnen Bewusstsein zu bringen, es geht darum, das Rebellische zu erkennen, das untrennbar zur Unterdrückung gehört, das Rebellische, das in uns allen ist, und zu versuchen, dessen Wellenlänge zu treffen, zu versuchen, es in ein Treffen der Würden einzubinden. Es geht nicht darum, die Menschen vollständig zu überzeugen, sondern darum, etwas in ihnen zu berühren. Das ist sicherlich die Frage, die hinter jedem antikapitalistischen politischen Handeln stehen sollte: Wie erzeugen wir Resonanzen mit den Würden um uns herum? Diese Frage gerät leicht aus dem Blick, wenn wir uns geschlossene, identitäre Begriffe für unseren Kampf zu eigen machen.

Wie erzeugen wir Resonanzen mit den Würden um uns herum?

Zuerst brauchen wir eine geschärfte Sensibilität, um die vielen Formen des Rebellischen gegen Unterdrückung, und folglich die Zurückweisung jedes Dogmatismus, zu erkennen. Wir müssen das Unhörbare hören, das Unsichtbare sehen.

Eine Welt der Würde kann nicht eine Welt des „Ich weiß, Du weißt nicht" sein. Es ist eine Welt geteilten Nicht-Wissens. Was uns vereint ist, das wir wissen, dass wir die Welt verändern müssen, aber wir wissen nicht, wie. Dies bedeutet eine Politik des fragenden Zuhörens, aber es bedeutet auch permanentes Experimentieren. Wir wissen nicht, wie wir mit den Würden um uns herum in Berührung kommen sollen, also lasst uns experimentieren!

Lasst uns experimentieren, aber im Kopf behalten, dass die einzig sinnvolle Kunst, und die einzig sinnvolle Gesellschaftstheorie, jene Kunst (oder Gesellschaftstheorie) ist, die sich selbst als Teil des Kampfes den Kapitalismus zu brechen, die die gegenwärtige Gesellschaft zu überwinden versteht. Dies bedeutet, das, was wir tun, als (zweifelsohne ketzerischen) Teil einer Bewegung zu verstehen, oder als Bewegung von Bewegungen. Und immer mit dem zentralen Prinzip der Asymmetrie. Wir wollen nicht sie sein, wir wollen nicht sein wie sie.

Fragend schreiten wir voran.

Aus dem Englischen übersetzt von Jens Kastner und Lars Stubbe.

Literatur:

Marx, Karl (1989): Das Kapital. Kritik der politischen Ökonomie, Erster Band, Berlin (Dietz Verlag), 33. Aufl.

* Vortrag, gehalten an der Primera Cátedra Latinoamericana de Historia y Teoría del Arte Alberto Urdaneta, Museo de Arte Universidad Nacional, Bogotá, Kolumbien, am 17. September 2007.

On Poetry and Revolution*

John Holloway

It is an honour and an excitement to be in a different world, a strange world of artists. When I was trying to think what I could possibly say about art to artists, I remembered that a few months ago, someone described me as the poet of the altermundista movement. I do not know why he said that, but I was very flattered, even though I knew that the person who said it intended it as an insult, or at least a disqualification. He meant it as an insult because he was saying that revolutionary theory should not be confused with poetry. Poetry is dangerous because it has to do with a beautiful but unreal world, whereas revolutionary theory is about the real world of hard struggle. In this real world of struggle, poetry and art and beauty do not play an important role: revolutionary struggle confronts ugliness with ugliness, guns with guns, brutality with brutality. There will be time for poetry and beauty and art after the revolution.

    I do not agree with that argument. On the contrary, I want to argue that revolutionary theory and practice must be artistic, or else it is not revolutionary, and also that art must be revolutionary or it is not art.

    (Forgive me if I speak of revolution. I know that it is a word that is out of fashion. It is just that I take as a starting point that we all know that capitalism is a catastrophe for humanity, and that if we do not succeed in getting rid of it, if we do not succeed in changing the world radically, it is very possible that we humans will not survive for very long. That is why I speak of revolution.)

Famously, Adorno said that after Auschwitz it was impossible to write poetry. We do not have to think back the sixty years to Auschwitz to understand what he meant. We have enough horrors closer at hand, especially in the world of today (Abu Ghraib, Guantánamo). In this world, to think of creating something beautiful seems a terrible insensitivity, almost a mockery of those who, at this very moment, are being tortured, brutalised, raped, killed. How we can write poetry or paint pictures or give talks when we know what is happening around us?

But then what? Ugliness against ugliness, violence against violence, power against power, is no revolution. Revolution, the radical transformation of the world cannot be symmetrical: if it is, there is no transformation, simply the reproduction of the same thing with different faces. Asymmetry is the key to revolutionary thought and practice. If we are struggling to create something different, then our struggle too must be something different.

Asymmetry is all-important because what we are fighting against is not a group of people but a way of doing things, a form of organising the world. Capital is a social relation, a form in which people relate to one another. Capital is the enemy, but this means that the enemy is a certain form of social relations, a form of social organisation based on the suppression of our determination of our own doing, on the objectification of the subject, on exploitation. Our struggle for a different world has to mean opposing different social relations to the ones that we are fighting against. If we struggle symmetrically, if we accept the methods and forms of organisation of the enemy in our struggle, then all we are doing is reproducing capital within our opposition to it. If we fight on the terrain of capital, then we lose, even if we win.

But what is this asymmetry, this otherness, that we oppose to capital?

In the first place, asymmetry means refusal, refusal of capital and its forms. No, we do not accept. No we do not accept that the world should be driven by profit. No, we refuse to subordinate our lives to money. No we shall not fight on your terrain, we shall not do what you expect us to do. No!

Our No is a threshold. It opens to another world, to a world of other doing. No, we shall not shape our lives according to the requirements of capital, we shall do what we consider necessary or desirable. We shall not labour under the command of capital, we shall do something else. To one type of activity we oppose a very different type of activity. Marx referred to the contrast between these two types of activity as the "two-fold character of labour" and he insisted that this two-fold character of labour is "the pivot on which a comprehension of political economy turns" (Marx 1965: 41) – and therefore of capitalism. He refers to the two sides of labour as "abstract labour" on the one hand, and "concrete or useful labour" on the other. Abstract labour refers to the abstraction which the market imposes on the act of creation: it is emptied of all concreteness, abstracted from its particular characteristics, so that one labour is just the same as another. It is alienated labour, labour that is alienated or abstracted or separated from the people who perform it. (The concept of abstract labour has nothing to do with the material or immaterial nature of the labour.) Concrete or useful labour refers to the creative activity that exists in any society and that is potentially unalienated, free from alien determination. To make the distinction a bit more clear, we shall speak of abstract labour on the one hand, and useful-creative doing on the other.

Our No opens the door to a world of useful-creative doing, a world based on use value not on value, a world of a doing that pushes towards self-determination. Where is this world? Orthodox Marxist theory tells us that it exists in the future, after the revolution, but this is not true. It exists here and now, but it exists in the cracks, in the shadows, always on the edge of impossibility. Its core is useful-creative doing, the push towards self-determination which exists in, against and beyond abstract labour. It exists in abstract labour in the daily activity of all of us who sell our labour power in order to survive, against in the constant revolt against abstract labour both from within employment and in the refusal to enter into employment, and it exists beyond abstract labour in the attempts of millions and millions of people all over the world to dedicate their lives, individually or collectively, to what they consider necessary or desirable.

If capitalism is understood as a system of command, then these attempts, these doings that go against and beyond abstract labour, can be understood as cracks in the system. It is people saying, individually, collectively, sometimes massively "No, we shall not do what money commands, we, in this place, at this moment, shall do what we consider to be necessary or desirable, and we shall create the social relations that we want to have." These cracks may be so small that nobody sees them (the decision of a painter say to devote her life to painting, whatever the consequences) or they may be bigger (the creation of an alternative school, or a conference, for example) or they may be huge (the revolt of the zapatistas, or the piqueteros, or of the indigenous in Bolivia). These cracks are always contradictory (they can never be pure non-capitalist spaces in a capitalist world) and they always exist on the brink of impossibility, because they are standing out against the dominant flow of the world. As artists know perhaps better than anybody, it is difficult to exist on passion alone. And yet that is what many artists do: in spite of the difficulties, they put their creative doing before abstract labour, they put use value before value, they refuse to accept the logic of money and try to live. Not all, but many.

Despite the fact that they stand against the logic of the world, these cracks exist all over the place, and the more we focus on them, the more we see that the world is full of cracks, full of people refusing to conform, refusing to subordinate their lives. To speak of cracks has nothing to do with marginality: there is nothing more common than being anti-capitalist. Revolution is quite simply the recognition, creation, expansion and multiplication of these cracks. (I speak of cracks rather than autonomies to emphasise three points: first, that they are ruptures which are rooted in negation, that they go against the dominant flow; second, that they are ruptures in movement – cracks run, they expand or are filled; and third, that a world of cracks is a fragmented world, a world of particularities in which the cracks tend to join up, but do not necessarily tend towards unity.)

Our vision of the world changes as we enter into another world, a world based not on abstract labour but on useful-creative doing, not on value but on use value. This is the world of communism, but it is not (or not only) in the future, but a world that already exists here and now, in the cracks, as movement. The world of capitalism appears to be one-dimensional, but it is not. There is never a total flattening of alternatives. There is always another dimension, a dimension of resistance, of otherness – the world of communism that exists in the cracks, in the shadows, a subterranean world.

This half-invisible world is a world of pain, but not of suffering. It is a world of pain because the other world, the world of abstract labour, sits on top of it, suppresses and represses it. The world of abstract labour is a world of money, of things, of fetishised social relations, of the objectification of human subjects, objectification to the point of murder, rape and torture. Pain is at the centre of our world, but not suffering. Suffering implies the acceptance of objectification. But our world is the world of the subject struggling against her objectification, of the creator struggling against the negation of her creativity. Our pain is not the pain of suffering, but the pain of an anguished scream, the pain of hurt-and-rage, the pain that moves us to act.

Our pain is the pain of dignity.

In our heart there was so much pain, so much death and hurt, that it no longer fitted, brothers in this world that our grandparents gave us to carry on living and struggling. So great was the pain and the hurt that it no longer fitted in the heart of a few people and it overflowed and filled other hearts with pain and hurt, and the hearts of the oldest and wisest of our peoples were filled, and the hearts of the young men and women, all of them brace, were filled, and the hearts of the children, even the smallest, were filled, and the hearts of the animals and plants were filled with hurt and pain, and the heart of the stones, and all our world was filled with hurt and pain, and the wind and the sun felt the hurt and the pain, and the earth was in hurt and pain. All was hurt and pain, all was silence.

Then that suffering that united us made us speak, and we recognised that in our words there was truth, we knew that not only pain and suffering lived in our tongue, we recognised that there is hope still in our hearts. We spoke with ourselves, we looked inside ourselves and we looked at our history: we saw our most ancient fathers suffering and struggling, we saw our grandfathers struggling, we saw our fathers with fury in their hands, we saw that not everything had been taken away from us, that we had the most valuable, that which made us live, that which made our step rise above plants and animals, that which made the stone be beneath our feet, and we saw, brothers, that all that we had was DIGNITY, and we saw that great was the shame of having forgotten it, and we saw that DIGNITY was good for men to be men again, and dignity returned to live in our hearts, and we were new again, and the dead, our dead, saw that we were new again and they called us again, to dignity, to struggle. (Carta del CCRI, 1/2/1994)

Our world is not just a world of pain, but a world of dignity. Dignity is the refusal inside us, the refusal to submit, the refusal to be an object, and therefore it is more than mere refusal. If I refuse to be an object, then I assert that, in spite of everything that reduces me to the level of an object, I am still a subject and I create, I create differently. Dignity is the affirmation of useful-creative doing against the abstraction of labour, here and now and not in the future. Dignity is the affirmation that we are not victims. We are exploited, humiliated, repressed, tortured: but we are not victims. Why? Because in spite of everything, we still have that "which made our step rise above plants and animals": we still have something that goes beyond, something that overflows our humiliation, our objectification. There is a world of difference between a politics of dignity and a politics of the poor victim. Victims are the downtrodden masses, they need leaders, hierarchical structures. The world of victims is a world of power, a world that dovetails neatly with the structures of the state, the world of the party, the world of the monologue. But if we start from dignity, if we start from the subject that exists against and beyond her objectification, this takes us to a very different politics, a politics of dialogue not of monologue, of listening not of talking, a politics not of parties and hierarchical structures but of assemblies or councils, forms of organisation that seek to articulate the voices of dignity, a politics that seeks not to win the power-over symbolised by the state, but to strengthen the power-to-do that comes from below. A politics too of doing, not of complaining. Victims complain, dignity does.

Dignity means the recognition that we are self-divided, each and all of us. Dignity is a self-antagonism within us, a self-antagonism inseparable from living in a self-antagonistic society, a turning not only against capitalism but also against ourselves. We submit, but we do not. We allow ourselves to be treated as objects, but then raise our heads and say no, we are creative subjects. Breaking capital, we break ourselves. Dignity is an ec-stasy within us, a standing out and against and beyond. We would be victims if we did not have this ec-static dignity within us that keeps the stones beneath our feet. The stones are beneath our feet because they have no dignity. If we tread upon them, they remain trodden upon. Stones are identities: they are. Our ec-static dignity is our non-identity, or, better, our anti-identity, our refusal to simply be. Capital imposes an identity, tells us that we are. Our dignity replies that no, we are not: we are not, because we do, we create and, in doing so, we negate and create ourselves. We overflow all identities, all the roles and personifications and character-masks that capital imposes upon us. We overflow all classifications. Capital imposes classifications upon us, divides us into classes. Our struggle is a class struggle, but not strengthen our class identity but to break it, to dissolve classes, to free us from all classification. This is important ,because, among other things, it makes sectarianism impossible. Sectarianism is based upon identitarian (that is, capitalist) thought: it labels, conceives of people as fitting neatly within a classification. If our starting point is dignity, this means the acceptance that we and others are contradictory, self-antagonistic, overflowing, unclassifiable.

Overflowing identity, we overflow time itself, identitarian time, clock time. Our world of pain and dignity, our shadowy world of doing against-and-beyond labour is a world of the dead-not-dead, of the born-not-yet-born. Our dead are not dead, they are waiting. As both the Zapatistas and Walter Benjamin make clear, the dead are awaiting their redemption. We saw our fathers with fury in their hands and now it us up to us to redeem them. They did not manage to create a world of dignity in their lifetime, now it is up to us to redeem them. This world of dignity that our ancestors fought for is a world that does not yet exist, but that means that it exists not yet, as Ernst Bloch tells us. If the struggles of the past exist in the present of our world, so too does the future possible. It really exists not yet, in the cracks, in our dreams, in our struggles, in our breaks from the dominant world, in our creations that prefigure another world, in the always fragile existence of the possible future in the present.

Fragile, shadowy, half-invisible, teetering on the brink of impossibility: that is the world in which we live, poor mad rebels who have no certainties but one - our scream of No against capitalism, against this world that is destroying us and destroying all humanity. Sometimes it all seems hopeless. Our dignity is there all the time, but sometimes it seems to sleep, drugged by money, labour or fear. Our ec-stasy is always there, but sometimes it seems crushed under the weight of routine. Our non-identity is there, but sometimes it seems totally imprisoned within the iron cage of identity. The not-yet is there, but sometimes it seems tightly bound to the hands of the clock that go tick-tock, no-hope, no-hope.

How does our dignity wake? How does it touch other dignities? How do our dignities speak to one other? We are the "sin voz" (the "without voice"), as the Zapatistas put it. This is not just because we have no access to the radio and television, but also for a deeper reason. Our struggle, being anti-identitarian in the sense that it goes against and beyond identities, is also anti-conceptual in the same sense, a struggle that breaks through and beyond concepts, that pushes beyond the language of conceptuality. The concept identifies, encloses, and therefore is unable to capture that which breaks beyond identity. The language of dignity must be conceptual (to understand and to criticise what we are doing), but also it must go beyond the conceptual, must explore other forms of expression. Revolutionary theory, then, must be both rigorous and poetic.

Our world is a world in search of a language, not just now but constantly, in part because the other world, that of abstract labour, steals our language all the time, but also because we are always inventing new doings and new forms of struggle. Social theory, art and poetry are all part of this constant search.

It is probably the Zapatistas who have understood this search and the unity of aesthetics and revolution better than any other group. I refer not only to the language of the communiqués but to their profound sense of theatre and symbolism.

When they rose up on the first of January 1994, they not only expressed their own dignity, but brought our dignities to life. ""As more and more rebel communiqués were issued, we realised that in reality the revolt came from the depths of ourselves", as Antonio García de León commented. The dignity of the Zapatistas in Chiapas resonated with our slumbering dignities and awoke them.

A politics of dignity is a politics of resonance. We recognise the dignity in the people around us, in the seat next to us, in the street, in the supermarket, and try to find a way to resonate with it. It is not a question of educating the masses or bringing consciousness to them, it is a question of recognising the rebelliousness that is inseparable from oppression, the rebelliousness that is inside all of us, and of trying to find its wavelength, of trying to engage it in a meeting of dignities. It is not necessarily a question of convincing whole people but of touching something within them. This is surely the question that should be behind all anti-capitalist political action: how do we resonate with the dignities around us? This question easily gets lost when we adopt closed, identitarian conceptions of our struggle.

How do we resonate with the dignities that surround us?
First we need a sharp sensitivity to recognise the many forms of rebelliousness against oppression, and hence the rejection of all dogmatism. We have to hear the inaudible, see the invisible.

A world of dignity can not be a world of "I know, you don't know". It is world of shared not-knowing. What unites us is that we know that we must change the world, but we do not know how to do it. This means a politics of asking-listening, but it also means constant experimentation. We do not know how to touch the dignities that surround us, so let's experiment.

Let's experiment, but bearing in mind that the only art that makes sense, and the only social theory that makes sense, is an art (or social theory) that understands itself as part of the struggle to break capitalism, to overcome present society. This means understanding what we are doing as part (no doubt a heretical part) of a movement, or a movement of movements. And always with the central principle of asymmetry. We do not want to be them, we do not want to be like them.

Asking we walk.

Literature:
Marx, Karl (1965): The Capital. Volume 1, Moscow (Progress Publishers).

* Talk given in the Primera Cátedra Latinoamericana de Historia y Teoría del Arte Alberto Urdaneta, Museo de Arte Universidad Nacional, Bogotá, 17 de septiembre de 2007.

Ein Jahrhundert des Revolutionären Zivilen Ungehorsams

Kurzer Abriss des aktivistischen Zivilen Ungehorsams aus gewaltfrei-anarchistischer Sicht

Lou Marin

Mag Henry David Thoreau (1973) auch schon sehr früh, 1849, in seiner Schrift „Über die Pflicht zum Ungehorsam gegen den Staat" die wichtigste theoretische Grundlage zum individuellen Zivilen Ungehorsam gelegt haben, so waren es doch die von Mohandas K. Gandhi geprägten Kampagnen des explizit so benannten, massenhaften Zivilen Ungehorsams gegen das britische Kolonialreich im 20. Jahrhundert, die den Zivilen Ungehorsam zu einer effizienten, radikalen Aktionsstrategie für entrechtete Minderheiten und unterdrückte Mehrheiten werden ließen. Erst durch die Umsetzung auf der Aktionsebene wurde die theoretische Schrift Thoreaus zum Ausgangspunkt eines breiten- und massenwirksamen Aktionskonzepts des Zivilen Ungehorsams, welches das gesamte 20. Jahrhundert stark beeinflussen sollte. Es trug zum Sturz des größten Kolonialreichs, des British Empire, ebenso bei wie zur Abschaffung des institutionalisierten Rassismus, der Segregation, in den Südstaaten der USA und zum Zusammenbruch der staatssozialistischen Militarismen in Osteuropa.

Gandhi verwandelte dabei Thoreaus Aufruf zum individuellen Ungehorsam gegen den Staat in ein massenwirksames und aktivistisches Widerstandskonzept, das in Südafrika und Indien gleichzeitig für Frauenbefreiung und Befreiung von Rassismus und Kolonialismus sowie für eine antikapitalistische Selbstversorgungswirtschaft eingesetzt wurde. Der libertäre Anti-Kolonialist Gandhi (vgl. Marin 2008) blieb dabei der inhaltlichen Tendenz und ausdrücklichen Zielvorstellung

Thoreaus treu, wonach die beste Regierung diejenige sei, „welche am wenigsten regiert", was darauf hinauslaufe: „Die beste Regierung ist die, welche gar nicht regiert." (Thoreau 1973: 7)

Antikolonialismus und die Kampagne Zivilen Ungehorsams in Indien (1919-1922)

Durch die Kampagne des massenhaften Zivilen Ungehorsams in Transvaal/Südafrika 1913 und die erste große Kampagne des Zivilen Ungehorsams in Indien (1919-1922) wurden Gandhi und seine Konzepte der gewaltfreien direkten Aktion (satyagraha: Festhalten an der Wahrheit) und des Zivilen Ungehorsams weltweit bekannt und in den 1920er Jahren auch weltweit rezipiert, u.a. auch in breitem Ausmaß in der Weimarer Republik. (Vgl. Jahn 1993)

Oft übersehen wird bei diesen ersten Kampagnen des expliziten massenhaften Zivilen Ungehorsams im 20. Jahrhundert die hohe Frauenbeteiligung, ja die Prägung des Aktionscharakters durch die Tatsache, dass Frauen von Anfang an verantwortungsvolle Rollen übernahmen. „Bereits die erste größere satyagraha-Kampagne [...] 1913 in Südafrika wurde mit einem für jene Zeit unter InderInnen unglaublich hohen Anteil an Aktivistinnen durchgeführt. Elf Frauen aus der ‚Tolstoy Farm' und sechzehn AktivistInnen aus dem älteren ‚Phoenix'-ashram, darunter vier Frauen – Gandhis Ehefrau, Kasturba, mit inbegriffen –, nahmen daran teil. Sie protestierten gegen die sogenannten ‚Black Act'-Gesetze zum Migrationsstopp aus Indien; gegen das Verbot zur Überschreitung der Provinzgrenzen von Natal und Transvaal für die indische Minderheit; und gegen eine willkürliche Kopfsteuer, die jeder indische Arbeiter bezahlen musste, der von seinem fünfjährigen Kontraktarbeitsvertrag nach Ableistung entlassen wurde und dann in Südafrika bleiben wollte. Vor allem aber protestierten sie gegen diskriminierende Heiratsgesetze, die Ehen unter christlichen InderInnen bestätigten, diejenigen unter indischen MusliminInnen, Parsis/ZoroastrierInnen und Hindus jedoch rückwirkend für ungültig erklärten. Die sechzehn AktivistInnen aus Phoenix überquerten illegal die Grenze von Natal nach Transvaal und wurden dafür zu drei Monaten harter Zwangsarbeit verurteilt. An den unmenschlichen Bedingungen dieser Zwangsarbeit starben einige satyagrahis. Und die Frauen der ‚Tolstoy Farm', meist Ehefrauen ehemaliger Kontraktarbeiter, übernahmen Leitungsfunktionen beim ‚Newcastle-Marsch', den Gandhi mit 5000 streikenden Kohle-Bergarbeitern und ihren Familien von Natal nach Transvaal durchführte. Trotz zahlreicher Verhaftungen – auch Gandhi wurde festgenommen – konnte der Marsch nicht aufgehalten werden und wurde im Dezember 1913 durch einen Streik von 50000 Bergarbeitern unterstützt, der zur Stilllegung der Bergwerke führte. Der ‚Newcastle-Marsch' wurde für Gandhi zum beispielhaften Vorbild des Salzmarsches und wird etwa in der Oper des Komponisten Philip Glass, ‚Satyagraha', auch in diesem Sinne behandelt." (Marin 2008: 44f.) Glass wurde als 1968er Hippie sozialisiert und reiste, wie viele Intellektuelle seiner Generation, mehrfach nach Indien – ein erster Hinweis auf den Zusammenhang einer bestimmten Gandhi-Interpretation mit 1968.

Die hohe Frauenbeteiligung bei den Massenkampagnen Zivilen Ungehorsams in Indien von 1919 bis 1922 (Generalstreik 1919 und Kampagne für Nicht-Zusammenarbeit 1920-22), 1930/31 (Salzmarsch) und 1942 (Quit-India-Kampagne) charakterisiert die indische Unabhängigkeitsbewegung gleichzeitig als die Phase einer ersten breiten indischen Frauenbewegung.

Auf einen weiteren, weithin in Vergessenheit geratenen Aspekt, der sich bereits in der Aktionsbasis des Newcastle-Marsches unter den indischen Bergarbeiter-Familien herauskristallisierte und dann beim Generalstreik 1919 und der Kampagne für Nicht-Zusammenarbeit 1920-22 in Indien noch verdeutlichte, möchte ich hier hinweisen: den antikapitalistischen Charakter der frühen Massenaktionen des Zivilen Ungehorsams Gandhis. Die indische Kampagne für Nicht-Zusammenarbeit 1920-22 wurde innerhalb der libertären Arbeiterbewegung Europas (etwa in der IAMV, der Internationalen Antimilitaristischen Vereinigung; der niederländischen Solidaritätsgruppe Vrienden van India; bei Personen wie Henriette Roland Holst, Clara Wichmann, Bart de Ligt, Albert de Jong, Arthur Lehning, Pierre Ramus u.a.) auch als Alternative zum sowjetischen bewaffneten Revolutionskonzept von 1917 diskutiert (vgl. Jochheim 1977), weil sie nicht nur die britischen Kolonialherren, sondern auch die gesamte indische kapitalistische Klasse herausgefordert hatte:

„Als Gandhi 1920 seine Bewegung der Nicht-Zusammenarbeit gegen die Briten startete, waren die indischen Textilfabrikanten nahezu als gesamte Klasse gegen ihn. 1920 wurde in Bombay eine ‚Anti-non-cooperation Society' gegründet [...], unter ihren Geldgebern waren die Tatas [größte Unternehmerfamilie Indiens zur damaligen Zeit; heute großer Stahl-, LKW- und Auto-Produzent; d.A.]. Diese Gesellschaft versuchte, die Nicht-Zusammenarbeit durch ‚Counter-Propaganda' zu bekämpfen und sie arbeitete eng mit gemäßigten politischen Führungspersonen zusammen, die in Opposition zu Gandhi standen. Es ist bezeichnend, dass nicht ein einziger Industrieller den satyagraha-Schwur vom März-April 1919 unterzeichnete." (Nanda 1985: 136)

In der Kampagne für Nicht-Zusammenarbeit (oder: Non-Cooperation) 1920-22 bestand das Konzept der gewaltfreien Aktion für Gandhi aus der legalen, den Massen aktiv Beteiligter relativ leicht vermittelbarer Nicht-Zusammenarbeit mit den kolonialen Behörden und Institutionen und auch dem Aufgeben, der Demission oder dem Wechsel von privilegierten und gut bezahlten Berufen, die den Kolonialherren dienten oder mit ihnen in Verbindung standen. Für die Zuspitzung der Kampagne sorgten Aktionen Zivilen Ungehorsams, bei denen sich die AktivistInnen über mögliche Folgen und einsetzende Repression im Klaren waren. Gandhi charakterisierte die politische Aufgabe des Zivilen Ungehorsams im Rahmen der Nicht-Zusammenarbeits-Kampagne in einem zeitgenössischen Artikel seiner Zeitung Young India vom 23. März 1921 wie folgt:

„Zivil-Desobedienz bedeutet Bruch solcher gesetzlicher Vorschriften, die sittlich anfechtbar sind. Der Ausdruck ist meines Wissens von Thoreau geprägt worden. Er bezeichnete damit seinen eigenen Widerstand gegen die Erlasse eines der

Südstaaten der Union, in dem noch Sklaverei herrschte. Er hat einen meisterhaften Aufsatz über die Pflicht zur Zivil-Desobedienz hinterlassen. Doch war Thoreau vielleicht kein überzeugter Vorkämpfer der Non-Violenz. Vermutlich hat er seine Zivil-Desobedienz auf die Steuergesetze beschränkt, während unsere Zivil-Desobedienz vom Jahre 1919 jedem unsittlichen Gesetz gegenüber geltend gemacht wurde. In ihr dokumentierte sich die Missachtung der Gesetze durch den Resistenten in ‚ziviler', d.h. non-violenter Weise. [...] Non-Kooperation bedeutet die Entziehung der Zusammenarbeit (Ko-operation) mit dem Staat, der in den Augen des Non-Kooperationisten korrupt geworden ist, und schließt Zivil-Desobedienz strengster Art aus, wie wir sie oben beschrieben haben. Sie kann selbst von Kindern in ihrem Wesen erfasst und von den großen Massen ohne weiteres durchgeführt werden. [...] Doch ist Non-Kooperation wie Zivil-Desobedienz ein Bestandteil von Satyagraha, das alle Arten non-violenten Widerstandes um der Wahrheit willen umfasst." (Gandhi 1924: 241f.)

Ziviler Ungehorsam war für Gandhi also die illegale gewaltfreie Aktion neben einer für die Massen leichter durchführbaren gewaltfreien Aktion, die den Rahmen der Legalität nicht überschreitet. Beide zusammen bildeten das Gesamtkonzept der gewaltfreien Massenaktion (Satyagraha). In seiner libertären Gandhi-Interpretation weist der indische Sozialpsychologe Ashis Nandy (2008: 178ff.) darauf hin, dass Gandhi auch bei seinen Aktionskampagnen immer wieder experimentierte, den spontaneistischen, geradezu chaplinesken Ausdrucksformen auf der Basis eines vielfältigen und gleichwohl toleranten Volks-Hinduismus Raum zur Entfaltung ließ, was an einzelnen Beispielen des Salzmarsches sogar Parallelen zu späteren politisch-kulturellen Strömungen wie Situationismus und Surrealismus entstehen lässt und Ursache für ein tatsächliches Zusammentreffen zwischen Gandhi und Chaplin war (Marin 2008: 51ff.). Dieser Spontaneismus beinhaltende Ansatz des massenhaften Zivilen Ungehorsams schloss auch das Risiko gewaltsamer Abirrungen mit ein, die zwischen 1919 und 1922 zweimal durch Abbruch der Massenkampagnen korrigiert werden mussten. Jedenfalls ist der Aspekt des „Experiments" bei Gandhis Kampagnen nach Nandys Interpretation höher anzusetzen als Aspekte der Disziplin bei der Ausbildung von Satyagrahis in den Gandhi-Ashrams, die es auch gab. Trotzdem blieben die Massenkampagnen, besonders diejenigen des Salzmarsches von 1930/31 in bewundernswerter Weise weitgehend gewaltfrei und konnten durch ihre dadurch zum Ausdruck kommende höhere Moralität und Kultur nach Nandy die koloniale Ideologie, nach welcher die britische Gesellschaft aufgeklärter, historisch fortgeschrittener, moralisch und kulturell zivilisierter sei, schließlich entlegitimieren. Das hatte zwei unmittelbare Auswirkungen: Erstens entstand keine Eskalationsspirale aus Repression und Gegengewalt mit ständiger Erhöhung des Brutalisierungsniveaus. So kann Nandy (1987: 161), was die britische Repression im Kolonialland betrifft, feststellen: „Man könnte sogar sagen, es war Gandhis Methode, die seinen Gegnern eine relativ humane Reaktion entlockte" – auch im Vergleich mit anderen britischen Kolonialländern, wo die britische Repression zum Teil weitaus härter war. Und zweitens entstanden nun auch in

England selbst, in der englischen Mittelschicht wie in der Arbeiterbewegung – kulturell beschämt und davon überzeugt, dass der moralisch legitimierte Erziehungsanspruch des Kolonialismus widerlegt worden war – antikoloniale Bewusstseinsstrukturen und politische Strömungen, die den kulturellen Konsens im Herzen des britischen Kolonialismus, unter den aufstrebenden Mittelklassen, untergraben konnten. Damit war der Kolonialismus in seiner gesellschaftlichen Legitimation kulturell zersetzt, noch Jahre bevor formal die politische Unabhängigkeit Indiens gewährt wurde. Die Labour-Regierung Attlee wurde in Großbritannien nach dem Zweiten Weltkrieg in einer gesellschaftlichen Stimmung gewählt, in der die Forderung nach Dekolonisierung in der britischen Arbeiterbewegung weit verbreitet war, in der Mittelschicht Verständnis fand, und deshalb über reaktionäre Tendenzen, das britische Empire wieder herstellen zu wollen, wofür immerhin große Teile des Zweiten Weltkriegs vor allem in der Dritten Welt geführt worden waren, triumphierte – dies auch im Gegensatz übrigens zu den Stimmungen und Regierungen in Frankreich und den Niederlanden unmittelbar nach dem Krieg. Die drei Massenkampagnen Zivilen Ungehorsams in Indien können daher mit einiger Berechtigung als revolutionärer Ziviler Ungehorsam Gandhis charakterisiert werden. Besonders nach Gandhis Rückkehr nach Indien ging es ihm nicht mehr, wie noch in Südafrika, um gleiche Rechte innerhalb des Empire, sondern der Zivile Ungehorsam wurde zum Kampfmittel mit einer revolutionären Zielsetzung, dem Sturz des Empire und der indischen Unabhängigkeit.

Rezeption und Weiterentwicklung: Ziviler Ungehorsam in Westeuropa und Nordamerika in den 1950er und 1960er Jahren

Angesichts dieses historischen Erfolges nach einem fast 30 Jahre dauernden Kampf überrascht es nicht, dass der Zivile Ungehorsam der InderInnen auch von anti-kolonialen Befreiungsbewegungen nach dem Zweiten Weltkrieg sowie entstehenden Friedensbewegungen in Europa intensiv beobachtet, studiert und rezipiert wurde. Auf zwei dieser Bewegungen, die den Zivilen Ungehorsam gleichzeitig rezipierten und in eigener aktionistischer Praxis weiter entwickelten, sei hier kurz eingegangen.

In Großbritannien setzte direkt nach der formellen Entkolonialisierung eine Tendenz ein, die indischen Erfahrungen für eigene Zielsetzungen des beginnenden Kampfes gegen die atomare Bewaffnung zu nutzen. Gegen die Gefahr der Stationierung atomarer Waffen auf britischem Boden bildete sich Anfang der 1950er Jahre eine gewaltfreie Aktionsgruppe mit dem bezeichnenden Namen „Operation Gandhi". Sie führte am 11. Januar 1952 die wahrscheinlich erste Sitzblockade in Europa, vor dem Eingang des britischen Verteidigungsministeriums, durch. Die zehn Blockierer wurden verhaftet und zu einer geringen Geldstrafe verurteilt. Diese Form des Zivilen Ungehorsams wurde in den folgenden Jahren immer weiter entwickelt und war schließlich die prägende Aktionsform der direkten gewaltfreien Aktionen des „Direct Action Committee" und des von ihm gebildeten „Committee of 100" um den politischen Intellektuellen und Philosophen Bertrand Russell. Ihm gelang der Durchbruch zum massenhaften zivilen Ungehorsam auch in Europa. Das Commitee of 100 sammelte Selbstverpflichtungserklärungen von AktivistInnen und Russell schrieb: „Vorgeschlagen wird, dass keine Demonstration oder sonstige Aktion unternommen wird ohne mindestens 2000 Teilnehmer" (zit. nach Ebert 1984b: 209). So entstanden in den Jahren 1960-62 regelmäßige massenhafte Sitzproteste im Stadtzentrum Londons „bis zum bislang größten Massensitzprotest auf dem Trafalgar Square in London am 17. September 1961. Damals nahmen 5000-7000 Demonstranten an dem Sitzprotest teil; 1317 wurden festgenommen und in Polizeiwagen abtransportiert." (Ebert 1984b: 206) Mit dieser Methode wurden 1960-62 auch britische und US-amerikanische Militärstützpunkte blockiert, bevor die Bewegung Rückschläge erlitt und versandete.

Die Afrikanischen AmerikanerInnen in den Südstaaten der USA rezipierten den Zivilen Ungehorsam der indischen Unabhängigkeitsbewegung ebenfalls vornehmlich in den 1950er Jahren. Viele schwarze AktivistInnen informierten sich durch Indienreisen direkt vor Ort über die indische Widerstandstradition. James Lawson etwa verbrachte drei Jahre in Indien, bevor er Ende der fünfziger Jahre Trainings in gewaltfreier Aktion in den Südstaaten der USA durchführte (vgl. Carson 2004: 68f.). Rosa Parks, die 1955 mit ihrer Aktion den legendären Busboykott von Montgomery initiierte, hatte an der Highlander Folk School in Monteagle, Tennessee, an einem Seminar über Zivilen Ungehorsam teilgenommen, das der indische gandhianische Sozialist Ram Manohar Lohia gab, der 1951 auf Einladung von StudentInnen dieser Universität für Schwarze in den USA weilte. „Lohia hatte AktivistInnen der Highlander Folk School mit Gandhis Ideen und Praktiken über gewaltfreien zivilen Ungehorsam bekannt gemacht und forderte sie dazu auf, sie anzuwenden." (Rudolph 2006: 110) Diese Rezeption initiierte die Aktionen des massenhaften Zivilen Ungehorsams der Schwarzenbewegung in den Südstaaten der USA, für die zwar Martin Luther King, Jr., bekannt wurde, die aber ihre Massenbasis in der schwarzen studentischen Organisation Student Nonviolent Coordinating Committee (SNCC) hatten. Wie in Großbritannien kam es zu einem Höhepunkt der Aktionen des massenhaften Zivilen Ungehorsams in den Südstaaten der USA zu Anfang der 1960er Jahre: 1960 besetzten schwarze StudentInnen massenhaft rassistisch getrennte öffentliche Einrichtungen, Bars, Cafés, Restaurants, Wartehallen auf Bus- und Eisenbahnhöfen usw. Es folgten Aktionen Zivilen Ungehorsams gegen die so genannte „Rassentrennung" in US-amerikanischen Überlandbussen („Freedom Rides") und eine Reihe von Protestmärschen durch ländliche Regionen, in denen der Rassismus am stärksten verwurzelt war oder in denen BürgerrechtlerInnen umgebracht worden waren. Als King am 4. April 1968 ermordet wurde, hatte er sich in der Auseinandersetzung mit den StudentInnen des SNCC selbst radikalisiert, öffentlich den Vietnamkrieg verurteilt, eine moralische Kapitalismuskritik entwickelt und in Memphis eine Streikwelle schwarzer Müllarbeiter unterstützt (vgl. Carson 2004).

Ziviler Ungehorsam um 1968

Die massenhaften Aktionen Zivilen Ungehorsams der afrikanisch-amerikanischen StudentInnen und des britischen Committee of 100 machten weltweit Furore und erwiesen sich als beispielhafte Vorbilder für das, was die StudentInnen von 1968 dann vorläufig und etwas unpassend als „begrenzte Regelverletzung" bezeichnen sollten. Besonders in den Anfängen der westdeutschen StudentInnenbewegung bis zum Attentat an Rudi Dutschke am 11. April 1968 bezog sich die 68er Revolte oftmals explizit auf die angelsächsische Tradition des Zivilen Ungehorsams. In Berlin ging aus dem Arbeitskreis 28 der Kritischen Universität ein deutschsprachiges „Komitee der 100" hervor, das am 3. Februar 1968 einen Sitzprotest von rund 1000 StudentInnen gegen die griechische Militärdiktatur vor der Griechischen Militärmission in Berlin durchführte. Zur Mobilisierung wurden 50000 Flugblätter mit einer Selbstverpflichtungserklärung verteilt, in der die Bereitschaft zu gewaltfreiem Verhalten erklärt wurde (Ebert 1984a: 62). Direkt nach der Ermordung Martin Luther Kings erklärte der Allgemeine Studentenausschuss der Freien Universität Berlin: „Martin Luther King entwickelte mit seinen Freunden die Kampfformen, die heute hier angewandt werden und deren amerikanische Namen sit-in, teach-in noch an ihre Herkunft erinnern" (zit. nach Ebert 1984a: 22f.). Und sogar noch am 17.4.1968, nach dem Attentat auf Dutschke und den zum Teil gewaltsamen Aktionen gegen das Springer-Hochhaus, gab das Aktionskomitee der Arbeiter, Schüler und Studenten in der Technischen Universität Berlin eine Presseerklärung zur Strategie ab: „Prinzipiell ist unsere Praxis aufklärerisch und damit grundsätzlich gewaltfrei" (zit. nach Ebert 1984a: 27). Doch nun setzte die Auseinandersetzung um Gegengewalt innerhalb der StudentInnenbewegung umfassend ein, fand sozusagen in jedem einzelnen Kopf statt.

Es ist interessant für das Verständnis des Zivilen Ungehorsams von 1968 im Vergleich zu späteren Formen des Zivilen Ungehorsams in den Jahren 1970-2000, einen damals geschriebenen Aufsatz des Theoretikers Theodor Ebert heranzuziehen. In der Frage der Gewaltanwendung bei direkten Aktionen setzte sich Ebert 1968 kritisch mit dem Begriff „Gegengewalt" von Herbert Marcuse (vgl. Marcuse 1966) auseinander und wollte ihn durch eine Konzeption der „Gegenmacht" ersetzen, die dann durch massenhafte direkte gewaltfreie Aktion ausgeübt werde (vgl. Ebert 1984a: 18). In diesem Zusammenhang schrieb Ebert als Zugeständnis an Marcuse:

„Wenn demokratische, legale Wege zur Änderung der sozialen Verhältnisse fehlen oder infolge umfassender Manipulation verschlossen sind, wird die bloße Mahnung zu Friedfertigkeit und Gewaltverzicht zur Ideologie, die objektiv im Dienst der Herrschenden steht. Diese Kritik Marcuses an dem Establishment nahe stehenden Predigern der Gewaltlosigkeit war nötig" (Ebert 1984a: 18). Der vom Frankfurter Mitglied des Sozialistischen Deutschen Studentenbundes (SDS) Hans-Jürgen Krahl nach den Anti-Springer-Demonstrationen propagierten Devise, revolutionäre Gewalt sei Notwehr, versuchte Ebert einen revolutionären Zivilen Ungehorsam entgegensetzen. Dabei griff er auf die revolutionäre Interpretation zurück, die Gandhi dem Zivilen Ungehorsam Anfang der 1920er Jahre gegeben hatte: Wenn sich das Establishment „zu keinen oder nur zu symbolischen Zugeständnissen bereit findet, kann und braucht die außerparlamentarische Opposition nicht länger bei Dramatisierungsmethoden stehen zu bleiben; sie kann dann zu Zwangsmaßnahmen greifen, welche die Fortsetzung der ungerechten Herrschaft unmöglich machen und neue Institutionen schaffen, welche demokratische Gegenmacht ausüben" (Ebert 1984a: 43). Und: „Die außerparlamentarische Opposition ist zur Zeit allenfalls zum demonstrativen zivilen Ungehorsam fähig, jedoch nicht zu einem revolutionären zivilen Ungehorsam, der das bestehende System lähmen würde. [...] Wenn der Kreis derer, die auf diese Weise zivilen Ungehorsam leisten, die Zahl von mehreren Tausend überschreitet, kann dies nicht nur die Justizmaschine blockieren, sondern auch die materiellen und prestigemäßigen Kosten für die Herrschenden so erhöhen, dass es ihnen bequemer erscheint, auf die Durchführung dieser Gesetze zu verzichten" (Ebert 1984a: 50, 52). Ganz in der Begrifflichkeit der studentischen Systemkritik spricht Ebert von der „formaldemokratischen" Struktur der Bundesrepublik, von der er eine inhaltliche Demokratie als utopische Zielsetzung des Kampfes absetzt. An Rudi Dutschkes Konzept vom „langen Marsch durch die Institutionen" kritisiert er nicht das Ziel der revolutionären Umwälzung, sondern die Inspiration Dutschkes durch das Denken in Kategorien Maos und des bewaffneten Kampfes:

„Wenn man aber weniger auf dieses Selbstverständnis und mehr auf die Praxis achtet, kann man mit noch größerer Berechtigung behaupten, dass die Studenten auch Gandhi-Schüler sind. Die ‚Graswurzelrevolution', das heißt, die radikale Umwandlung einer Gesellschaft durch die sukzessive Demokratisierung ihrer Institutionen von unten nach oben war seine Revolutionskonzeption, in deren Sinne er [...] eine genossenschaftliche Räterepublik" (Ebert 1984a: 53) angestrebt habe. Gandhis Revolutionskonzept liege der APO zudem auch deshalb näher, weil sie den langen Marsch durch die Institutionen, so Ebert weiter, „nicht territorial, sondern sozial verstand" (Ebert 1984a: 53). Doch dies werde von den StudentInnen nicht bewusst aufgenommen: „Diese Strategie des gewaltfreien Aufstandes ist nicht nur unbekannt; ihre Rezeption ist emotional blockiert. [...] Da der SDS sich in seiner Sozialkritik fast ausschließlich an marxistischen Denkern zu orientieren gelernt hat, war es für ihn nahe liegend, sich auch diejenigen Theoretiker und Praktiker der Revolution zum Vorbild zu nehmen, die sich ausdrücklich auf Karl Marx beriefen. In einem Umkehrschluß wurden alle anderen Strategen des sozialen Wandels wie Gandhi und King, die sich aufgrund ihrer religiösen Kritik am historischen Materialismus nie als Marxisten bezeichnet hatten, ohne eingehende Prüfung als bürgerlich und liberal eingestuft. Dabei entging dem SDS und auch anderen Meinungsführern der außerparlamentarischen Opposition, dass Gandhi und King in ihrer Analyse des Kapitalismus und Imperialismus mit marxistischen Theoretikern weitgehend übereinstimmen oder sich zumindest in ihrem theoretischen Ansatz nicht im Widerspruch zu ihnen befinden" (Ebert 1984a: 23f.).

Damit positioniert sich Ebert 1968 noch ganz im Rahmen des revolutionären Zivilen Ungehorsams und seines sozialen Antikapitalismus, der schon Basis der indischen Bewegung Anfang der 1920er Jahre gewesen war. Interessant ist eine bereits damals auftretende Ambivalenz im Aufsatz Eberts: Einerseits hebt er Formen des „politischen Happenings", des „Sozialistischen Straßentheaters" usw. hervor, mit denen die protestierenden StudentInnen erstarrte Protestformen der 1950er Jahre kulturell aufgebrochen haben, und kann sogar schreiben: „Die Spontaneität dieses Demokratisierungsprozesses ist seine große Stärke, denn bei einer ‚Graswurzelrevolution' hat es einen geringen repressiven Effekt, wenn man die höchsten Halme abschneidet" (Ebert 1984a: 54). Andererseits kritisiert Ebert aber das Übergewicht der theatralischen, spontaneistischen gegenüber den ernsthaften, disziplinierten Aktionsformen bei den StudentInnen und plädiert für „disziplinierten zivilen Ungehorsam" (Ebert 1984a: 40). Die Schwarzen der amerikanischen Bürgerrechtsbewegung und die AtomwaffengegnerInnen des „Committee of 100" hätten „aus einer Gewissensverpflichtung heraus" demonstriert „und nicht, weil das Demonstrieren ‚spannend ist und Spaß macht'" (Ebert 1984a: 31). Hier deutet sich ein Gegensatz zwischen Spontaneismus und Disziplin/Schematismus an, der für die weitere Entwicklung des Zivilen Ungehorsams in Europa noch bedeutend werden und zu Konflikten und unterschiedlichen Konzepten führen sollte.

Zunächst muss jedoch auf den massenhaften Zivilen Ungehorsam in Diktaturen verwiesen werden, der mit dem Widerstand der StudentInnen und ArbeiterInnen von Prag 1968 eine Art Initialzündung erfuhr. Die weitgehende Gewaltfreiheit der tschechoslowakischen Bewegung gegen die sowjetische Besatzung gelang ganz ohne disziplinarische Maßnahmen, Trainings oder gar Ausbildung von AktivistInnen und war so massenhaft und spontaneistisch, dass sie sogar in einem der letzten Texte der französischen Situationistischen Internationale vom September 1969 als beispielhaft und wegweisend dargestellt wurde:

„Das tschechoslowakische Experiment hat die außerordentlichen Kampfmöglichkeiten gezeigt, über die eine konsequente und organisierte revolutionäre Bewegung eines Tages verfügen kann. Gerade die vom Warschauer Pakt gelieferte Ausrüstung (um eine eventuelle imperialistische Invasion in die Tschechoslowakei zu vereiteln!) wurde von den tschechoslowakischen Journalisten benutzt, um 35 Untergrundsender aufzubauen, die mit 80 Hilfssendern verbunden waren. So wurde die sowjetische Propaganda – die für eine Besatzungsarmee doch so nötig ist – an der Basis sabotiert; so konnte auch die Bevölkerung mehr oder weniger alles wissen, was im Land vor sich ging und den Anweisungen der liberalen Bürokraten oder einigen radikalen Elementen Folge leisten, die die Sender kontrollierten. Prag wurde, nachdem der Rundfunk dazu aufgefordert hatte, die Operationen der russischen Polizei zu sabotieren, in ein echtes ‚Straßenlabyrinth' verwandelt, in dem alle Straßen ihre Namen und alle Häuser ihre Nummern verloren hatten, um stattdessen mit Parolen im besten Stil des Pariser Mai bedeckt zu werden. Es war ein Zuhause der Freiheit geworden, das jeder Polizei trotzte, ein Beispiel für revolutionäre Zweckentfremdung des polizeilichen Urbanismus." (Situationistische Internationale 1995: 289f.)

Hier war auch die von Ebert so beklagte emotionale Blockade der StudentInnen verschwunden: „Die Kritik des Leninismus [...] war der Höhepunkt der theoretischen Kritik, der in einem bürokratischen Land erreicht wurde. Selbst Dutschke wurde von den tschechischen revolutionären Studenten lächerlich gemacht, und seinen ‚Anarcho-Maoismus' wiesen sie verächtlich als ‚absurd, komisch und nicht einmal wert, von fünfzehnjährigen Kindern beachtet zu werden' zurück." (Situationistische Internationale 1995: 288)

Es waren die tschechischen StudentInnen und ArbeiterInnen, die den revolutionären Zivilen Ungehorsam in seiner spontaneistischen, graswurzelrevolutionären Form, wie von Ebert 1968 gefordert, am eindrucksvollsten durchführten. Zwar scheiterten sie unmittelbar in ihrem Widerstand gegen die sowjetische Besatzung. Aber die kulturelle und moralische Überlegenheit war so erdrückend und blieb als emanzipative Erinnerung so stark im Bewusstsein der AktivistInnen haften, dass sich Prag 1968 bei der erstbesten Gelegenheit wiederholte, als innerhalb des sowjetischen Systems eine innere Machtkrise die Repressionsfähigkeit der sowjetischen Truppen in Osteuropa lockerte. So setzte die revolutionäre massenhafte Bewegung Zivilen Ungehorsams von Prag 1989 nur das um, was längst kulturell hegemonial geworden war. Zusammen mit den Bewegungen in der DDR, Polen und anderen osteuropäischen Ländern machte sie 1989 zum Jahr des Zivilen Ungehorsams gegen Diktaturen, das auch Ausläufer und Konsequenzen für den Sturz des Apartheid-Regimes in Südafrika und die Überwindung der Militärdiktaturen in Lateinamerika hatte.

Feminismus und Antimilitarismus: Ziviler Ungehorsam in den Neuen Sozialen Bewegungen der 1970er und 1980er Jahre

Im Westen allgemein und in Westdeutschland im Besonderen hat sich der Zivile Ungehorsam in einem langwierigen Prozess trotz der emotionalen Blockade der StudentInnen von 1968 etwas verspätet doch noch durchgesetzt, und zwar in den 1970er und 1980er Jahren im Rahmen der neuen sozialen Bewegungen, vor allem bei der Frauenbewegung (Kampagne: „Ich habe abgetrieben" – eine klassisch durchgeführte Aktion Zivilen Ungehorsams gegen geltendes Gesetz), der radikalen Ökologiebewegung (Bauplatzbesetzungen gegen AKWs), der Friedensbewegung (Blockaden vor Militäreinrichtungen wie in Großengstingen 1982 und Mutlangen ab 1983, Verweigerungskampagnen, Manöverstörungen im Fulda Gap) oder beim Volkszählungsboykott (1983-1987). TheoretikerInnen und AktivistInnen aus gewaltfreien Aktionsgruppen und anderen Bezugsgruppen, die an einem systemüberwindenden revolutionären Zivilen Ungehorsam festhalten wollten, hatten sich nun allerdings weniger mit marxistischen (oder linksradikalen) Konzepten der Gegengewalt und dafür mehr und mehr mit reformistischen Neuinterpretationen des Zivilen Ungehorsams auseinanderzusetzen.

Den Auftakt zu dieser Tendenz bildete schon 1970 ein politischer Essay der Philosophin Hannah Arendt, „Ziviler Ungehorsam", der die Erfahrungen der afrikanisch-amerikanischen Bürgerrechtsbewegung, der Anti-Vietnamkriegsbewegung und der Studentenbewegung in den USA auswertete und interpretierte. Arendts Reflexion blieb gegenüber dem revolutionären zivilen Ungehorsam gleichwohl noch ambivalent. Einerseits – und ganz im Gegensatz zu allen nachfolgenden reformistischen Auslegungen des Zivilen Ungehorsams – unterschied Arendt zwischen zivilem und kriminellem Ungehorsam und betonte dadurch, dass der Zivilen Ungehorsam Leistende zwar das Risiko eingehe, für seine Tat Repression zu erleiden oder ins Gefängnis geworfen zu werden, dass er dies aber keineswegs freiwillig und als integraler Bestandteil des Zivilen Ungehorsams tun müsse: „‚Die Idee, dass die Verbüßung einer Strafe die Gesetzesverletzung rechtfertige, leitet sich nicht von Gandhi und der Tradition des zivilen Ungehorsams her, sondern von Oliver Wendell Holmes und der Tradition des Rechtsrealismus. [...] Auf dem Gebiet des Strafrechts ist eine solche Doktrin offensichtlich absurd. Die Annahme ist unsinnig, dass Mord, Vergewaltigung oder Brandstiftung gerechtfertigt seien, wenn man nur die Strafe bereitwillig verbüße.' Es ist höchst bedauerlich, dass in den Augen vieler Leute ein ‚Element der Selbstaufopferung' als der beste Beweis für die ‚Intensität des inneren Engagements', die ‚Ernsthaftigkeit des Verweigerers und seine Gesetzestreue' gilt, denn besessener Fanatismus ist zumeist ein Kennzeichen von Übergeschnappten und verunmöglicht in jedem Fall eine rationale, sachbezogene Diskussion." (Arendt 1986: 131) Mag sein, dass diese harsch vorgetragene Kritik mit Arendts Erfahrungen bei der Sammlung von Berichten der Judenrettung im Europa des Nationalsozialismus zusammenhängt, in der ein Sich-Stellen der GesetzesbrecherInnen einem sofortigen Todesurteil gleich gekommen wäre (Arendt 1964). Andererseits aber ist Arendt im zweiten Teil ihres Essays „Ziviler Ungehorsam" sehr daran gelegen, die als organisierte Minderheit handelnden AktivistInnen des Zivilen Ungehorsams mit dem „Geist der Gesetze" (Arendt 1986: 145) der US-Gründerväter zu versöhnen, insbesondere mit den ur-amerikanischen Traditionen des Konsenses, der ein Recht auf Dissens freiwilliger Vereinigungen mit einschließt, und mit der Legitimation eines verfassungsmäßigen Widerstandsrechts und einer „horizontale(n) Version des Gesellschaftsvertrags" (Arendt 1986: 145ff.) nach John Locke. So sucht sie nach einem „Ort" (Arendt 1986: 144) in der Verfassung für den Zivilen Ungehorsam, nach dessen „politische(r) Institutionalisierung" (Arendt 1986: 158), obwohl ihr eigentlich bewusst ist, dass „‚der Rechtsbruch nicht gesetzlich gerechtfertigt werden (kann)', selbst wenn dieser Verstoß in der Absicht begangen wird, der Verletzung eines anderen Gesetzes vorzubeugen" (Arendt 1986: 157).

In der westdeutschen Friedensbewegung der 1980er Jahre übernahmen dann einzelne Kampagnen für Zivilen Ungehorsam Schlagworte der Verrechtlichung wie „Ziviler Ungehorsam als aktiver Verfassungsschutz" (Rechtswissenschaftler E. Küchenhoff) oder erklärten den Zivilen Ungehorsam zur „sozialen Erfindung der Demokratie" (Ebert 1984b) – nun aber bei Ebert nicht mehr vor dem Hintergrund der Charakterisierung der bestehenden Demokratie als einer Formaldemokratie, sondern einer wie durch ein Wunder ohne Revolution seit 1968 Wirklichkeit gewordenen Demokratie! Im Rahmen mehrjähriger Verfahren wurde die Aktionsform der Blockade vom Verfassungsgericht schließlich zu einer verfassungsgemäßen Form der Demonstration herabgewürdigt.

Die veränderte Situation lässt sich an einem weiteren Aufsatz von Theodor Ebert (1984b) diskutieren. Ebert hat nun – wie so viele 1968er vor und nach ihm – die Seiten gewechselt und ist das geworden, was er damals selbst kritisiert hat, „ein dem Establishment nahe stehender Prediger der Gewaltlosigkeit." Von revolutionärem Zivilen Ungehorsam ist nun bei Ebert nicht mehr die Rede: „Wenn man also Nutzen und Nachteil des zivilen Ungehorsams für die repräsentative Demokratie untersuchen möchte, dann muß man dieses Thema demokratie-immanent angehen. Dies ist auch nahe liegend, weil das Konzept des zivilen Ungehorsams ursprünglich in Demokratien entwickelt wurde und im Unterschied zum allgemeinen Konzept des gewaltfreien Widerstands eine demokratiespezifische Variante der gewaltfreien Aktion darstellt" (Ebert 1984c: 255). Das ist nun ganz neu und widerspricht völlig der von Gandhi gemachten Einteilung in legale Aktion und illegale Aktion (Ziviler Ungehorsam) der gewaltfreien Aktion. Ebert weiter: „Nach Auffassung der International Encyclopedia of Social Sciences hat ‚civil' in Verbindung mit ‚disobedience' fünf untereinander gleichberechtigte Bedeutungen: 1. eine allgemeine Bürgerpflicht wahrnehmen; 2. nicht-militärisch gewaltfrei; 3. höflich, zivilisiert; 4. öffentlich (im Unterschied zu privat); 5. am Gemeinwohl orientiert. Aus dieser Auslegung von ‚zivil' spricht die Anerkennung des zivilen Ungehorsams als gelegentlicher demokratischer Pflichtübung" (Ebert 1984c: 260). Der Zivile Ungehorsam ist jetzt nicht mehr eine „Zwangsmaßnahme", die die „materiellen Kosten" für die Herrschenden erhöhen soll, sondern er ist nur noch demonstrativ, dramatisierend: „Die gewaltfreie, direkte Aktion dramatisiert einen Konfliktgegenstand so, dass er nicht mehr länger ignoriert werden kann" (Ebert 1984c: 265). Aktionen Zivilen Ungehorsams werden schließlich von Ebert selbst als „dramatische Aktion" (Ebert 1984c: 267) charakterisiert. Wer aber nur dramatisiert, ändert nicht selbst, sondern überlässt die Entscheidung freiwillig anderen, in diesem Fall den verfassungsmäßigen rechtsstaatlichen Organen.

Als sich im Rahmen der europaweiten Friedensbewegung gegen die Stationierung von Mittelstreckenraketen in Westdeutschland die SPD mit Schmidt als Pro-Stationierungspartei ab 1982 nicht mehr an der Regierung halten konnte, streckte eine angeblich gewandelte SPD ihre Fühler in die oppositionellen Bewegungen aus und versuchte, Aktionskonzepte, darunter den Zivilen Ungehorsam, staatlich zu vereinnahmen und mit dem Rechtsstaat zu versöhnen. Hier haben wir es nicht mehr wie bei Thoreau mit „Ungehorsam gegen den Staat" zu tun, sondern mit Zivilem Ungehorsam „im Rechtsstaat" (Glotz 1983). Das bedeutete, wie damals in der Zeitung Graswurzelrevolution (1984: 10f.) kritisiert wurde, „dass es bei der Diskussion in der Sozialdemokratie nicht um die Unterstützung von Formen zivilen Ungehorsams geht, sondern um ihre Funktionalisierung." Der damalige SPD-Parteistratege Peter Glotz führte aus: „Was wir brauchen, ist der Prozess der stets neu erforderlichen Versöhnung von Legalität und Legitimität. In der Staatsform, die wir uns ausgesucht haben, ist Recht ein auf Konsens angelegtes – und angewiesenes – Ordnungsprogramm" (Glotz 1983: 8). Hier geht es um die sozialdemokratische Integration ins System unter Ausschaltung von Legitimationen für die illegale Aktion des Zivilen Ungehorsams. Den zivilen Ungehorsam leistenden Bürgerinitiativen, so die Kritik der Graswurzelrevolution an Glotz, würde so einzig und allein die Funktion zugewiesen, „als eine Art Frühwarnsystem für die politischen Entscheidungsträger zu dienen" (1984: 10). Der Staatsbürger bzw. die Staatsbürgerin erfüllt somit ihre staatsbürgerliche Pflicht. Die oftmalige Verwendung der deutschsprachigen Übersetzung „bürgerlicher Ungehorsam" anstatt „ziviler Ungehorsam" verstärkte dieses Verständnis in den damaligen Diskussionen noch. Es ging ganz zentral um die Frage, ob das staatliche Gewaltmonopol als legitim und als fortschrittliche Kulturleistung anerkannt werden sollte oder nicht. Glotz dazu: „Der eilfertige Rückzug auf das Gewissen gefährdet die Kulturleistung des staatlichen Gewaltmonopols" (Glotz 1983: 12). Gegen dieses Staatsverständnis von Peter Glotz und auch Jürgen Habermas (1985: 79-99) argumentierte die Graswurzelrevolution (1984: 11) wie folgt: „Der Staat ist nicht durch Gesellschaftsvertrag oder durch die individuelle Übereinkunft über eine Anzahl von gemeinsam zu regelnden Angelegenheiten entstanden, wie dies letztlich z.B. auch Habermas unterstellt. Staat bedeutet historisch im Wesentlichen: Das Monopol, Gewalt auszuüben mit dem Ziel, eine bestimmte gesellschaftliche Gruppe zur herrschenden zu machen oder sie an der Macht zu halten. Daraus resultiert das usurpierte Recht, sachliche oder Geldmittel (Steuern) zur Erhaltung dieses Apparates den Unterworfenen abzunötigen. Der Staat ist der offene oder gebändigte Kriegszustand gegen die Gesellschaft. [...] Wenn nun Gesellschaftsmitglieder ihren Willen auf dem Wege des Ungehorsams gegen den Staat kundtun, so ist das eine Zurücknahme von durch den Staat usurpierten Entscheidungskompetenzen durch die Gesellschaft. Man mag nun mit Habermas einwenden, dass eine solche Argumentation die Gewalt in der Gesellschaft freisetzt und Glotz würde sicherlich die ‚Kulturleistung des staatlichen Gewaltmonopols' gefährdet sehen. Genau an dieser Stelle aber findet auch das Gewaltfreiheits-Postulat des zivilen Ungehorsams seinen Platz: dem staatlichen Gewaltapparat kann nur mittels der Ablehnung des Prinzips des Staates, eben der Gewalt, eine glaubhafte Alternative entgegengesetzt werden. Ziviler Ungehorsam gefährdet also das staatliche Gewaltmonopol, weil er es durch friedliche Regelungen und Verhaltensweisen ersetzt, Staat so wirklich überflüssig macht. Wer demgegenüber selbst Gewalt gegen den Staat setzt, will nur Staat – wenn auch einen anderen."

Doch auch auf der Aktionsebene, unter den AktivistInnen des Zivilen Ungehorsams selbst, gab es Kontroversen, die an die Bewusstseinsstrukturen dieses reformistischen Verständnisses von Zivilem Ungehorsam anschlossen. Besonders in einer „Kampagne ziviler Ungehorsam bis zur Abrüstung" verbreitete sich im Laufe der 1980er Jahre bei mehreren aufeinander folgenden Blockaden in Mutlangen, deren öffentlichen Begründungen und dem sich schematisch wiederholenden Ablauf ein sozialdemokratisches Verständnis des Zivilen Ungehorsams, was wiederum von anderen gewaltfreien Aktionsgruppen und AutorInnen aus dem Umfeld der Graswurzelrevolution als Schematismus, Ritualisierung, Disziplinierung der Aktion und der AktionsteilnehmerInnen und zunehmende Berechenbarkeit der Aktionen des Zivilen Ungehorsams kritisiert wurde. Aus der Perspektive eines revolutionären Zivilen Ungehorsams hatte Mitte der 1980er Jahre im Vergleich zu den spontaneistischen Unberechenbarkeiten bei direkten gewaltfreien Aktionen und politischen Happenings während der 1968er Revolte die Variante der disziplinierten und disziplinierenden Aktion Terrain gewonnen. Gleichzeitig hat dies zu einer Verarmung der phantasievollen und künstlerischen Ausdruckskraft der Bewegung beigetragen. Ein Autor der Graswurzelrevolution kritisierte:

„Die Blockaden sollen zeigen, wie ernst es den Blockierern ist. Wie zeigt man das? Ziviler Ungehorsam weiß auch dafür eine Antwort: Seine ‚Mittel sind nicht Macht und Gewalt, sondern Argumente und Leidensbereitschaft'. [...] Anzugreifen ist ein Harmoniedenken, das vor lauter Dialogbereitschaft nicht mehr zwischen Freund und Feind unterscheidet. Es gibt keine Gegner mehr sondern nur noch Gesprächspartner. Wenn die Friedensbewegung von sich aus darauf verzichtet, Gegenmacht zu entfalten (das wäre die Aufgabe massenhaften Zivilen Ungehorsams!), bleibt sie im Wortsinne ohnmächtig" (Bröckling 1986: 9). Hier wird nur Eberts Begrifflichkeit von 1968 in einer Zeit wiederholt, in der dieser zu solcher Begrifflichkeit nicht mehr in der Lage ist. Weiter in der Kritik an der „Kampagne Ziviler Ungehorsam bis zur Abrüstung": „Anzugreifen ist eine Leidensmystik in den Erklärungen der Kampagne. Politischer Kampf bringt Nachteile und Risiken mit sich, das zu leugnen wäre naiv. Die herrschenden Mächte lassen sich nicht ungestraft kritisieren. Wer aber diese Nachteile und Risiken, wer Leiden zum ‚Mittel' des Widerstandes stilisiert, verkennt nicht nur die Realität (W. Biermann sang es in seiner ‚Ermutigung', die oft auch während der Blockaden zu hören war: ‚Die Herrschenden erzittern, sitzt Du erst hinter Gittern, doch nicht vor Deinem Leid...'), er ist auch zynisch gegenüber den Opfern, die sich ihr Leiden nicht freiwillig ausgesucht haben. Anzumerken ist noch die erschreckende Banalität der ‚Ästhetik des Widerstandes' in Mutlangen. Sie erschöpft sich im Beschwören des atomaren Untergangs, frommen Liedern und Betroffenheitslyrik. [...] Wenn es stimmt, dass die künstlerischen Kräfte, die eine Bewegung freisetzt, Gradmesser ihres emanzipatorischen Potentials sind, dann steht es nicht gut um Mutlangen und die Friedensbewegung" (Bröckling 1986: 9).

Auch gegen eine in solchem sozialdemokratischen Verständnis des Zivilen Ungehorsams verbreitete Parole unter manchen AktivistInnen: „Die Polizei ist nicht unser Gegner" (Saathoff/Uebelacker 1983: 22) wurde in der Graswurzelrevolution argumentiert:

„Dem sich gewaltfrei Wehrenden tritt die Polizei nicht [...] als neutrales Vollzugsorgan, sondern als Teil einer der Konfliktparteien entgegen. [...] Es ist richtig, jederzeit den politisch Verantwortlichen Verhandlungen über unsere politischen

Forderungen anzubieten. Völlig verkehrt, überflüssig, schädlich sind jedoch Verhandlungen mit politisch nicht verantwortlichen Polizisten über unsere Aktionsformen! Sie führen dazu, unsere Direkten Aktionen zu von der Polizei kalkulierbaren Landkartenspielen verkommen zu lassen. [...] Wer durch Diskussionen mit der Gegenseite die Mittel der Auseinandersetzung in den Vordergrund rückt, gar Verhandlungen mit der Polizei darüber führt, erklärt sich damit einverstanden, dass unsere politische Auseinandersetzung in ein polizeiliches Problem umgewandelt wird. Man kann sich unserer Meinung nach nicht auf die ‚Klassiker' der Gewaltfreiheit berufen, um Verhandlungen über Aktionsformen zu rechtfertigen. Der richtige Grundsatz der Dialogbereitschaft bezieht sich auf den Dialog über inhaltliche Forderungen. Hat Gandhi, bevor er zum Salzmarsch aufbrach, mit der britischen Exekutive konferiert? Hat sich M.L. King, bevor er zum Busboykott aufrief, mit dem Polizeichef von Montgomery an einen Tisch gesetzt, um gemeinsam über geeignete Aktionsformen zu sinnen?" (Saathoff/Uebelacker 1983: 22f.)

Vermeidung von Sackgassen: Ziviler Ungehorsam in den 1990er Jahren und den ersten Jahren des 21. Jahrhunderts

Diesem Potential zu kritischer Reflexion und Selbstkritik innerhalb der Reihen gewaltfreier Aktionsgruppen ist es allerdings auch zu verdanken, dass schematisierende Sackgassen in den Kampagnen Zivilen Ungehorsams während der westdeutschen Friedensbewegung in Frage gestellt werden konnten und bei der Blockade des Bundestags anlässlich der Abstimmung über die Asylrechtsänderung 1993, bei den Aktionen gegen Golf- und Jugoslawienkriege in den neunziger Jahren, bei den direkten gewaltfreien Aktionen gegen Atomtransporte nach Gorleben und jüngst bei den Aktionskampagnen gegen die G7 und G8-Gipfeltreffen weitgehend überwunden wurden, wodurch sich phantasievolle und unberechenbare Aktionen des massenhaften Zivilen Ungehorsams in sozialen Bewegungen wieder neu entfalten konnten. Die theoretischen und praktischen Grundlagen eines sozialdemokratischen, dramatisierend-demonstrativen, disziplinarischen, staatsorientierten und instrumentellen Verständnisses von Zivilem Ungehorsam haben sich in den ersten Jahren des 21. Jahrhunderts allerdings auch Think Tanks in den USA angeeignet, die besonders in Osteuropa und Asien vermittels finanzieller Unterstützung der USA für kleine Gruppen vor Ort (z.B. „Otpor"/"Widerstand" in Serbien) Regierungen durch Kampagnen Zivilen Ungehorsams gestürzt haben, wo sich diese in ihrer Politik als den Interessen der USA zuwiderlaufend erwiesen. Eine ganze Reihe von angeblichen gewaltlosen Revolutionen mit medial griffigen Etiketten wie „Zedernrevolution" (Libanon), „orangene Revolution" (Ukraine), „Rosenrevolution" (Georgien), „Tulpenrevolution" (Kirgisien) sind willkommene „Regime Changes" im Sinne der US-Regierung. Sie werden mit Mitteln aus US-Forschungsinstitutionen und Stiftungen finanziert, die oft der Demokratischen Partei nahe stehen. Auch die Soros Foundation des milliardenschweren US-Investmentbankers George Soros ist beteiligt. Oft wird die strategische Absicht verborgen hinter der vorgeblich selbstlosen Bereitstellung von strategischen Hilfsmitteln und

Ratgebern für Zivilen Ungehorsam aus Friedensinstituten um den inzwischen wie Ebert reformistisch und systemtreu gewordenen bekanntesten Theoretiker des Zivilen Ungehorsams in den USA, Gene Sharp (2003). Es sollte zu denken geben, wenn das „Freedom House" des Ex-CIA-Chefs und Rumsfeld-Beraters James Woolsey der serbischen Oppositionsgruppe „Otpor" 5000 Exemplare des Buches von Sharp „From Dictatorship to Democracy" (Sharp 2003) zukommen lässt, um Kampagnen des Zivilen Ungehorsams zu organisieren (Eiselberg 2006: 6). Dagegen wurden auffälliger Weise Initiativen für gewaltlosen Widerstand gegen Diktaturen, die in Osteuropa und Zentralasien im Sinne der US-Interessen handeln (Aserbeidschan zum Beispiel, mit deren Regierung lukrative Ölverträge für US-Multis bestehen), nicht unterstützt und konnten u.a. deshalb auch keine Massenwirksamkeit entfalten. Dies ist sicherlich nicht die alleinige Ursache für die entstandenen Massenbewegungen in Osteuropa und Zentralasien, aber doch ein weithin unterschätzter, gewichtiger Faktor. Hier gilt es, daran zu erinnern, dass die Kampagnen des Zivilen Ungehorsams von Gandhi Anfang der 1920er Jahre einen antikapitalistischen Charakter hatten, und durch diese Erinnerung den Zivilen Ungehorsam heute vor Strategien systemintegrativer Vereinnahmung und imperialistischer Instrumentalisierung zu retten, die von US-Think Tanks als die billigere Alternative interessengeleiteter Weltpolitik zu militärischen Interventionen wie denen im Irak und in Afghanistan eingeschätzt werden und somit in Zukunft wohl noch weitaus stärker an Bedeutung gewinnen werden (vgl. Eiselberg 2006: 6-7). Der Kampf um Begriffe, Verständnis und Bewusstseinsstrukturen um das Konzept des Zivilen Ungehorsams, der Kampf gegen seine Instrumentalisierung durch staatliche Interessen geht weiter! Aber dieser Kampf ist zugleich auch deutliches Zeichen für die Relevanz und Bedeutung des Zivilen Ungehorsams für die sozialen Kämpfe im 21. Jahrhundert!

Literatur:

Arendt, Hannah (1964): Eichmann in Jerusalem. Ein Bericht von der Banalität des Bösen, München (Piper Verlag).
Arendt, Hannah (1986): Ziviler Ungehorsam [1970], in: dies.: Zur Zeit. Politische Essays, Berlin (Rotbuch Verlag), S. 119-159.
Bröckling, Ulrich (1986): Kampagne Ziviler Ungehorsam bis zur Abrüstung. Widerstand als Ritual? – Kritische Anmerkungen, in: Graswurzelrevolution Nr. 103, 4/1986, S. 8-9.
Carson, Clayborne (2004): Zeiten des Kampfes. Das Student Nonviolent Coordinating Committee (SNCC) und das Erwachen des afro-amerikanischen Widerstands in den sechziger Jahren, Nettersheim (Verlag Graswurzelrevolution).
Ebert, Theodor (1984a): Die außerparlamentarische Opposition und die gewaltfreie Macht [1968], in: ders.: Ziviler Ungehorsam. Von der APO zur Friedensbewegung, Waldkirch (Waldkircher Verlag), S. 12-58.
Ebert, Theodor (1984b): Ziviler Widerstand gegen die Raketenbasen. Lehren der 60er Jahre – Aktionsformen für 1983 [1982], in: ders.: Ziviler Ungehorsam. Von der APO zur Friedensbewegung, Waldkirch (Waldkircher Verlag), S. 204-216.
Ebert, Theodor (1984c): Ziviler Ungehorsam – eine soziale Erfindung der Demokratie [1983], in: ders.: Ziviler Ungehorsam. Von der APO zur Friedensbewegung, Waldkirch (Waldkircher Verlag), S. 253-275.
Eiselberg, Thomas S. (2006): Globalizing Nonviolence? ‚Gewaltfreie Revolution' in Osteuropa und Zentralasien im Auftrag nationaler Interessen der USA?, in: Graswurzelrevolution Nr. 306, 2/2006, S. 6-7.
Gandhi, Mahatma (1924): Jung Indien. Aufsätze aus den Jahren 1919 bis 1922. Auswahl von Romain Rolland und Madeleine Rolland, Erlenbach-Zürich (Rotapfel-Verlag).

Glotz, Peter (Hg.) (1983): Ziviler Ungehorsam im Rechtsstaat, Frankfurt a. M. (Suhrkamp).
Graswurzelrevolution (1984): Ziviler Ungehorsam und Sozialdemokratie [Artikel nicht namentlich gezeichnet], Nr. 81, 1/1984, S. 10-11.
Habermas, Jürgen (1984): Ziviler Ungehorsam – Testfall für den demokratischen Rechtsstaat, in: ders.: Die neue Unübersichtlichkeit, Frankfurt a. M. (Suhrkamp), S. 79-99.
Jahn, Beate (1993): Politik und Moral. Gandhi als Herausforderung für die Weimarer Republik, Kassel (Verlag Weber, Zucht & Co.).
Jochheim, Gernot (1977): Antimilitaristische Aktionstheorie, Soziale Revolution und Soziale Verteidigung. Zur Entwicklung der Gewaltfreiheitstheorie in der europäischen antimilitaristischen und sozialistischen Bewegung 1890-1940, unter besonderer Berücksichtigung der Niederlande, Frankfurt a. M. (Haag & Herchen).
Nanda, B.R. (1985): Gandhi and his Critics, New Delhi (Oxford University Press).
Nandy, Ashis (1987): From Outside the Imperium: Gandhis Cultural Critique of the West, in: ders.: Traditions, Tyranny and Utopias. Essays in the Politics of Awareness, New Delhi (Oxford University Press), pp. 127-62.
Nandy, Ashis (2008): Der Intimfeind. Verlust und Wiederaneignung der Persönlichkeit im Kolonialismus, Nettersheim (Verlag Graswurzelrevolution).
Marcuse, Herbert (1966): Repressive Toleranz, in: Wolff, Robert, Barrington Moore und Herbert Marcuse: Kritik der reinen Toleranz, Frankfurt a. M. (Suhrkamp), S. 91-128.
Marin, Lou (2008): Einleitung: Zur Rezeption von M.K. Gandhis libertärem Anti-Kolonialismus, in: Nandy, Ashis: Der Intimfeind. Verlust und Wiederaneignung der Persönlichkeit im Kolonialismus, Nettersheim (Verlag Graswurzelrevolution), S. 7-62.
Saathoff, Günter und Stephan Uebelacker (1983): Zwischen Gegnerschaft und Kumpanei. Unterwerfung unter das staatliche Gewaltmonopol: Gespräche, De-Eskalation, Staatsverträge, in: Graswurzelrevolution Nr. 78, 8/1983, S. 19-23, 37.
Sharp, Gene (2003): From Dictatorship to Democracy. A conceptual framework for Liberation, Boston (The Albert Einstein Institution).
Situationistische Internationale (1995): Reform und Gegenreform in der bürokratischen Macht [1969], in: dies.: Der Beginn einer Epoche. Texte der Situationisten, Hamburg (Edition Nautilus), S. 284-292.
Thoreau, Henry David (1973): Über die Pflicht zum Ungehorsam gegen den Staat, in: ders.: Über die Pflicht zum Ungehorsam gegen den Staat und andere Essays, Zürich (Diogenes Verlag), S. 7-35.
Rudolph, Lloyd I. (2006): Gandhi in the Mind of America, in: ders. und Susanne Rudolph Hoeber: Postmodern Gandhi and Other Essays, London & Chicago (Chicago University Press), S. 92-139.

One Century of Revolutionary Civil Disobedience

A brief sketch of activist civil disobedience from a nonviolent-anarchist perspective

Lou Marin

Although Henry David Thoreau (1849) may have laid the most important theoretical foundation of individual civil disobedience very early on, in his 1849 essay "Resistance to Civil Government," later entitled "Civil Disobedience," civil disobedience became a strategy of efficient and radical action for disenfranchised minorities and oppressed majorities only with the 20th century campaigns of what was explicitly called civil disobedience against the British colonial empire, campaigns shaped by the ideas of Mohandas K. Gandhi. Only with this realization on the level of action did Thoreau's theoretical text become the point of departure for a concept of action involving broad social groups and the masses that would exercise a strong influence throughout the 20th century. It contributed to the overthrow of the world's largest colonial empire, the British Empire, but also to the abolition of institutionalized racism, called segregation, in the American South, and to the collapse of the state-socialist militarist regimes of Eastern Europe.

Gandhi turned Thoreau's call to individual disobedience against the state into a concept of mass activist resistance that was used in South Africa and India to advance simultaneously the liberation of women, liberation from racism and colonialism, and an anti-capitalist economy of self-sufficiency. In so doing, the libertarian anti-colonialist Gandhi (Marin 2008: 7-62) remained faithful to what was both a tendency evident in Thoreau's work and his explicit idea of an ultimate goal: that "[t]hat government is best which governs least"—and, thus Thoreau, this means in the end that "that government is best which governs not at all." (Thoreau 1849: 189)

Anti-colonialism and the campaign of civil disobedience in India (1919-1922)

The campaign of mass civil disobedience in Transvaal, South Africa (1913) and the first grand campaign of civil disobedience in India (1919-1922) earned Gandhi and his conceptions of non-violent direct action (satyagraha: holding on to truth) and civil disobedience worldwide notoriety and, in the 1920s, a worldwide reception, including a broad-based reception in the Weimar Republic (cf. Jahn 1993).

Historians of these first campaigns of explicit mass civil disobedience of the 20th century often fail to note the strong involvement of women—that the character of these actions was indeed shaped by the fact that women took on responsible roles from the very beginning. "Already the first larger satyagraha campaign [...] in South Africa in 1913 was undertaken with women representing a share of the total number of activists that was incredibly high by the standards among Indians of the time. Eleven women from 'Tolstoy Farm' and sixteen activists from the older 'Phoenix' ashram, including four women—among them Gandhi's wife, Kasturba—participated in this campaign. They protested against the so-called 'Black Act,' which imposed a ban on migration from India; against the law prohibiting the Indian minority from crossing the provincial border between Natal and Transvaal; and against an arbitrary poll tax levied on every Indian worker who was discharged after fulfillment of his five-year contract worker's term and wished to remain in South Africa. But their protest was directed above all against discriminating marriage laws that confirmed marriages between Christian Indians while retroactively declaring those among Indian Muslims, Parsis/Zoroastrians, and Hindus invalid. The sixteen activists from Phoenix illegally crossed the border from Natal into Transvaal; for this infraction, they were sentenced to three months of heavy labor. A number of satyagrahis died as a consequence of the inhuman conditions of this forced labor. And the women from 'Tolstoy Farm,' most of them wives of former contract workers, took on leadership functions during the 'Newcastle March' from Natal to Transvaal undertaken by Gandhi and 5,000 striking coalminers and their families. Despite numerous arrests—Gandhi himself was arrested—there was no stopping this march, and in December 1913 it gained the support of 50,000 miners, whose strike led to a shutdown of the mines. To Gandhi's mind, the 'Newcastle March' became an exemplary model for the Salt March; it is also treated as such for instance in the opera 'Satyagraha' by composer Philip Glass." (Marin 2008: 44f.) Glass was socialized as a 1968 hippie and, like many intellectuals of his generation, traveled to India a number of times—a first indication of the link between 1968 and a certain interpretation of Gandhi.

The strong involvement of women in the mass campaigns of civil disobedience in India between 1919 and 1922 (the general strike of 1919 and the campaign for non-cooperation of 1920-22), in 1930/31 (the Salt March), and in 1942 (the Quit

India campaign) renders the Indian independence movement simultaneously the period of a first broad-based Indian women's movement.

There is another largely forgotten aspect I would like to point out here, one that already emerged in the activist platform of the Newcastle March formed by Indian miners' families and became even more distinct with the general strike of 1919 and the campaign for non-cooperation of 1920-22 in India: the anti-capitalist nature of Gandhi's early mass actions of civil disobedience. Within the libertarian workers' movement in Europe (thus within the IAMV, the International Antimilitarist Union; the Dutch solidarity group Vrienden van India; and between individuals such as Henriette Roland Holst, Clara Wichmann, Bart de Ligt, Albert de Jong, Arthur Lehning, Pierre Ramus, et al.), the Indian non-cooperation campaign of 1920-22 was discussed also as an alternative to the concept of armed revolution put into action by the Soviets in 1917 (cf. Jochheim 1977) because it had challenged not merely the British colonial masters but also the entire Indian capitalist class:

"When Gandhi launched his non-cooperation movement against the British in 1920, the Indian millowners almost as a class opposed him. An 'Anti-non-cooperation Society' came up in Bombay in 1920 [...] its financiers included the Tatas [at the time India's leading family of entrepreneurs; today an important producer of steel, trucks, and cars; L.M.]. This society sought to combat non-cooperation through 'counter-propaganda', and worked in close cooperation with the Moderate leaders who were opposing Gandhi. It is significant that not a single industrialist signed the satyagraha pledge in March-April 1919 [...]" (Nanda 1985: 136).

During the campaign for non-cooperation between 1920 and 1922, Gandhi's concept of nonviolent action consisted in the refusal to cooperate with colonial authorities and institutions, an action that was legal and relatively easily communicated to the masses, as well as individual decisions to abandon, resign, or switch privileged and well-paid professions that served the colonial masters or placed the professional in relationships with them. A sharper edge was added to this campaign with actions of civil disobedience; those who participated in the latter were conscious of the potential consequences and the repression that would follow. In a contemporary article written for his newspaper Young India and published on March 23, 1921, Gandhi characterized the political task of civil disobedience within the framework of the non-cooperation campaign as follows:

"Civil-Disobedience is civil breach of unmoral statutory enactments. The expression was, so far as I am aware, coined by Thoreau to signify his own resistance to the laws of a slave state. He has left a masterly treatise on the duty of Civil Disobedience. But Thoreau was not perhaps an out and out champion of non-violence. Probably, also, Thoreau limited his breach of statutory laws to the revenue law i.e. payment of taxes. Whereas the term Civil Disobedience as practised in 1919 covered a breach of any statutory and unmoral law. It signified the resister's outlawry in a civil i.e. non-violent manner. [...] Non-cooperation predominantly implies withdrawing of cooperation from the State that in the non-cooperator's view has become corrupt and excludes Civil Disobedience of the fierce type described above. By its very nature, Non-cooperation is even open to children of understanding and can be safely practised by the masses. […] Non-cooperation, too, like Civil Disobedience is a branch of Satyagraha which includes all nonviolent resistance for the vindication of truth." (Gandhi 1923: 90)

For Gandhi, then, civil disobedience was illegal non-violent action accompanying a more mass-compatible non-violent action that remained within legal bounds. Taken together, these two formed the comprehensive concept of non-violent mass action (satyagraha). In his libertarian interpretation of Gandhi, the Indian social psychologist Ashis Nandy (1983: 104-5) points out that Gandhi also kept experimenting during his action campaigns and, on the basis of a multiform and nonetheless tolerant popular Hinduism, allowed room for spontaneist and almost Chaplinesque forms of expression to unfold; this liberality even gave rise, in individual examples during the Salt March, to events that anticipated later political-cultural currents such as Situationism and Surrealism and led to a later actual encounter between Gandhi and Chaplin (Marin 2008: 51ff.). This spontaneist component in Gandhi's approach to mass civil disobedience also implied the risk of a degeneration into violence, which, in the years between 1919 and 1922, twice made it necessary to abort the mass campaigns. In any case, thus Nandy's interpretation, the "experimental" aspect to Gandhi's campaigns must be seen as more important than the aspects of discipline in the training of satyagrahis at the Gandhi ashrams, though there were such aspects. Nonetheless, these mass campaigns, especially those of the Salt March in 1930/1931, admirably remained to a large extent free of violence, and by giving expression, thus Nandy, to a superior moral and cultural development, they ultimately succeeded in delegitimizing the colonial ideology that British society was more enlightened, had made greater historical progress and attained a higher degree of moral and cultural civilization. There were two immediate consequences: first, there was no spiral of escalation between repression and counter-violence, with steadily rising levels of brutalization. Nandy (1987: 161) can therefore state with regard to British repression in its colony: "One might even say, it was Gandhi's technique which elicited from his opponents a relatively humane response"—that also in comparison with other British colonies, where British repressive measures were sometimes far stronger. And second, England now also saw the rise, among the middle class as well as the Labour movement—which was culturally embarrassed and convinced that colonialism's claim to a pedagogical role and its moral justification had been defeated—of anti-colonial structures of consciousness and political currents that were able to undermine the cultural consensus at the heart of British colonialism, among the rising middle classes. The social legitimacy of colonialism had thus been corroded even years before India was granted political independence. The Labour government under Attlee was elected amid a social atmosphere in post-World War II Great Britain in which the demand for decolonization was widespread in the British Labour movement and met with sympathy among the middle class, permitting it to triumph over reactionary tendencies that called for a reconstruction of the British Empire, an Empire for which, after all, World War II had in large part been fought, especially in the Third World—a demand for decolonization, incidentally, that contrasted with the moods and government policies in France and the Netherlands immediately after the war. The three mass campaigns of civil disobedience in India, then, can arguably be characterized as Gandhi's revolutionary civil disobedience. Especially after his return to India, Gandhi no longer sought, as he still had in South Africa, to achieve equal rights within the Empire; instead, civil disobedience became a means in a struggle for revolutionary goals, a struggle to overthrow the Empire and attain Indian independence.

Reception and further development: civil disobedience in Western Europe and North America during the 1950s and 1960s

Given this historical achievement crowning a struggle that lasted almost 30 years, it is little wonder that anti-colonial liberation movements after World War II as well as the emerging peace movements in Europe closely observed, studied, and adopted for themselves the Indians' civil disobedience. In the following, I will briefly discuss two of these movements that both adopted civil disobedience and developed it further in the framework of their own actionist praxis.

In Great Britain, a tendency emerged immediately after formal decolonization had been concluded to draw on the experiences in India for the domestic purposes of the incipient struggle against the buildup of nuclear arms. In the early 1950s, a non-violent action group, which styled itself not incidentally "Operation Gandhi," formed to fend off the danger that nuclear weapons would be deployed on British soil. On January 11, 1952, it performed what was probably Europe's first sit-in outside of the British Ministry of Defence. The ten protesters were arrested and sentenced to small fines. Over the course of the following years, this form of civil disobedience was continually developed and became the characteristic form chosen for direct non-violent actions by the "Direct Action Committee" and its successor, the "Committee of 100" around the political intellectual and philosopher Bertrand Russell. Through the work of the Committee of 100, civil disobedience flourished into a mass-participation form of protest also in Europe. The "Committee of 100 collected pledges from activists; Russell proposed that no demonstration or other action be undertaken without at least 2000 participants (see Ebert 1984b: 209). As a result, between 1960 and 1962, mass sit-ins regularly took place in central London, "culminating in the largest-ever mass sit-in protest on Trafalgar Square, London, on September 17, 1961. On that day, between 5000 and 7000 demonstrators participated in the sit-in protest; 1317 were arrested and taken away in police vehicles." (Ebert 1984b: 206) The same method was also applied between 1960 and 1962 in blockades of British and American military bases before the movement suffered setbacks and petered out.

The 1950s were also the main period of reception of the Indian independence movement's civil disobedience among African-Americans in the American South.

Many black activists traveled to India in order to gather first-hand knowledge of the Indian tradition of resistance. James Lawson, for instance, spent three years in India before offering training in non-violent action in the American South in the late fifties (cf. Carson 1995: 22). Rosa Parks, whose action initiated the legendary 1955 Montgomery Bus Boycott, had participated in a seminar on civil disobedience at Highlander Folk School in Monteagle, Tennessee taught by the Indian Gandhian and socialist Ram Manohar Lohia, who was in the US in 1951 at the invitation of students at this black college. "Lohia had familiarized Highlander Folk School leaders with Gandhi's ideas and practices about non-violent civil disobedience and urged them to use them." (Rudolph 2006: 110) This reception gave rise to the actions of mass civil disobedience of the African-American Civil Rights Movement in the American South, which, though they made Martin Luther King, Jr., famous, had their basis in the black student organization Student Nonviolent Coordinating Committee (SNCC). As in Great Britain, the actions of mass civil disobedience in the American South culminated in the early 1960s: in 1960, black students staged mass occupations of public facilities, bars, coffee shops, restaurants, waiting halls at bus and railway stations, etc. that were subject to racist segregation. The next stage saw actions of civil disobedience against the so-called "racial segregation" on American interstate buses ("Freedom Rides") and a series of protest marches through rural regions were racism's roots were strongest or where civil rights workers had been killed. When King was murdered on April 4, 1968, his exchanges with the students of the SNCC had radicalized him, too; he had publicly denounced the Vietnam war, developed a morally founded critique of capitalism, and lent his support to a strike campaign mounted by black garbage collectors in Memphis (cf. Carson 1995).

Civil disobedience around 1968

The mass actions of civil disobedience staged by African-American students and the British Committee of 100 garnered worldwide attention and turned out to be exemplary models for what the students of 1968 were to call, with a provisional and not altogether adequate term, "limited infraction." Especially in the early phase of the West German student movement, before the attempted assassination of Rudi Dutschke on April 11, 1968, the revolt of '68 frequently invoked explicitly the Anglo-Saxon tradition of civil disobedience. In Berlin, a German-language "Committee of 100" formed around "Arbeitskreis 28" at the Kritische Universität (Critical University); on February 3, this Committee staged a sit-in by ca. 1000 students directed against the Greek military dictatorship outside the Greek military mission in Berlin. In order to mobilize participants, the organizers distributed 50,000 flyers containing a pledge that declared their determination to limit themselves to non-violent behavior (Ebert 1984a: 62). Immediately after the assassination of Martin Luther King, the Free University of Berlin's student union executive committee declared: "Martin Luther King and his friends developed the forms of struggle that are being used here today; their names—sit-in, teach-in—are still reminiscent of this origin" (quoted in Ebert 1984a: 22f.). And even on April 17, 1968, after the attempted assassination of Dutschke and the attacks against the Springer publishing house's headquarters, which had in part been violent, the action committee of workers and high-school and college students at the Technical University of Berlin issued a press release on questions of strategy: "Our practice is, as a matter of principle, educational and hence fundamentally non-violent" (quoted in Ebert 1984a: 27). But at this point the altercations within the student movement over the question of counter-violence fully set in, taking place, as it were, inside every individual mind.

For an understanding of the civil disobedience of 1968 in comparison with later forms of civil disobedience in the years between 1970 and 2000, a contemporary essay by the theorist Theodor Ebert is of interest. Regarding the question of the use of violence during direct actions, Ebert, in 1968, critically engaged Herbert Marcuse's concept of "counter-violence" (cf. Marcuse 1965), seeking to replace it with a conception of "counter-power," which would be exercised by mass direct non-violent action (Ebert 1984a: 18). In this context, Ebert concedes to Marcuse that

"[W]hen democratic, legal paths toward changing the social conditions are absent or blocked due to comprehensive manipulation, the mere appeal to peaceableness and the renunciation of violence becomes an ideology that objectively serves those in power. This was Marcuse's necessary critique of the preachers of non-violence affiliated with the establishment" (Ebert 1984a: 18). Against the slogan propagated by Hans-Jürgen Krahl, a Frankfurt member of the Socialist German Student Union, after the demonstrations against Springer, that revolutionary violence was self-defense, Ebert argued in favor of a revolutionary civil disobedience. His argument drew on the revolutionary interpretation Gandhi had given to civil disobedience in the early 1920s: if the establishment "is prepared to make no or only symbolic concessions, the extra-parliamentary opposition can no longer, nor needs to, limit itself to methods of dramatization; it can then resort to measures of compulsion that render the continued exercise of unjust power impossible and create new institutions that exercise democratic counter-power" (Ebert 1984a: 43). And: "the extra-parliamentary opposition is currently capable at best of demonstrative civil disobedience but not of a revolutionary civil disobedience that would paralyze the existing system [...] If the group of those who perform civil disobedience in this way grows beyond a number of multiple thousands, this may not only block the judicial machinery but also raise the material cost to those in power as well as the expense of prestige to such an extent that it may appear to them more convenient to forgo the implementation of these laws" (Ebert 1984a: 52, 52). Arguing firmly within the terminology of the students' systemic critique, Ebert speaks of the Federal Republic's "formally democratic" structure, which he contrasts with a substantive democracy as the utopian goal of the struggle. With regard to Rudi Dutschke's concept of the "Long March through the Institutions" he criticizes not the goal of revolutionary overthrow but the fact that Dutschke is inspired by thinking in Mao's categories and those of armed struggle:

"Yet if one pays attention less to this self-conception than to their practice, one is even more justified in saying that the students are also Gandhi's disciples. Gandhi's conception of revolution was that of a 'grassroots revolution,' that is to say, a radical transformation of a society by successively democratizing its institutions from the bottom up; in accordance with this conception," Gandhi, thus Ebert, had striven to establish "a republic of cooperative councils" (Ebert 1984a: 53). Gandhi's conception of revolution was closer to that entertained by the extra-parliamentary opposition also because, thus Ebert further, the latter understood the Long March through the institutions to be one "not in a territorial but in a social sense" (Ebert 1984a: 53). Yet the students, he wrote, failed to consciously apperceive that fact: "This strategy of non-violent insurrection is not only unknown; its reception is emotionally blocked. [...] Since the SDS has learnt to follow in its critique of the social state of affairs almost exclusively the lead provided by Marxist thinkers, it is not surprising that it would also adopt as its guides those theorists and practicians of the revolution who explicitly invoked Karl Marx. Conversely, all other strategists of social change, such as Gandhi and King, who, because of their religiously motivated critique of historical materialism, had never been self-identified Marxists, are classified as bourgeois and liberals without further examination. The SDS, as well as other leaders of opinion among the extra-parliamentary opposition, thus failed to perceive that Gandhi's and King's analyses of capitalism and imperialism are largely in agreement with those of Marxist theorists, or at least not in contradiction with the theoretical underpinnings of the latter" (Ebert 1984a: 23f.)

In 1968, Ebert thus takes a position firmly within the framework of revolutionary civil disobedience and the social anti-capitalism associated with it that had already been the basis of the Indian movement of the early 1920s.

It is interesting to note an ambivalence that appears already at this time in Ebert's essay: on the one hand, he highlights forms of "political happening," of "socialist street theater," etc., with which the student protesters disrupted the petrified culture of 1950s forms of protest; he can even write that "[t]he spontaneity of this process of democratization is its great strength, for the repressive effect of cutting the tallest blades of grass in a 'grass-roots revolution' is small" (Ebert 1984a: 54). Yet on the other hand, Ebert criticizes the preponderance within the student movement of theatrical and spontaneist forms of action over serious and disciplined ones, arguing in favor of "disciplined civil disobedience" (Ebert 1984a: 40). The black members of the American Civil Rights Movement and the opponents of nuclear armament of the "Committee of 100," thus Ebert, participated in demonstrations "out of an obligation to their conscience and not because demonstrating 'is exciting and fun'" (Ebert 1984a: 31). An antagonism begins to emerge here between spontaneism and discipline/schematism that will be of great significance for the further development of civil disobedience in Europe and lead to the formation of distinct and conflicting conceptions.

First, however, reference must be made to the mass civil disobedience in dictatorships ignited, as it were, by the resistance of students and workers in Prague in 1968. The Czechoslovak movement against the Soviet occupation needed no disciplinary or educational measures, let alone specially trained activists, in order to remain largely non-violent; it drew such mass participation and was so spontaneist that even one of the last texts by the French Situationist International, in September, 1969, presented it as exemplary and seminal:

"The Czechoslovakian experience has shown the extraordinary possibilities of struggle that a consistent and organized revolutionary movement will one day have at its disposal. Equipment provided by the Warsaw Pact (in anticipation of a possible imperialist invasion of Czechoslovakia!) was used by the Czech journalists to set up 35 clandestine broadcasting stations linked with 80 emergency backup stations. The Soviet propaganda—so necessary for an occupation army—was thus totally undermined; and the population was able to know just about everything that was happening in the country and to follow the directives of the liberal bureaucrats or of the radical elements that controlled certain stations. For example, in response to a radio appeal aimed at sabotaging the operations of the Russian police, Prague was transformed into a veritable "labyrinth-city": all the streets lost their names, all the houses lost their numbers and were covered with inscriptions in the best style of May 1968 Paris. Defying all the police, Prague became a home of freedom, an example of the revolutionary detournement of repressive urbanism." (Situationist International 1981: 262)

Gone, too, was here what Ebert had lamented as the students' emotional blockade: "The critique of Leninism [...] was [...] the highest point of theoretical critique attained in a bureaucratic country. Dutschke himself was ridiculed by the revolutionary Czech students and his 'anarcho-Maoism' scornfully rejected as 'absurd, laughable and not even deserving the attention of a fifteen-year-old.'" (Situationist International 1981: 261)

The Czech students and workers offered the most impressive exercise of revolutionary civil disobedience in its spontaneist, grass-roots revolutionary form as called for by Ebert in 1968. True, their resistance against the Soviet occupation was an immediate failure. But their cultural and moral superiority was so overwhelming and left such a powerful impression of an emancipatory movement in the minds of activists that Prague, 1968 was repeated as soon as the opportunity arose—when an internal crisis of power within the Soviet system weakened the ability of Soviet troops in Eastern Europe to exercise repression. In this sense, the revolutionary mass movement of civil disobedience in Prague in 1989 only put into action what had long attained cultural hegemony. Together with the movements in East Germany, Poland, and other countries in Eastern Europe, it rendered 1989 the year of civil disobedience against dictatorships, with repercussions and consequences reaching as far as the overthrow of the Apartheid regime in South Africa and the victories over military dictatorships in Latin America.

Feminism and anti-militarism: civil disobedience in the New Social Movements of the 1970s and 1980s

In the West in general and in West Germany in particular, civil disobedience prevailed, in a protracted process, over the emotional disconnect of the students of 1968 to become a widely used form of protest in the New Social Movements of the 1970s and 1980s, especially in the Women's Movement (the "I had an abortion" campaign was a classical display of civil disobedience against an established legal standard), the radical environmentalist movement (occupations of construction sites of future nuclear power plants), the peace movement (blockades of the access roads to military sites such as Großengstingen in 1982 and Mutlangen from 1983 onward, campaigns in support of conscientious objectors to the obligatory military service, disruptions of maneuvers at the Fulda Gap training area), or during the general census boycott (1983-1987). However, theorists and activists organized in non-violent action groups and other relevant associations who sought to hold on to the project of a revolutionary civil disobedience that would vanquish the system were compelled to contend less with Marxist (or radical-leftist) concepts of counter-violence and more and more with reformist reinterpretations of civil disobedience.

This tendency emerged as early as 1970, in a political essay by the philosopher Hannah Arendt entitled "Civil Disobedience," which assessed and interpreted the experiences of the African-American Civil Rights Movement, the movement against the Vietnam War, and the student movement in the US. Arendt's reflections, however, retained an ambivalent attitude toward revolutionary civil disobedience. On the one hand—and in clear contrast with all subsequent reformist interpretations of civil disobedience—Arendt distinguished between civil and criminal disobedience, emphasizing that while the participant in civil disobedience runs the risk of suffering repression in response to his act or to be thrown in prison, it is by no means necessary that he do so of his own free volition and as an integral component of civil disobedience: "'The idea that paying the penalty justifies breaking the law derives, not from Gandhi and the tradition of civil disobedience, but from Oliver Wendell Holmes and the tradition of legal realism. ... This doctrine ... is plainly absurd ... in the area of criminal law. ... It is mindless to suppose that murder, rape or arson would be justified if only one were willing to pay the penalty.' It is most unfortunate that, in the eyes of many, a 'self-sacrificial element' is the best proof of 'intensity of concern,' of 'the disobedient's seriousness and his fidelity to law,' for single-minded fanaticism is usually the hallmark of the crackpot and, in any case, makes impossible a rational discussion of the issues at stake." (Arendt 1972: 66-67) It is possible that this harshly phrased critique relates to Arendt's experiences during her collection of accounts of how Jews were saved in Europe under National-Socialist occupation, where for those who broke the law to surrender to the authorities would have been tantamount to an immediate death sentence (Arendt 1963). On the other hand, however, the second part of her essay on "Civil Disobedience" very much seeks to reconcile the organized minority of civil disobedience activists to the American founding fathers' "spirit of the laws" (Arendt 1972: 85) and in particular to the fundamentally American traditions of consensus, which include the right of voluntary associations to dissent, and to the legitimation of a constitutional right to resistance and a Lockian "horizontal version of the social contract" (Arendt 1972: 86). She thus seeks to find a "niche" (Arendt 1972: 83) within the constitution for civil disobedience, "[t]he establishment of civil disobedience among our political institutions" (Arendt 1972: 101), even though she is fully aware that "'the law cannot justify the violation of the law,' even if this violation aims at preventing the violation of another law" (Arendt 1972: 99).

In the West German peace movement of the 1980s, certain campaigns then adopted juridicalizing terms for civil disobedience such as "civil disobedience as active protection of the constitution" (the legal scholar E. Küchenhoff), or declared civil disobedience to be "the social invention of democracy" (Ebert 1984b)—but now, thus in Ebert, no longer against the backdrop of an existing democracy pronounced to be merely formal in nature; instead, the idea was that democracy had since 1968 become reality without a revolution, as though by a miracle! Over the course of trials that lasted for a number of years, the blockade as a form of direct action breaking the law was finally downgraded by Germany's Federal Constitutional Court to the status of a constitutional form of demonstration.

How the situation had changed can be discussed on the basis of a second essay by Theodor Ebert (1984b). By this time, Ebert—like so many of those involved in 1968 before and after him—has switched sides and become what he himself had criticized years earlier, a "preacher of non-violence affiliated with the establishment." In this second essay by Ebert, there is no more talk of revolutionary civil disobedience: "If, then, the intention is to examine the benefits and drawbacks of civil disobedience to representative democracy, the question must be approached in a way that remains immanent to democracy. Nor is that surprising, given that the concept of civil disobedience was originally developed in democracies and, as distinct from the general concept of non-violent resistance, represents a variant of non-violent action specific to democracies" (Ebert 1984c: 255). That is an entirely new idea, and in perfect contradiction with Gandhi's classificatory division of non-violent action into legal action and illegal action (civil disobedience). Ebert further writes: "According to the International Encyclopedia of the Social Sciences, 'civil' in conjunction with 'disobedience' has five equally legitimate meanings: 1. in recognition of general obligations of citizenship; 2. non-military and non-violent; 3. polite, civilized; 4. public (as opposed to private); 5. oriented toward the common good. This interpretation of 'civil' bespeaks the recognition that civil disobedience is sometimes a democratic obligation" (Ebert 1984c: 260). Civil disobedience is no longer a "measure of compulsion" intended to "raise the material cost to those in power" but now only a demonstrative and dramatizing measure: "Non-violent direct action dramatizes a matter of conflict in such a way that it can no longer be ignored" (Ebert 1984c: 265). Ultimately, Ebert directly characterizes the civil disobedience action as "dramatic action" (Ebert 1984c: 267). But one who merely dramatizes does not himself effect a change, instead voluntarily leaving those decisions to others—in this case, to the constitutional organs of the lawful state.

From 1981 onward a pan-European peace movement was rising against the deployment of medium-range ballistic missiles. In West Germany, this movement led to the ouster of the pro-deployment Social Democrats under Schmidt in 1982. Subsequently, a supposedly reformed Social Democratic Party tentatively extended its reach into oppositional movements and sought to co-opt concepts of action including that of civil disobedience for the state, to reconcile them with the lawful state. Here, we are dealing no longer, as in Thoreau, with "resistance to civil government" but with civil disobedience "within the lawful state" (Glotz 1983). This meant, as a writer for the journal Graswurzelrevolution (1984: 10f.) criticized at the time, "that the discussion within the Social Democracy is not about support for forms of civil disobedience but about their functionalization." Peter Glotz, at the time the party's leading strategist, wrote that "[w]hat we need is the indefinite process of an ongoing reconciliation between legality and legitimacy. In the form of government we have chosen, the law is a program of order designed to produce—and dependent on—consensus" (Glotz 1983: 8). At issue is here a Social-Democratic integration into the system and, conversely, the elimination of arguments that legitimize the illegal action of civil disobedience. In this way, thus Glotz's critic in Graswurzelrevolution, citizens' initiatives engaging in civil disobedience would be assigned the sole function "of serving as a sort of early-warning system to the politicians appointed to make the decisions" (1984: 10). In so doing, the citizen discharges his or her civic duty. The fact that 'civil disobedience' was often rendered in German as "bürgerlicher" (the Bürger is both the citizen and the bourgeois) instead of "ziviler Ungehorsam" also served to bolster this interpretation in the debates at the time. At their center stood the question of whether or not the state's monopoly on the use of force ought to be recognized as legitimate and as a progressive cultural achievement. Glotz on this question: "The hasty retreat to the position of conscience endangers the cultural achievement of the state's monopoly on the use of force" (Glotz 1983: 12). Against this conception of the state articulated by Glotz as well as Jürgen Habermas (1985: 95-116), Graswurzelrevolution (1984: 11) argued as follows: "The state has not come into being by virtue of a social contract or of individual agreements on a number of issues to be cooperatively settled, as Habermas, for instance, ultimately also supposes. Historically, the state means primarily the monopoly to exercise force in order for a specific social group to acquire or retain dominance. The result is the usurped right to extort from the subjects the material or financial means (taxes) to sustain this apparatus. The state is the open or restrained state of war against society. […] If, then, members of the social body express their volition by way of disobedience against the state, this means that society is taking back powers of decision-making the state had usurped. One may object at this point, with Habermas, that such an argument unleashes the violence within society; Glotz would surely see the 'cultural achievement of the state's monopoly on the use of force' in danger. Yet this is precisely also where the postulate of non-violence in civil disobedience has its place: a credible alternative to the state's apparatus of force can be offered only by rejecting the principle of the state, that is, by rejecting violence. Civil disobedience, then, endangers the state's monopoly on the use of force because it replaces it with peaceful settlements and modes of behavior, truly rendering the state superfluous. Those who, by contrast, oppose the state with their own violence wish for nothing but state—albeit a different one."

Yet even on the level of action, among the activists of civil disobedience themselves, there were controversies that took up the structures of consciousness behind this reformist interpretation of civil disobedience. During the 1980s, especially among the "campaign of civil disobedience until disarmament," a Social-Democratic interpretation of civil disobedience spread over the course of a number of successive blockades of the Mutlangen missile site, in the public statements of their motivation and in their schematically repetitive procedures; an interpretation which other non-violent action groups and authors around Graswurzelrevolution in turn criticized as a schematization, ritualization, and disciplining of the actions and the participants in it and as an increasing calculability of the actions of civil disobedience. From the perspective of revolutionary civil disobedience, the model of disciplined and disciplining action had by the mid-1980s gained ground against the spontaneist incalculability entailed by the direct non-violent action and political happening of the 1968 revolt. At the same time, this process contributed to an impoverishment of the movement's imagination and artistic expressivity. One author in Graswurzelrevolution criticized that

"[t]he blockades are to demonstrate how serious those who perform them are about this. How do you demonstrate that? Civil disobedience has an answer to this question, too: its 'means are not power and violence but arguments and the willingness to suffer.' […] What must be attacked is a thinking focused on harmony that forgoes to distinguish between friend and enemy, so great is its willingness to engage in dialogue. There are no more enemies, only partners in dialogue. If the peace movement voluntarily renounces the development of counter-power (that would be the mission of mass civil disobedience!), it remains quite literally powerless" (Bröckling 1986: 9). This merely repeats Ebert's terminology of 1968 at a time when Ebert himself is no longer capable of using these terms. The critique of the "campaign of civil disobedience until disarmament" continues: "What must be attacked is a mysticism of suffering in the campaign's public statements. Political struggle entails drawbacks and risks; to deny that would be naïve. The powers that be will not be criticized with impunity. Yet those who stylize these drawbacks and risks, stylize suffering into a 'means' of resistance, not only misapprehend reality (Wolf Biermann sang in his 'Encouragement,' a song also often played during the blockades: 'Those in power tremble once you're behind bars, but not for fear of your suffering ...'); they also display cynicism toward the victims who have not freely chosen their suffering. What remains to be noted is the shocking banality of the 'aesthetic of resistance' in Mutlangen. Its means are limited to invocations of nuclear catastrophe, pious songs, and lyrical effusions of solicitude. [...] If it is correct that the artistic powers unleashed by a movement are an indicator of its emancipatory potential, then Mutlangen and the peace movement are not in a good way." (Bröckling 1986: 9)

Graswurzelrevolution also argued against a slogan indicative of such a Social-Democratic interpretation of civil disobedience spreading among some activists, that "The police is not our enemy" (Saathoff/Uebelacker 1983: 22):

"Those who offer non-violent opposition do not confront the police [...] as a neutral executive organ but as a part of one of the conflicting parties. [...] It is right that we should at any time offer those in positions of political responsibility negotiations over our political demands. By contrast, negotiations with the police, who are not politically responsible, over the forms of our actions are completely wrong, superfluous, and deleterious! Their consequence is that our direct actions degenerate into games played out on a map and calculable to the police. [...] Those who, by negotiating with the other side, foreground the means of this conflict, even negotiating them with the police, give their consent that our political conflict be transformed into a problem of public safety. We believe that no invocation of the 'classic authors' of non-violence can justify negotiations over forms of action. The principle of willingness to engage in dialogue, which remains correct, refers to a dialogue over substantive demands. Did Gandhi confer with the British executive before setting out on the Salt March? Did M.L. King, before he called for the Bus Boycott, sit down with the chief of police in Montgomery to contemplate appropriate forms of action together with him?" (Saathoff/Uebelacker 1983: 22f.)

Avoiding dead ends: civil disobedience in the 1990s and the first years of the 21st century

Yet it was also owing to this capacity for critical self-reflection and self-critique among the members of non-violent action groups that schematizing dead-ends in the civil disobedience campaigns of the West-German peace movement could be questioned, and largely overcome during the blockade of the German Parliament, the Bundestag, on the occasion of the vote on the restrictive asylum law revision of 1993, the actions against the Gulf and Yugoslavian wars during the 1990s, the direct non-violent actions against nuclear waste transports to Gorleben, and most recently the action campaigns against the G7 and G8 summit meetings, once again unleashing imaginative and unpredictable actions of mass civil disobedience of social movements. During the first years of the 21st century, however, the theoretical and practical foundations of a Social-Democratic, dramatic-demonstrative, disciplinary, state-oriented, and instrumental interpretation of civil disobedience have been appropriated also by think tanks in the US, which organized campaigns of civil disobedience, with financial support from the United States for small local groups (such as "Otpor"/"Resistance" in Serbia), in order to topple governments, especially in Eastern Europe and Asia, whose policies turned out to run counter to US interests. A whole series of supposedly non-violent revolutions bearing made-for-the-media labels such as "Cedar Revolution" (Lebanon), "Orange Revolution" (Ukraine), "Rose Revolution" (Georgia), "Tulip Revolution" (Kyrgyzstan) are "regime changes" welcomed by the US government. They are paid for with funds from US research institutions and foundations often affiliated with the Democratic Party. One such player is the Soros Foundation set up by US investment banker and billionaire George Soros's. The strategic interests that drive such involvement are often concealed behind ostensibly altruistic support in the form of strategic assistance and advisors in matters of civil disobedience drawn from peace institutes around the most prominent American theorist of civil disobedience, Gene Sharp (2003), who has by now, like Ebert, become a reformist loyal to the system. It is certainly indicative when the organization "Freedom House" led by the former CIA chief and Rumsfeld adviser James Woolsey donates 5000 copies of Sharp's book "From Dictatorship to Democracy" (Sharp 2003) to the Serbian oppositional group "Otpor" in order to organize campaigns of civil disobedience (Eiselberg 2006: 6). By contrast, initiatives of non-violent resistance against dictatorships in Eastern Europe and Central Asia that act in accordance with US interests (such as Azerbaijan, with whose government US-based multinational companies have signed lucrative oil contracts) conspicuously received no such support, which was one reason why they failed to draw mass participation. While this is certainly not the only cause behind the mass movements that have arisen in Eastern Europe and Central Asia, it is surely one important and largely underestimated factor. It is important in this context to remember that Gandhi's campaigns of civil disobedience in the early 1920s were anti-capitalist in character—such historical memory would serve today to protect civil disobedience against strategies that seek to appropriate it, integrate it into the system, and make it an instrument of imperialism; strategies which US think tanks see as a cheaper alternative in the service of self-interested global policies to military interventions such as those in Iraq and Afghanistan, and which will thus probably gain even greater importance in the future (cf. Eiselberg 2006: 6-7). The struggle over concepts, interpretations, and structures of consciousness around the concept of civil disobedience, the struggle against its instrumentalization for the interests of the state continues! But his struggle is simultaneously also a clear indication of the relevance and significance of civil disobedience to the social struggles of the 21st century!

Translated from the German by Gerrit Jackson.

Literature:

Arendt, Hannah (1963): Eichmann in Jerusalem. A Report on the Banality of Evil, New York (Viking).
Arendt, Hannah (1972): Civil Disobedience [1970], in: Arendt, Crises of the Republic, New York (Harcourt Brace Jovanovich), pp. 49-102.
Bröckling, Ulrich (1986): Kampagne Ziviler Ungehorsam bis zur Abrüstung. Widerstand als Ritual? – Kritische Anmerkungen, in: Graswurzelrevolution Nr. 103, 4/1986, pp. 8-9.
Carson, Clayborne (2004): In Struggle. SNCC and the Black Awakening of the 1960s, Cambridge, Mass. (Harvard University Press).
Ebert, Theodor (1984a): Die außerparlamentarische Opposition und die gewaltfreie Macht [1968], in: Ebert, Theodor: Ziviler Ungehorsam. Von der APO zur Friedensbewegung, Waldkirch (Waldkircher Verlag), pp. 12-58.
Ebert, Theodor (1984b): Ziviler Widerstand gegen die Raketenbasen. Lehren der 60er Jahre – Aktionsformen für 1983 [1982], in: Ebert, Theodor: Ziviler Ungehorsam. Von der APO zur Friedensbewegung, Waldkirch (Waldkircher Verlag), pp. 204-216.
Ebert, Theodor (1984c): Ziviler Ungehorsam – eine soziale Erfindung der Demokratie [1983], in: Ebert, Theodor: Ziviler Ungehorsam. Von der APO zur Friedensbewegung, Waldkirch (Waldkircher Verlag), pp. 253-275.
Eiselberg, Thomas S. (2006): Globalizing Nonviolence? ‚Gewaltfreie Revolution' in Osteuropa und Zentralasien im Auftrag nationaler Interessen der USA?, in: Graswurzelrevolution Nr. 306, 2/2006, pp. 6-7.
Gandhi, Mahatma (1923): Notes: Satyagrah, Civil Disobedience, Passive Resistance, Non-co-operation, in: Young India, Ahmedabad, March 23rd, 1921, pp. 89-90.
Glotz, Peter (Hg.) (1983): Ziviler Ungehorsam im Rechtsstaat, Frankfurt a. M. (Suhrkamp).
Graswurzelrevolution (1984): Ziviler Ungehorsam und Sozialdemokratie [anonymous contributor], Nr. 81, 1/1984, pp. 10-11.
Habermas, Jürgen (1985): Civil Disobedience: Litmus Test for the Democratic Constitutional State, tr. J. Torpey, Berkeley Journal of Sociology 30, pp. 95-116.
Jahn, Beate (1993): Politik und Moral. Gandhi als Herausforderung für die Weimarer Republik, Kassel (Verlag Weber, Zucht & Co.).
Jochheim, Gernot (1977): Antimilitaristische Aktionstheorie, Soziale Revolution und Soziale Verteidigung. Zur Entwicklung der Gewaltfreiheitstheorie in der europäischen antimilitaristischen und sozialistischen Bewegung 1890-1940, unter besonderer Berücksichtigung der Niederlande, Frankfurt a. M. (Haag & Herchen).
Nanda, B.R. (1985): Gandhi and his Critics, New Delhi (Oxford University Press).
Nandy, Ashis (1983): The Intimate Enemy. Loss and Recovery of Self under Colonialism, New Delhi (Oxford University Press).
Nandy, Ashis (1987): From Outside the Imperium: Gandhis Cultural Critique of the West, in: Nandy, Ashis: Traditions, Tyranny and Utopias. Essays in the Politics of Awareness, New Delhi (Oxford University Press), pp. 127-62.
Marcuse, Herbert (1965): Repressive Tolerance, in: Wolff, Robert, Barrington Moore, and Herbert Marcuse: A Critique of Pure Tolerance, Boston (Beacon), pp. 95-137.
Marin, Lou (2008): Einleitung: Zur Rezeption von M.K. Gandhis libertärem Anti-Kolonialismus, in: Nandy, Ashis: Der Intimfeind. Verlust und Wiederaneignung der Persönlichkeit im Kolonialismus, Nettersheim (Verlag Graswurzelrevolution), pp. 7-62.
Saathoff, Günter, and Stephan Uebelacker (1983): Zwischen Gegnerschaft und Kumpanei. Unterwerfung unter das staatliche Gewaltmonopol: Gespräche, De-Eskalation, Staatsverträge, in: Graswurzelrevolution Nr. 78, 8/1983, pp. 19-23, 37.
Sharp, Gene (2003): From Dictatorship to Democracy. A conceptual framework for Liberation, Boston (The Albert Einstein Institution).
Situationist International (1981): Reform and Counterreform in Bureaucratic Power [1969], in: Situationist International Anthology, Berkeley, CA (Bureau of Public Secrets), pp. 256-256.
Thoreau, Henry David (1849): Resistance to Civil Government [Civil Disobedience], in: Elizabeth Peabody (ed.): Aesthetic Papers, Boston and New York (Peabody and Putnam), pp. 189-211.
Rudolph, Lloyd I. (2006): Gandhi in the Mind of America, in: Rudolph, Lloyd, and Susanne Hoeber Rudolph: Postmodern Gandhi and Other Essays, London & Chicago (Chicago University Press), pp. 92-139.

Ziviler und Sozialer Ungehorsam gleich Verweigerung plus Utopie?

Ulrike Laubenthal

Freitag, 1. Juni 2007: 600 Kriegsgegner und Kriegsgegnerinnen besiedeln den geplanten Bombenabwurfplatz in der Kyritz-Ruppiner Heide. Sie nehmen einen alten Kommandoturm in Besitz und streichen ihn im Handumdrehen mit der „zivilen" Farbe rosa, hängen Transparente und Fahnen auf, errichten Zelte. Musiker und Musikerinnen spielen Stücke von Haydn, Weill, Bach, Pasquay und anderen. Über 100 Clowns treiben ihren Spaß und verjagen damit einen Jeep der Bundeswehr, der sich in die Nähe der Aktion gewagt hatte. Unter den Teilnehmern und Teilnehmerinnen befinden sich auch zahlreiche Menschen aus dem europäischen Ausland, die sich mit Euromärschen und Fahrradkarawanen auf dem Weg nach Rostock befinden. Die Aktivisten und Aktivistinnen übernachten auf dem Platz. Am Samstagmorgen fährt die Mehrzahl dann weiter zur Großdemonstration gegen den G8-Gipfel in Rostock.

Ziviler Ungehorsam erlebt zurzeit eine neue Blüte. Die globalisierungskritische Bewegung entdeckt für sich alte, erprobte Formen gemeinsamen politischen Handelns neu, die in den letzten Jahren nur von verhältnismäßig kleinen Kreisen praktiziert wurden.

Es kann noch sehr spannend werden in den nächsten Jahren. Mehr und mehr Menschen leben prekär, gewohnte Sicherheiten schwinden dahin. Kriegseinsätze der Bundeswehr in aller Welt, die vor 20 Jahren noch zu einem großen Aufschrei geführt hätten, sind auf dem Umweg über Sanitäts – und Minensucheinsätze nach und nach im Bewusstsein von mehr und mehr Menschen als normal und akzeptabel verbucht worden. Sie dürften in den nächsten Jahren noch massiv zunehmen. Im Inland wird derweil das Militär in immer mehr gesellschaftlichen Bereichen präsent. Überwachungs- und Unterdrückungsmethoden, die noch vor kurzem völlig undenkbar gewesen wären, werden mit erstaunlicher Geschwindigkeit und von der Öffentlichkeit beinahe unbemerkt „normal".

Mag sein, dass die sozialen Bewegungen angesichts dieser Veränderungen eine Randerscheinung bleiben, weil sich gerade in Zeiten zunehmender Verunsicherung viele doch zuerst darum kümmern, die eigenen Schäfchen ins Trockene zu bringen. Mag aber auch sein, dass wir tatsächlich eine wachsende, mächtiger werdende emanzipatorische Bewegung erleben, die durch Sozialen Ungehorsam an Macht gewinnt. Dann wären für mich die spannenden Fragen:

Wird diese Bewegung sich nur den bestehenden globalisierten staatlichen und wirtschaftlichen Strukturen verweigern, oder wird sie Utopien und handfeste Konzepte für eigene tragfähige Entscheidungs- und Subsistenz-Wirtschafts-Strukturen entwickeln und umsetzen?

Wird diese Bewegung den üblichen Eskalationsschemata gesellschaftlicher Konflikte folgen, wonach bei zunehmender Intensität der Konfliktaustragung immer mehr Regeln des menschlichen Miteinanders außer Kraft gesetzt, Menschenrechte einander abgesprochen werden? Oder wird diese Bewegung dadurch etwas Besonderes sein, dass sie Menschenrechte und Verabredungen für ein solidarisches und menschenwürdiges Miteinander auch und gerade in Zeiten des Kampfes, auch und gerade gegenüber dem politischen Gegner einhält?

Werden mehr und mehr diejenigen auf allen Seiten an Einfluss gewinnen, die jung, stark, männlich und ungebunden sind, während Frauen, Kindern, Alten und Menschen mit Behinderung die Rolle der zu beschützenden und zu benützenden Opfer zufällt? Oder werden wir Organisationsformen finden, in denen alle, ob stark oder schwach, alt oder jung, Mann, Frau oder Zwitter Einfluss auf die Entwicklung haben? Zunächst mal eine Begriffsklärung: Unter Zivilem Ungehorsam verstehe ich eine begrenzte Regelverletzung, eine Weigerung, an einem Unrecht mitzuwirken, ein Unrecht hinzunehmen, in einem ungerechten System zu funktionieren.

Ihre besondere Wirkungskraft bezieht diese Form politischen Handelns nach meinem Verständnis aus dem Umstand, dass die zivil Ungehorsamen Verantwortung übernehmen. Üblich ist es ja in politischen Auseinandersetzungen, Verantwortung abzuschieben, sich selber für unschuldig an allem Schlechten, für hilflos zu erklären („da kann man nichts machen") und von den anderen, „den Verantwortlichen", eine Änderung zu fordern. Ganz anders das, was Thoreau in seinem viel zitierten Aufsatz „Über die Pflicht zum Ungehorsam gegen den Staat" beschreibt und was seitdem vielerorts praktiziert wurde: „Mach dein Leben zu einem Gegengewicht, um die Maschine aufzuhalten. Jedenfalls muss ich zusehen, dass ich mich nicht zu dem Unrecht hergebe, das ich verdamme." (Thoreau 1973: 18) Wer Gesetze bricht aus einer eigenen Gewissensentscheidung, aus einer Einsicht in die eigene Mitverantwortung heraus, geht auf die politischen Gegner nicht aggressiv zu, sondern affirmativ: Nicht die Anklage gegen andere Personen steht im Vordergrund, sondern die Kritik an einem Unrecht und die eigene Übernahme von Verantwortung zu seiner Überwindung. Diejenigen, die am Unrecht festhalten, werden eingeladen, ebenfalls Verantwortung für ihr eigenes Handeln zu übernehmen. Diese Haltung entspricht der, die Burkhard Bläsi auf der Grundlage seiner empirischen Forschungen zur „Gütekraft" beschreibt. Er beschreibt zwei Säulen mit Verhaltensweisen, die diese Kraft freisetzen, die auch „Kraft der Gewaltfreiheit", „Kraft der Wahrheit" oder von Gandhi „Satyagraha" genannt wurde. Eine Säule nennt er „Paroli bieten", dazu gehört, am Ort des Unrechts präsent zu sein, den eigenen Standpunkt beharrlich deutlich zu machen, ggf. auch Nachteile in Kauf zu nehmen. Die andere Säule, „Vertrauensaufbau", beinhaltet nicht verletzendes Verhalten, Empathie, Offenheit und die Ermunterung zum Perspektivenwechsel. (Bläsi 2001) Die Kombination von „Paroli bieten" und „Vertrauensaufbau" kann beim Gegenüber Achtung erzeugen. Sie erzeugt eine emotionale Betroffenheit und ggf. ein Anerkennen gemeinsamer Werte; im optimalen Fall wird das Gewissen aktiviert und treibt das Gegenüber zu einer Änderung seines/ihres eigenen Verhaltens oder seiner/ihrer Ansichten.

Beim Zivilen Ungehorsam sind wir am Ort des Geschehens und machen unsere Forderungen deutlich; zugleich tun wir das auf eine Art, die allen anderen Beteiligten zu verstehen gibt, dass wir sie als Menschen achten. Der Zivile Ungehorsam ist in besonderer Weise eine Einladung zum Perspektivenwechsel: Indem wir uns einem ungerechten Gesetz verweigern, werden alle, die mit seiner Durchsetzung beauftragt sind, unmittelbar gefordert, selber Stellung zu beziehen. Würden wir sie physisch angreifen, dann gäbe es für sie keinen Zweifel, dass sie im Recht sind, wenn sie sich verteidigen. Stattdessen verweigern wir unsererseits dem Unrecht die Kooperation, sind dabei verletzlich und nehmen mögliche Nachteile in Kauf. Mit dieser Haltung ermuntern wir unser Gegenüber dazu, sich der eigenen Rolle bewusst zu werden und selber eine Gewissensentscheidung zu treffen.

Hinter einer Aktion Zivilen Ungehorsams mag eine Vision davon stehen, wie unser Zusammenleben ohne das konkrete bekämpfte Unrecht aussehen kann – z.B. wie wir unsere Lebensmittelversorgung ohne Gentechnik sichern oder wie wir in einer Gesellschaft mit offenen Grenzen solidarisch leben können. In manchen Fällen mag eine solche Vision nicht vorhanden sein, sondern lediglich die Einsicht treiben, dass ein bestimmtes Handeln Unrecht ist und deshalb beendet werden muss. Unabhängig von dieser konkreten Vision in Bezug auf ein spezifisches Unrecht verbindet sich mit Zivilem Ungehorsam eine Utopie von einem anderen Zusammenleben – eine Vorstellung von einer Gesellschaft, in der viele Einzelne gemeinsam Verantwortung übernehmen und ihr Gewicht in die Waagschale werfen, um zu einer am Gewissen orientierten Politik zu kommen. Im Idealfall wirkt eine Aktion Zivilen Ungehorsams in zwei Richtungen: Zum einen für eine bestimmte Sache, zum anderen für selbstbestimmte, nichthierarchische Strukturen.

Eine alte Streitfrage in Sachen Ziviler Ungehorsam ist die nach der grundsätzlichen Akzeptanz des Staates und der Regierung. Thoreau wendet sich in seinem

Aufsatz nicht grundsätzlich gegen Regierungen, aber er findet, die beste Regierung sei die, welche am wenigsten regiert. Gandhi forderte von seinen MitstreiterInnen, dass sie außer der einen Regel, gegen die Ungehorsam geleistet wird, alle anderen Regeln und Gesetze peinlich genau befolgen und damit die Autorität der Regierung grundsätzlich anerkennen. Doch viele von denen, die Zivilen Ungehorsam leisten, sind AnarchistInnen und stellen den Staat grundsätzlich in Frage. Ob auch das unter den „klassischen" Begriff des Zivilen Ungehorsams fällt oder ob es etwas darüber hinaus Gehendes ist, dazu möchte ich das Thoreau-Zitat noch einmal ausführlicher betrachten: „Wenn die Ungerechtigkeit einen Ursprung hat, ein Zahnrad oder einen Übertragungsriemen oder eine Kurbel, wovon sie ausschließlich herstammt, dann kannst du vielleicht erwägen, ob die Kur vielleicht schlimmer wäre als das Übel; wenn aber das Gesetz so beschaffen ist, dass es notwendigerweise aus dir den Arm des Unrechts an einem anderen macht, dann, sage ich, brich das Gesetz. Mach dein Leben zu einem Gegengewicht, um die Maschine aufzuhalten. Jedenfalls muss ich zusehen, dass ich mich nicht zu dem Unrecht hergebe, das ich verdamme." (Thoreau 1973: 18) Wenn ich zu der Überzeugung gelange, dass ein bestimmtes politisches System ein Unrechtssystem ist, dann kann ich es selbstverständlich zu meiner Sache machen, dieses System zu überwinden, und kann dazu die Mittel des Zivilen Ungehorsams anwenden. Vielleicht bin ich dazu sogar moralisch verpflichtet, wenn ich durch ein Mittragen des Systems schuldig würde. Die Mittel des Zivilen Ungehorsams sind auch in diesem Fall die, Verantwortung zu übernehmen und die eigene Beteiligung an dem Unrecht zu beenden.

Mir kommt es manchmal so vor, als sei in der Vorstellungskraft vieler Menschen Ziviler Ungehorsam reduziert auf Blockaden. Wo ein Unrecht passiert und das Demonstrieren allein nicht mehr ausreicht, da wird blockiert. Die Steigerungsform davon – wenn das Ziel eine Systemveränderung ist – wären in dieser Logik: Blockaden überall, nichts geht mehr. Tatsächlich hätte eine relativ kleine Gruppe von Menschen die Macht, eine Gesellschaft weitgehend lahm zu legen, und könnte damit Veränderungen sozusagen erpressen. Mir fallen dazu die Geschichten aus Nordirland ein, wo sich alljährlich im Juli katholische und protestantische EinwohnerInnen gegenseitig das Leben schwer machen: Blockiert Ihr unsere Parade zur Erinnerung an den Sieg Wilhelms von Oranien, dann blockieren wir euren Kirchgang. Blockiert ihr unseren Kirchgang, dann blockieren wir den Schulweg eurer Kinder usw. Aber das ist nicht die Idee hinter dem Zivilen Ungehorsam. Wenn wir es für notwendig halten, ein Atomwaffendepot zu schließen, dann macht es Sinn, hin zu gehen und die Zufahrt zu blockieren. Wenn wir ein politisches System ändern wollen, dann macht es keinen Sinn, hier und da und überall auf der Straße zu sitzen, sondern wir müssen erst mal schauen, wo wir selber als Teil dieses Systems funktionieren, und unsere Kooperation einstellen. Das geht beim Wahlboykott los und hört beim Steuerboykott noch lange nicht auf. Um es mit Gustav Landauer zu sagen: „Einen Tisch kann man umwerfen und eine Fensterscheibe zertrümmern, aber die sind eitle Wortemacher und gläubige Wortanbeter, die den Staat für so ein Ding oder einen Fetisch halten, den man zertrümmern kann, um ihn zu zerstören. Staat ist ein Verhältnis, ist eine Beziehung zwischen den Menschen, ist eine Art, wie die Menschen sich zueinander verhalten; und man zerstört ihn, indem man andere Beziehungen eingeht, indem man sich anders zueinander verhält." (aus: „Aufruf zum Sozialismus", zit. n. Wolf 1988: 60)

Spannend wird diese Frage aktuell unter anderem deshalb, weil im Rahmen der globalisierungskritischen Bewegung sehr viel mehr Menschen zum Zivilen Ungehorsam bereit sind, als das in den letzten Jahren zu anderen Themen der Fall war. Nachdem in den 1980er Jahren Tausende von Menschen in Westeuropa gegen die Atomraketenstationierung Ungehorsam leisteten, waren es in den 1990er Jahren nur kleine Gruppen von Unentwegten, die gegen Atomanlagen, Militärstützpunkte und Abschiebehaftanstalten ungehorsame Aktionen machten und dafür teilweise immer wieder ins Gefängnis gingen. Große Aktionen Zivilen Ungehorsams fanden nur bei den Castor-Transporten im Wendland statt, mit einem Höhepunkt 1997 (Die Initiative X-tausendmal quer blockierte mit über 6000 Menschen den Verladekran). Block G8 in Heiligendamm hat da ein neues Kapitel aufgemacht. In diesem Zusammenhang ist das Wort „Sozialer Ungehorsam" aufgetaucht, wie ich es verstehe eine aktuelle Ausformung des Zivilen Ungehorsams, die sich durch breite Beteiligung und durch grundsätzliche Systemkritik auszeichnet. Beides ist für sich genommen nichts Neues, aber in dieser Kombination besonders. Welche Möglichkeiten entstehen, wenn Tausende zusammen kommen, die sich nicht nur in einem einzelnen Punkt einem Unrecht entgegenstellen, sondern grundsätzlich eine andere Gesellschaft wollen?

Ziviler Ungehorsam, so habe ich behauptet, hat immer auch die utopische Komponente eines Entwurfs für eine andere Gesellschaft. In den Zusammenhängen, die in den letzten Jahren Zivilen Ungehorsam geleistet haben, haben wir viel gelernt über Regeln des Miteinanders, über Kommunikation, über Konsensfindung auch in großen Gruppen. All das blieb auf überschaubare Kreise beschränkt, und es war nie das Hauptthema. Das Nachdenken über Entwürfe für herrschaftsfreie Strukturen auf großer gesellschaftlicher Ebene blieb theoretisch. Anders könnte es in Zukunft werden: Eine Bewegung, die Herrschaftsstrukturen mit Mitteln des Zivilen Ungehorsam in Frage stellen will, muss Visionen für ein anderes Miteinander entwickeln. Denn Ziviler Ungehorsam beschränkt sich ja gerade nicht auf das Kritisieren und Fordern von anderen, sondern es geht immer auch darum, im eigenen Handeln Alternativen zum Unrecht zu leben. Und eine Bewegung, die immer größer wird und keine Herrschaftsstrukturen will, muss schon aus diesem Grund Konzepte für ein herrschaftsfreies Miteinander weiter entwickeln.

Als ich in den 1980er Jahren erstmals an Aktionen Zivilen Ungehorsams in Mutlangen teilnahm, da agierten wir in sehr überschaubaren Gruppen. Blockaden fanden oft in Gruppen von zehn bis dreißig Personen statt, manchmal auch zu zweit oder zu dritt. Zu großen Blockaden kamen vielleicht mal ein paar hundert Menschen zusammen. Bei den Castor-Blockaden im Wendland habe ich andere Dimensionen kennen gelernt: In einer Gruppe von zweihundert Leuten würden viele gar nicht erst mit einer Blockade anfangen, weil sie fürchten würden, viel zu schnell wieder von der Polizei geräumt zu sein. Block G8 mit den großen Massenblockaden hat hier im Juni 2007 wiederum neue Maßstäbe gesetzt.

Was bedeutet es, in solchen großen Gruppen Zivilen Ungehorsam zu leisten? An dieser Stelle noch zwei Zitate von Thoreau (1973: 9): „Man sagt, dass vereinte Masse kein Gewissen hat und das ist wahr genug; gewissenhafte Menschen aber verbinden sich zu einer Vereinigung mit Gewissen." Und: „In den Handlungen von Menschenmassen ist die Tugend selten zu Hause." (Thoreau 1973: 14) Wie kann es gelingen, dass sich Tausende von Menschen in einer Großaktion tatsächlich von ihrem Gewissen leiten lassen? Wie können wir verantwortungsvoll mit der Eigendynamik umgehen, die ein Handeln in solch großen Gruppen entwickelt? Manche Aktionsgruppen legen Wert darauf, dass nur diejenigen an der Aktion teilnehmen, die sich gründlich vorbereitet haben. Andere akzeptieren auch ein Einsteigen von Kurzentschlossenen, und bei vielen Aktionen wird gerade darauf gesetzt, dass eine Sache so viel Dynamik entwickelt, dass immer mehr Menschen spontan einsteigen. Wenn jetzt im Zuge der globalisierungskritischen Proteste der Zivile Ungehorsam in Form des „Sozialen Ungehorsams" eine neue Blüte erlebt, dann sicher zu einem großen Teil dadurch, dass Menschen sich im unmittelbaren Erleben ihrer Macht bewusst werden als Masse, die den Gehorsam verweigert und nach ihrem eigenen Drehbuch agiert.

Eine Menschenmenge, die ihre Freiheit entdeckt hat, zu tun was immer ihr beliebt, und dabei einigermaßen koordiniert handelt, kann eine große Macht entfalten.

Aber Ziviler Ungehorsam bedeutet nicht einfach nur, dass alle machen was sie wollen und dass keine Regeln mehr gelten. „Wo kämen wir denn hin, wenn alle das tun, was sie für richtig halten?", habe ich mal einen Richter sagen hören in seiner Begründung eines Urteils gegen einen Totalverweigerer. Ja, wo kämen wir hin? Wenn alle das tun, was sie für richtig halten, also alle ihrem Gewissen folgen, dann kommen wir jedenfalls woanders hin als dann, wenn alle das tun, wozu sie gerade Lust haben oder was sie gerade für sich nützlich finden. Ziviler Ungehorsam hat mit Gerechtigkeit zu tun, mit Menschenrechten, mit Rücksichtnahme auf andere. Damit aus einer Menschenmenge eine „Vereinigung mit Gewissen" entsteht, braucht sie Verabredungen, sowohl für den Umgang untereinander als auch für den Umgang mit den politischen GegnerInnen. Einzelne müssen die Möglichkeit haben, zu durchschauen was geschieht, ihre eigenen Kriterien bei der Planung einzubringen, sich Gehör zu verschaffen, wenn sie gegen eine Entwicklung Bedenken haben.

Dabei möchte ich nicht ausschließlich auf das Prinzip setzen „Wenn dich etwas stört, dann sprich die Person an, die es tut, und setze dich direkt mit ihr auseinander, dazu brauchst du keine Regel und keine Gruppenentscheidung". Das klingt zwar erst mal sehr verlockend: Keine Hierarchien, kein Delegieren von Verantwortung an Institutionen. Aber es birgt das Risiko, dass die Einzelnen letztlich allein bleiben. Ein Beispiel aus einem Aktionscamp: Jemand kann nicht schlafen, weil am Lagerfeuer noch Leute Lärm machen. Er geht hin und spricht sie an, stellt aber fest, dass sie betrunken sind und sehr aggressiv reagieren. Am nächsten Tag möchte derjenige, der in seinem Schlafbedürfnis gestört wurde, im Plenum Regeln für solche Fälle verabreden, wird aber zurückgewiesen: Regele das direkt mit den Leuten, die dich stören.

Es gibt keine soziale Begegnung ohne Regeln. Wenn keine Regeln vereinbart werden, nach denen dann gemeinschaftlich und solidarisch gehandelt wird, dann gelten – wie im beschriebenen Fall – die Regeln der Stärkeren. Das ist nicht Anarchie, sondern Faustrecht – nicht Herrschaftslosigkeit, sondern die Herrschaft der Starken.

Oft ist es auch so, dass wir mit verschiedenen Vorstellungen davon zusammenkommen, welche ungeschriebenen Gesetze im Umgang miteinander und mit politischen Gegnerinnen „selbstverständlich" gelten. Die daraus resultierenden Konflikte sind deswegen so schmerzhaft, weil sie an unsere in jeweils eigenen Aktionszusammenhängen gewonnenen Sicherheiten und unser Selbstverständnis rühren. Deshalb gehört für mich zu Visionen des Zivilen Ungehorsams auch eine Vision, wie wir gemeinsam in größer und bunter werdenden Zusammenhängen Regeln des Miteinanders aushandeln.

Besonders viel verhandelt wurde ja in den Monaten vor und auch nach dem G8-Gipfel in Rostock um Regeln des Umgangs mit denen, die „auf der anderen Seite" stehen. Gewaltfreiheit, für manche selbstverständliches und grundlegendes Prinzip des politischen Handelns, ist für andere ein Korsett, eine Einschränkung der eigenen Handlungsfreiheit. Ich denke, dass dahinter zwei verschiedene Vorstellungen von Wirkungsmechanismen liegen:

Die einen setzen auf die oben beschriebene Wirkung, auf das Gewissen aller Beteiligten durch die Kombination aus „Vertrauensaufbau" und „Paroli bieten", wofür ein klares Bekenntnis zur Gewaltfreiheit unabdingbar ist. Die größte Kraft entwickelt diese Art politischen Wirkens genau dann, wenn alle Beteiligten sich zu jeder Zeit sicher sein können, dass von den AktivistInnen keinerlei Bedrohung für ihre Würde, ihre Freiheit, ihre körperliche Unversehrtheit ausgeht.

Die anderen setzen auf die besondere Macht, die durch massenhafte, gemeinsame, potentiell unbegrenzte Regelverletzungen entsteht. Gerade das Moment des Unberechenbaren – alles kann passieren – führt auf Seiten der AktivistInnen zu einem sonst selten gekannten Machtgefühl und auf Seiten ihres Gegenübers zu Verunsicherung, Angst, Ohnmacht.

Das Problem, das ich bei dieser Art von Dynamik sehe, ist: Das hat überhaupt nichts Neues und Revolutionäres, Zukunftsweisendes an sich, sondern es ist Teil einer uralten Dynamik, die in der Geschichte immer wieder zur Eskalation von gesellschaftlichen Konflikten geführt hat. Angst und Verunsicherung lösen bei den meisten Menschen (wenn sie nicht gerade Aktive Gewaltfreiheit üben) entweder Fluchtverhalten oder Aggression aus – und je mehr jemand in die Enge getrieben ist, umso wahrscheinlicher wird die Aggression. Wenn in einer ohnehin schon aufgewühlten Situation jemand Regeln verletzt, die sein/ihr Gegenüber als grundlegende Regeln des Miteinander betrachtet, dann wird das als unfair empfunden und dient als Rechtfertigung für Gegengewalt. Diese Dynamik läuft natürlich auf beiden Seiten ab, die sich so wunderbar gegenseitig hochschaukeln können.

In den 1990er Jahren hatten wir es mit einer relativ kleinen Bewegung zu tun, die mit Mitteln des gewaltfreien Zivilen Ungehorsams ihren politischen Forderungen Nachdruck verlieh. Im neuen Jahrtausend erleben wir eine wachsende Bewegung, die unter dem Stichwort „Sozialer Ungehorsam" eine Menge der Techniken des Zivilen Ungehorsams aufgreift, ohne sich aber seiner Geschichte und der Erfahrungen, aus denen heraus diese Techniken entwickelt wurden, sehr bewusst zu sein.

Hierzu ein Beispiel: Um als Menschenmenge eine Demonstrationsroute durchzusetzen, an einen Blockadeort zu gelangen oder die Räumung eines Platzes zu verhindern, bringt es mehr, gut organisiert und friedlich ggf. durch Polizeiketten „sickernd" dahin zu gehen, wo man hin will, als die Polizei zu bekämpfen. Der Wirkungsmechanismus: An Schlachten können sich nur die körperlich fitten Beteiligen, am Durchfließen von Polizeiketten alle, die gehen können. PolizistInnen, die angegriffen werden (unabhängig davon ob sie selber vorher angegriffen haben), betrachten daraufhin ihre eigene Gewaltanwendung als gerechtfertigt und notwendig. PolizistInnen, an denen nur Leute friedlich vorbei gehen, haben deutlich mehr Hemmungen, zuzuschlagen. Die Grenzen dieser Methode: In dem Moment, wo aus einer derart agierenden Menge heraus PolizistInnen oder andere bedroht oder angegriffen werden, oder auch schon, wenn die Situation unüberschaubar und bedrohlich für die Polizei wird, kann die Sache jederzeit kippen. Je mehr Macht die DemonstrantInnen auf ihrer Seite haben, umso wichtiger wird es, dem Gegenüber klar zu signalisieren, dass ihr Leben und ihre Würde nicht gefährdet sind. (Auf den Philippinen haben die DemonstrantInnen z.B. auf dem Höhepunkt der People's Power-Bewegung die gegen sie eingesetzten Soldaten mit Lebensmitteln, Getränken und Zigaretten versorgt.)

Ein zweites Beispiel. Eine starke Einbindung einer Bewegung in die Gesellschaft bedeutet Schutz. So war es z.B. für die globalisierungskritischen Proteste in Rostock wichtig, dass fast alle Organisationen, Gruppen, Initiativen der im emanzipatorischen Sinne tätigen politischen Gruppen in Deutschland hinter den Protesten standen. Der Wirkungsmechanismus: Eine Regierung hat umso mehr Machtmittel gegenüber einer sozialen Bewegung, je mehr sie sich politisch leisten kann. Je mehr eine Bewegung in der Bevölkerung verankert ist, umso höher ist der politische Preis dafür, gegen diese Bewegung mit Gewalt vorzugehen. Grenzen dieses Mechanismus: die Regierung hat über gezielte Öffentlichkeitsarbeit die Möglichkeit, Bewegungen in der Bevölkerung zu diskreditieren. Dazu muss sie zeigen, dass eine Bewegung allgemein anerkannte Werte und Regeln verletzt. Das ist sehr schwer, wenn eine Bewegung sich ganz klar den Prinzipien Aktiver Gewaltfreiheit verpflichtet hat. Es wird deutlich einfacher, wenn auch nur Teile der Bewegung zu gewaltsamen Aktionen greifen. Dies mag anders sein, wenn in der Bevölkerung die Meinung verbreitet ist, dass solche Aktionen berechtigt und sinnvoll sind. Tatsächlich könnten wir es in den nächsten Jahren, angesichts der Verarmung immer breiterer Bevölkerungsgruppen, mit Situationen zu tun bekommen, wo ein größer werdender Teil der Bevölkerung revolutionäre Gewalt befürwortet. Das dürfte dann aber auch nicht dazu führen, dass die Herrschenden den politischen Preis für ein Niederschlagen der Aufstände zu hoch finden – gewaltsamen Aufständen nachzugeben, hat vermutlich einen höheren Preis.

Werden wir es schaffen, dem Krieg nach innen und außen, der Prekarisierung, dem Kampf um die natürlichen Ressourcen, den fortschreitenden Umweltkatastrophen etwas Substantielles entgegenzusetzen?

Ich sehe ein gewisses Risiko, dass die derzeit wachsenden und mächtiger werdenden sozialen Bewegungen, wenn sie sich auf einen Machtkampf im herkömmlichen Sinne – sei es auch mit Mitteln des Sozialen Ungehorsams – einlassen, sich im Laufe der Zeit mit der Zuspitzung des Konflikts einfach zu einer Art Bürgerkriegspartei im dann immerwährenden Krieg gegen die Konzerne und Staaten entwickeln.

Zugleich sehe ich die große Chance, dass die jetzt wachsenden sozialen Bewegungen einen Quantensprung nach vorne machen könnten, indem sie sich der Herausforderung stellen, nicht nur gegen die neoliberale Globalisierung und die davon profitierenden Konzerne zu sein, sondern tatsächlich eigene, tragfähige, auf gesellschaftlicher Ebene (und nicht nur in kleinen Gruppen) funktionierende Strukturen zu schaffen. Wenn innerhalb von großen sozialen Bewegungen Räume entstehen, in denen wir uns nicht mehr an die hergebrachten Regeln halten, und wenn wir in diesen Räumen unsere eigenen, solidarischen Regeln des Miteinander entwickeln; wenn zugleich alle, die zunächst als unsere GegnerInnen auftreten, feststellen, dass es innerhalb dieser neuen, solidarischen Strukturen und Umgangsweisen auch für sie einen Platz gibt – dann könnte eine solche Bewegung es schaffen, den Kampf aufzunehmen und zugleich den Krieg zu verweigern. Sie könnte die gesellschaftlichen Normen und Werte, die sie als Grundlage des gesellschaftlichen Zusammenlebens vorschlägt, sozusagen einseitig selber implementieren, im Umgang untereinander und gerade auch mit politischen GegnerInnen.

Ich wünsche mir, dass die sozialen Bewegungen des 21. Jahrhunderts ihre besondere Qualität des breiten und grundsätzlich systemkritischen Ungehorsams verbinden mit einem deutlichen Anknüpfen an die Traditionen, Werte und Erfahrungen des Zivilen Ungehorsams im 19. und 20. Jahrhundert. Dann würde es richtig spannend werden.

Literatur:

Bläsi, Burkhardt (2001): Konflikttransformation durch Gütekraft. Interpersonale Veränderungsprozesse. Studien zur Gewaltfreiheit Bd. 4, Münster (Lit-Verlag).
Thoreau, Henry David 1973: Über die Pflicht zum Ungehorsam gegen den Staat, in: ders.: Über die Pflicht zum Ungehorsam gegen den Staat und andere Essays, Zürich (Diogenes Verlag), S. 7-35.
Wolf, Siegbert (1988): Gustav Landauer zur Einführung, Hamburg 1988 (Junius Verlag).

Civil and social Disobedience = Refusal plus Utopia?

Ulrike Laubenthal

Friday, 1 June 2007: Six hundred anti-war activists inhabit the planned bombing rage in the Kyritz Ruppiner heath. They occupy an old command tower, in a flash paint it in the "civil" color pink, hang banners and flags, set up tents. Musicians play Haydn, Weill, Bach, Pasquay, etc. More than one hundred clowns have their fun and in doing so chase away a jeep from the German army that dared venture close to the action. Among the participants are also numerous Europeans from outside of Germany who are on their way with the Euro Marches and Bicycle Caravans to Rostock. The activists spend the night at the site and on Saturday morning most continue on their way to the major demonstration against the G8 summit in Rostock.

Civil disobedience is currently experiencing a fresh, new awakening. The anti-globalization movement is making its own re-discovery of old, tried forms of common political action that have been practiced in the past several years by only relatively small circles.

Things might really get going in the near future. More and more people are living precariously; the certainties that people are accustomed to are fading away. The army's involvement in wars throughout the world, which would have caused a major outcry just twenty years ago, is being registered in the minds of more and more people as normal and acceptable through the detour of medical services and landmine search and removal missions. These missions will most likely increase massively in upcoming years. Domestically, military presence will also be felt in ever more social realms. Methods of surveillance and suppression, which were entirely unthinkable just a short while ago, have become "normal" with amazing speed, practically unnoticed by the public realm.

In light of these changes, it may well be that social movements remain a peripheral phenomenon. In times of increasing uncertainty, many people first make sure their own homes are secure. But we may also see a growing emancipatory movement that becomes increasingly powerful, gaining strength through social disobedience. If so, then for me, the interesting questions are:

Will this movement simply refuse the existing globalized state and economic structures or will it develop and implement utopias and sound concepts to build its own workable structures for decision making and subsistence-based economies?

Will this movement follow the normal escalation schemes of social conflicts whereby ever more rules of humane coexistence are abolished and human rights denied as the intensity of the conflict increases? Or, will this movement prove to be something special by recognizing human rights and agreements for a humane cooperation based on solidarity, also, and especially in times of struggle, also, and especially, with regard to political opponents?

Will the influence of those who are young, strong, male, and unattached continue to grow on all sides, while women, children, the elderly, and disabled are assigned the role of victim in need of protection, and in danger of being utilized? Or will we discover organizational forms in which everyone, whether strong or weak; old or young; man, woman, or other-gendered will have an influence in the development?

At this point, I would like to introduce an explanation of terms: I understand civil disobedience as a limited breach of rules, a refusal to participate in an injustice, to accept an injustice, or to function within an unjust system.

In my opinion, this form of political action draws its exceptional effectiveness from the fact that those practicing civil disobedience accept responsibility. Normally, responsibility is handed over in political confrontations: people declare themselves innocent of all that is bad, they're helpless ("it's impossible to do anything") and they demand that change comes from the others, "the responsible ones." In his oft-cited essay "On the Duty of Civil Disobedience," Thoreau describes an entirely different position that has since been practiced in many places: "Let your life be a counter-friction to stop the machine. What I have to do is to see, at any rate, that I do not lend myself to the wrong which I condemn" (Thoreau 1848). Those who break laws based on matters of conscience, from a sense of one's shared responsibility, do not approach political opponents with aggression, but rather, affirmation. Rather than a condemnation of others, at the forefront are the critique of an injustice and one's own acceptance of responsibility in overcoming it. Those who embrace this injustice are likewise invited to take responsibility for their actions.

This position corresponds with the one Burkhard Bläsi outlines based on his empirical research on "Gütekraft" ("power of goodness"). He describes two pillars, each comprising a mode of behavior that releases this power, which is also called "the power of non-violence," "the power of truth," or as Gandhi calls it, "Satyagraha." He names one pillar "resisting", which encompasses being present at the site of an injustice, persistently clarifying one's own standpoint, and if necessary, also accepting any disadvantages. The other pillar, "building trust," includes non-hurtful behavior, empathy, openness, and encouragement to change one's perspective (Bläsi 2001). The combination of "resisting" and "building trust" generates respect from one's opponent. The combination of the two generates an emotional involvement and recognition of common values: in optimal cases, opponents experience an awakening of their own conscience, driving them to change their behavior or views.

When practicing civil disobedience, we are at the site of action, making our demands clear. At the same time, we are doing so in a way that lets everyone else involved know that we respect them as people. Civil disobedience is, in a special way, an invitation to change one's perspective: our refusal to accept an unjust law, is a direct challenge to all who are entrusted with its implementation to take a position. If we were to physically attack them, they would have no doubts about defending themselves. Instead, for our part, we refuse to cooperate with the injustice and are thereby vulnerable and accept possible disadvantages. With this position, we encourage our opponents to be aware of their own roles, and to arrive at their own decisions on a matter of conscience.

Behind an action of civil disobedience there might be a vision of how our coexistence could look without the concretely fought injustice—for example, how we can guarantee our food supplies without gene technology, or how we might live in solidarity in a world with open borders. In some cases, such a vision might not be available, but instead, civil disobedience is driven simply by the insight that a certain action is unjust and therefore must be put to a stop. Apart from such concrete visions pertaining to a specific injustice, associated with civil disobedience is a utopia of another way of living together—an idea of a society in which a multitude of individuals take shared responsibility, and put themselves entirely on the line to arrive at conscience-oriented politics. In the ideal case, an action of civil disobedience works on two areas: first, on a particular matter at hand, and second, on self-determined, non-hierarchical structures.

An old dispute in matters of civil disobedience is that of the fundamental acceptance of the state and government. In his essay, Thoreau does not turn against governments, in principle, but he considers the best government to be the one that governs least. Gandhi demands that his comrades follow all rules and laws meticulously, other than the one rule against which disobedience is practiced. He thereby basically recognizes the authority of the government. However, many of those who practice civil disobedience are anarchists and question the very principle of the state. With regard to whether this falls under the "classical" concept of civil disobedience or if it is something that goes beyond it, I would like to expand on the previous quote from Thoreau, "If the injustice has a spring, or a pulley, or a rope, or a crank, exclusively for itself, then perhaps you may consider whether the remedy will not be worse than the evil; but if it is of such a nature that it requires you to be the agent of injustice to another, then I say, break the law. Let your life be a counter-friction to stop the machine. What I have to do is to see, at any rate, that I do not lend myself to the wrong which I condemn (Thoreau 1848). If I arrive at the conviction that a certain political system is an unjust system, then I can naturally make it my business to overcome this system and apply the means of civil disobedience to do so. Perhaps I am even morally obligated as I would be guilty by sharing in the responsibility for the system. The means of civil disobedience in this case are also accepting responsibility and ending one's own participation in the injustice.

Sometimes it seems to me that in many people's minds, civil disobedience is limited to blockades. In situations where an injustice occurs and demonstrations alone are not sufficient, blockades occur. The next higher form according to this logic—if the goal is to change the system—would then be blockades everywhere, stop everything. In truth, a relatively small group of people have the power to bring society to a standstill, and could thereby cause change through extortion, so to speak. What comes to mind are the stories from Northern Ireland, where every year in July, Catholic and Protestant residents make each others' lives difficult: If you blockade our parade commemorating the victory of William of Orange, we will block your path to Church. If you block us from going to church, then we'll block your children from going to school, and so on. But that is not the idea behind civil disobedience. When we consider it necessary to close an atomic weapons depot, then it makes sense to go there and block the entrance. When we want to change a political system, then it doesn't make any sense to sit here and there and everywhere on the street. We first have to see where we function as part of this system and put an end to our own cooperation. This begins with boycotting elections and continues long after tax boycotts. In the words of Gustav Landauer: "One can overthrow a table and smash a window pane, but those who consider the State to be such a thing or fetish that one can smash in order to destroy it, are simply vain talkers, devoutly in awe of words. State is a relation, it is a relationship between people, it is how people behave towards one another; and one does destroy it by entering into another relationship, by behaving differently towards one another." Quoted from Wolf 1988: 60)

This issue becomes interesting today, among other reasons, because a great deal more people are willing to practice civil disobedience in the context of the anti-globalization movement than they were in the context of other issues in recent years. In the 1980s, thousands of people in Western Europe practiced disobedience against the nuclear missile stations, whereas in the 1990s only small groups of untiring activists—some of whom went to prison again and again—staged disobedient actions against nuclear facilities, military bases, and deportation centers. The only large actions of civil disobedience were at the Castor transports in Wendland, with a peak in 1997 (the initiative X-tausendmal quer blocked the loading crane with over 6,000 people.) Block G8 in Heiligendamm began a new chapter. The term "social disobedience" surfaced in this context, which, as I understand it, is a topical form of civil disobedience that is characterized by broad participation and a fundamental critique of the system. Both of these characteristics are not new, per se, but special in this combination. What possibilities arise at the convergence of thousands who are striving, in principle, for a different society and are not merely opposing an injustice centered on one single point?

Civil disobedience, as I purported, always also contains the utopian component of a draft for another society. In the contexts in which civil disobedience has been practiced in recent years, we have learned a great deal about the rules of working together, about communication, and about reaching a consensus even in large groups. That all remained limited to manageable circles and was never the main topic. Contemplation of designs for non-authoritarian structures at a larger societal level remained theoretical. In the future, things could be different: a movement that questions authoritative structures via the means of civil disobedience must develop visions for a different way of working together. Civil disobedience, after all, is not limited to criticizing and making demands of others, it is also always about living out alternatives to an injustice through one's own actions. A steadily growing movement that does not want to include any authoritarian structures must, for this reason alone, further develop concepts for non-authoritarian cooperation.

When I first participated in civil disobedience actions in Mutlangen in the 1980s, we moved in very manageable groups. Blockades often took place in groups of ten to thirty, and sometimes there were just two or three people. For the larger blockades, a few hundred people gathered, at most. At the Castor blockades in Wendland, I learned of different dimensions. With a group of two hundred people, many wouldn't even begin a blockade for fear of being dispersed by the police much too quickly. With their huge, mass blockades in June 2007, Block G8 once again set a new standard.

What does it mean to practice civil disobedience in such large groups? Two more quotes from Thoreau are applicable here: "It is truly enough said that a corporation has no conscience; but a corporation of conscientious men is a corporation with a conscience." And: "There is but little virtue in the action of masses of men" (Thoreau 1848). How can thousands of people in a large-scale action actually let themselves be led by conscience? How can we deal responsibly with the self-dynamics that develop in such large groups? Some action groups insist that only people who have been thoroughly briefed participate in an action, others accept also people who have made a last minute decision to join, and for many actions the plan is to create dynamics that are so powerful that ever more people will spontaneously join in. Civil disobedience's current new awakening, in the course of the anti-globalization protests in the form of "social disobedience," is certainly due in large part to people who in directly experiencing their power, become aware of themselves as a mass that refuses to be obedient, one that acts according to its own script.

A mass of people that has discovered the freedom to do as it pleases, and in doing so, to act in a relatively coordinated way, can unfurl tremendous power.

But civil disobedience does not simply mean that everyone does what they want and that no more rules are valid. "Where would we be if everyone did what they thought was right?" I once heard a judge say in justifying his decision against a conscientious objector. Sure, where would we be? When everyone does what they consider right, that is, follow their conscience, we would, in any case, be somewhere different than if everyone did what they had a desire to do at the moment, or what they considered useful. Civil disobedience has to do with justice, with human rights, with consideration for others. So that a "corporation with a conscience" can arise from a crowd, the crowd needs agreements; ones for dealing with one another and also for dealing with political opponents. Individuals must be given the opportunity to look through what is happening, introduce their own criteria into the planning, and they must be paid attention to when they have objections to a development.

In this, I do not want to rely exclusively on the principle: "When something is bothering you, then talk to the person who is doing it, and confront them directly. For that, you don't need any rules or any group decisions." Perhaps it sounds quite tempting at first: no hierarchies, no delegating of responsibility to institutions. But it harbors the risk of an individual ultimately being left alone. One example from an action camp: Someone can't sleep because people are still making a lot of noise at the campfire. He or she goes over and confronts them only to realize that they are drunk and react quite aggressively. The next day, the person whose sleep was disturbed wants to agree at the plenum on rules for such cases but is turned away: work things out directly with the people that are bothering you.

There are no social encounters without rules. When no rules are agreed upon for dealing in a communal, solidarity-based way, then what applies—as in the case described—are the rules of whoever is strongest. That is not anarchy, it's the rule of force—it's not non-authoritarian but the authority of whoever is strongest.

Often it is also the case that we come together with differing ideas of which unwritten laws apply "self-evidently" in dealing with one another and with our political opponents. The resulting conflicts are so painful because they touch on our own certainties and self perceptions that we have gained from the contexts in which we have acted. For that reason, I consider a vision of how to negotiate the rules of cooperation together in larger and ever more diverse contexts as part of a vision of civil disobedience.

A great deal of negotiating over rules for dealing with those who are "on the other side" went on before and also after the G8 summit in Rostock. Non-violence, which is an obvious and fundamental principle of political action for some, is a corset for others, a limitation on their own freedom of action. I think that two different ideas on mechanisms of action are behind this:

The one relies on the previously described effect of the combination of "building trust," and "resisting" on the conscience of all involved, for which a clear profession of non-violence is indispensable. This type of political action develops its greatest power precisely when all involved can assume at all times that the activists present absolutely no threat to their dignity, freedom, or physical integrity.

The other relies on the particular power that arises through massive, mutual, potentially unlimited infringements of rules. Precisely that moment of unpredictability—anything could happen—leads, on the part of the activists, to an otherwise rare sense of power and on the part of their opponents to uncertainty, fear, and powerlessness.

The problem that I see in this kind of dynamic is that it has absolutely nothing new, revolutionary, or future-oriented about it, but instead, is part of an age old dynamic that has consistently led throughout history to the escalation of social conflicts. For most people who are not practicing active non-violence at the moment, fear and uncertainty trigger a reaction of fight or flight—and the more that someone is pushed into a corner, the more likely they are to become aggressive. When someone infringes rules that his or her opponent considers to be fundamental rules of cooperation in an already turbulent situation, then it is felt to be unfair and serves as justification for counter violence. This dynamic naturally works on both sides, each of which becomes skilled at pushing the others' buttons.

In the 1990s we were dealing with a relatively small movement that lent expression to its political demands through the means of non-violent civil disobedience. In the new millennium we are experiencing a growing movement that takes up a great deal of the techniques of civil disobedience under the key term "social disobedience," without any great awareness of civil disobedience's history or the experiences from which its techniques were developed.

An example: in order for a crowd of people to successfully follow a demonstration route to arrive at the site of a blockade, or to prevent the clearing of a square, it is much more advantageous to proceed as well organized and peaceful as possible, "oozing" through police cordons to arrive at where one wants, as opposed to fighting the police. The action mechanism: everyone who can walk can participate in flowing through police cordons whereas only the physically fit can join in battle. Police officers who are attacked (regardless of whether or not they made the first move), consequently consider their own use of violence as justified and necessary. Police officers who experience a friendly flow of people passing by have significantly more reservations about striking out. The borders of this method are reached at the moment where police officers or others are threatened or attacked by a crowd that is operating in this way; things can also turn at any moment when the situation has simply become unmanageable and threatening for the police. The more power that demonstrators have on their side, the more important it is to send clear signals to the opponent that their life and dignity are not in danger. (In the Philippines, for example, at the height of People's Power movement, demonstrators supplied the deployed soldiers with food, drinks, and cigarettes.)

Another example: A movement's strong integration into society means protection. At the anti-globalization protests in Rostock it was important, for example, that virtually all organizations, groups, and initiatives from active, emancipatory political groups in Germany stood behind the protests. The action mechanism: the more political space a government has, the more means of power it has against a social movement. The more a movement is anchored in the population, the higher the political price for proceeding with violence against this movement. The border of this mechanism runs along the government's chance to publicly discredit the movement among the population through well-targeted publicity stunts. For this, they must show that a movement infringes on generally recognized values and rules. That is difficult when a movement is clearly committed to the principle of active non-violence. Things are certainly different when broad public opinion stands behind such actions and finds them justified and sensible. Actually, in the near future, the impoverishment of ever larger groups within the population may lead to a situation whereby a growing share of the population approves of revolutionary violence. However, this will never lead to a situation in which rulers determine that defeating the revolt comes at too high a price—the price of succumbing to violent revolutions is presumably higher.

Will we be successful in offering something substantial to counter the wars aimed inward and outward, precarization, the battle for natural resources, and a steadily growing ecological catastrophe?

I see a certain risk if currently growing social movements, which are becoming ever more powerful, engage in a power struggle in the classical sense. Even a power struggle carried out with means of social disobedience, over the course of time, with the escalation of the conflict, bears the risk of their becoming sort of a group of combatants in an everlasting civil war against big business and the State.

At the same time, I see a great chance that today's growing social movements are capable of taking a quantum leap forward by confronting the challenge of actually creating their own, sustainable, functioning structures at a societal level (and not only in small groups) rather than merely opposing neoliberal globalization and the industries that profit from it. When spaces in which we no longer observe handed-down rules surface within major social movements, and when we develop our own, solidarity-based rules in these spaces; when at the same time, all who initially enter as our opponents realize that there is room for them within these new, solidarity-based structures and ways of behaving—then such a movement is capable of taking up the conflict and simultaneously refusing the war. Such a movement could, for its part, implement the social norms and values that it suggests as a base for social cooperation, in dealing with each other and also with political opponents.

My hope is that social movements of the twenty-first century combine their special quality of disobedience, one that includes a broad base and a fundamental critique of the system, with a clear linking to the traditions, values, and experiences of civil disobedience from the nineteenth and twentieth centuries. Things are then bound to really get going.

Translation from The German by Lisa Rosenblatt

Literature:

Bläsi, Burkhardt (2001): Konflikttransformation durch Gütekraft. Interpersonale Veränderungsprozesse. Studien zur Gewaltfreiheit vol. 4, Münster (Lit-Verlag).
Thoreau, Henry David (1848/9): On the Duty of Civil Disobedience, available from the 1848 lecture online: http://www.panarchy.org/thoreau/disobedience.1848.html
  And in the 1849 publication form Civil Disobedience, originally published as "Resistance to Civil Government" 1849, with annotated text: http://thoreau.eserver.org/civil.html
Wolf, Siegbert (1988): Gustav Landauer zur Einführung, Hamburg 1988 (Junius Verlag).

* an English translation of the second edition of "Aufruf zum Sozialismus" is avaible: Gustav Landauer, For Socialism, transl. David J. Parent, Telos Press: New York, 1978.

Vom zivilen zum sozialen Ungehorsam und zurück

Zur Begriffspolitik globalisierungskritischer Proteste[1]

Andrea Pabst

„I'm not saying that I would support an armed revolution, necessarily – I'm just saying that I wouldn't rule it out as an option. When you do, you fall into this trap of creating rules of protesting."
John K. Samson

Einleitung

Nach den Protesten gegen den G8-Gipfel in Genua 2001 erklärte Luca Casarini, einer der SprecherInnen der Tute Bianche in Italien, dass die Phase des zivilen Ungehorsams zu Ende sei und nun zum sozialen Ungehorsam übergegangen werden müsse (vgl. Azzellini 2001/2002). Diese Aussage wirft vor allem Fragen auf: Was ist gemeint mit zivilem Ungehorsam? Warum hat er sich erschöpft? Wie soll sozialer im Unterschied zu zivilem Ungehorsam aussehen? Wie soll der Übergang vom einen zum anderen stattfinden? Und für wen spricht Casarini hier eigentlich? Für die Tute Bianche, die AktivistInnen in weißen Overalls, die insbesondere durch die Proteste gegen die Welthandelsorganisation (WTO) und den Internationalen Währungsfond (IWF) in Prag 2000 bekannt wurden und sich in Genua in die „Ungehorsamen" umbenannten (Disobbedienti)? Oder spricht er für ‚die' globalisierungskritische Bewegung insgesamt? Handelt es sich um ein Resümee der Proteste in Genua oder wird ein globaler historischer Wandel von Protestformen konstatiert?

Diese Fragen verweisen auf die grundsätzliche Problematik, mit der dieser Beitrag konfrontiert ist: thematisiert werden mit zivilem Ungehorsam, sozialem Ungehorsam und deren Formen in ‚der' globalisierungskritischen Bewegung Begriffe, die jeder für sich Bibliotheken mit Begriffsdiskussionen füllen könnten bzw. dies bereits schon tun. Die Begriffe sind inhaltlich – wenn überhaupt – kaum einheitlich bestimmt. Zudem handelt es sich in besonderer Weise um politisch umkämpfte Begriffe. Die Begriffspolitik besteht in der akademischen Auseinandersetzung über angemessene Definitionen einerseits und der damit verbundenen politisch-strategischen Verwendung der Begriffe durch AktivistInnen andererseits. Dieses Kapitel stellt eine Annäherung an und Diskussion über das Verhältnis von Globalisierungskritik, zivilem und sozialem Ungehorsam dar. Im ersten Abschnitt werden die Begriffe des zivilen und sozialen Ungehorsams eingeführt. Wie sich dabei zeigt, hat sich der Begriff des sozialen Ungehorsams bis dato jedoch nicht durchgesetzt. Deshalb wird im Weiteren nur auf zivilen Ungehorsam rekurriert. Hinsichtlich globalisierungskritischer Proteste wird dies im zweiten Abschnitt exemplarisch anhand der Proteste gegen den G8-Gipfel in Heiligendamm 2007 dargestellt. Während es sich hier vor allem um zivilen Ungehorsam mit einer Vielzahl von Beteiligten handelt, werden im dritten Abschnitt über zivilen Ungehorsam und transnationale Friedensbewegung historisch vergleichend Aktionen kleinerer Gruppen fokussiert. Daran anschließend wird die strategische Verwendung des Begriffes ziviler Ungehorsam diskutiert.

Vom zivilen zum sozialen Ungehorsam?

Seit Mitte der 1990er Jahre ist zumindest im deutschen und anglo-amerikanischen Sprachraum ein deutliches Abflauen der wissenschaftlichen Beschäftigung mit zivilem Ungehorsam zu verzeichnen. Während ziviler Ungehorsam bis dahin sowohl ein politisches als auch rechtliches Problem darstellte und umfangreich diskutiert wurde, scheinen sich die Wogen seither etwas geglättet zu haben. Dies als Verweis auf eine gegenwärtig kaum noch spürbare politische Sprengkraft von zivilem Ungehorsam zu verstehen, könnte sich allerdings als vorschneller Trugschluss erweisen. Möglicherweise steckt die politische Brisanz heute eben gerade in der Auseinandersetzung mit zivilem Ungehorsam oder anders gesagt: Auseinandersetzungen mit zivilem Ungehorsam berühren vielleicht insbesondere politische Themen, die in der Sicherheitsmatrix seit den Terroranschlägen vom 11. September 2001 zu Tabus erklärt wurden. Nicht zuletzt der Terrorverdacht gegen den Soziologen Andrej Holm – begründet unter anderem mit seiner Forschung zu Gentrifizierung – zeigt, welche Konsequenzen kritische Wissenschaft haben kann.[2]

Hinsichtlich der akademischen Diskurse zu zivilem Ungehorsam seit den 1950er Jahren im anglo-amerikanischen Raum und ca. 15 Jahre später im deutschsprachigen Raum können allgemein enge und weite Definitionen unterschieden werden. Als enge Definition lässt sich exemplarisch Jürgen Habermas heranziehen: „Ziviler Ungehorsam ist ein moralisch begründeter Protest, dem nicht nur private Glaubensüberzeugungen oder Eigeninteressen zugrundeliegen dürfen; er ist ein öffentlicher Akt, der in der Regel angekündigt ist und von der Polizei in seinem Ablauf kalkuliert werden kann; er schließt die vorsätzliche Verletzung einzelner Rechtsnormen ein, ohne den Gehorsam gegenüber der Rechtsordnung im ganzen zu affizieren; er verlangt die Bereitschaft, für die rechtlichen Folgen der Normverletzung einzustehen; die Regelverletzung, in der sich ziviler Ungehorsam äußert, hat ausschließlich symbolischen Charakter – daraus ergibt sich schon die Begrenzung auf gewaltfreie Mittel des Protestes" (Habermas 1983: 35). Howard Zinns Erläuterung, es handle sich bei zivilem Ungehorsam um „the deliberate violation of law for a vital social purpose" sei hier demgegenüber als weite Definition genannt (Zinn 1968: 39).

Die Vorstellungen von zivilem Ungehorsam bewegen sich zwischen diesen engen und weiten Definitionen. Dies gilt auch für aktivistische Verständnisse von zivilem Ungehorsam, insofern sie überhaupt von akademischen unterschieden werden können. Howard Zinn z.b. beschäftigt sich nicht nur als Geschichtsprofessor mit zivilem Ungehorsam, sondern verteidigt ihn auch öffentlich. Bei einer Demonstration gegen den Vietnamkrieg 1971 in Boston erklärte er: „A lot of people are troubled by civil disobedience. As soon as you talk about committing civil disobedience they get a little upset. But that's exactly the purpose of civil disobedience, to upset people, to trouble them, to disturb them. We who commit civil disobedience are disturbed too and we need to disturb those who are in charge of the war (...)."[3]

Dem Adjektiv ‚zivil' gebührt besondere Aufmerksamkeit. Im Kriegsfalle wird zwischen Zivilisten und Kombattanten unterschieden, ‚zivil' also als Gegensatz zu ‚militärisch' verstanden. So gesehen liegt es nahe, anti-militaristischen Protest – wie er insbesondere im dritten Abschnitt dieses Kapitels behandelt wird – als zivilen Ungehorsam zu beschreiben. Abgesehen von den ständischen Assoziationen, die der Begriff ‚bürgerlich' weckt, ist der Bürger – der ‚citoyen' – seit der französischen Revolution vor allem der Staatsbürger (und mittlerweile auch die Staatsbürgerin). Die Eigenschaften, die mit ‚zivil' verbunden sind, leiten sich also von einem Status ab, der von Staats wegen bestimmt ist. Engere Definitionen von zivilem Ungehorsam, wie die von Habermas, beinhalten dem entsprechend auch die Akzeptanz der von staatlichen Gerichten verhängten Strafe für Akte des zivilen Ungehorsams (vgl. auch Laker 1986: 153ff). Diese staatsbürgerliche Konnotation macht ihn für Proteste – wie noch zu zeigen sein wird – oftmals problematisch.

Bei zivilem Ungehorsam handelt es sich also um einen Begriff, der auf einen umfangreichen sowohl akademischen als auch aktivistischen Diskurs verweisen kann. Angesichts der Vielfalt an Verständnissen ist die eingangs dargelegte Erklärung der italienischen Disobbedienti, der zivile Ungehorsam habe ausgedient, schwer dingfest zu machen. Die mit der Absage an den zivilen Ungehorsam verbundene Ausrufung des sozialen Ungehorsams bleibt gleichzeitig inhaltlich weitgehend unbestimmt. Roberto Bui vom Schriftstellerkollektiv Wu Ming bezeichnet sozialen Ungehorsam „als eine Art Taschenspielertrick (...), um sich in der Nach-Genua Zeit zurecht zu finden".[4] In den Kontexten, in denen der soziale Ungehorsam von Disobbedienti in Italien ausgerufen wurde, scheint es sich in erster Linie um ein Plädoyer für die Ausweitung des Ungehorsams auf alle gesellschaftlichen Bereiche zu handeln. Auslöser – so AktivistInnen von Tute Bianche – seien die Gewalterfahrungen von Genua gewesen, die einen zivilen Ungehorsam kaum noch als ausreichend oder angemessen erscheinen ließen (vgl. Azzellini/Ressler 2002). Nicht mehr nur unmittelbar an die Öffentlichkeit gerichtete direkte Aktionen wie z.B. Blockaden kommt damit Aufmerksamkeit zu. Als sozialer Ungehorsam wird auch die Unterstützung von ÄrztInnen verstanden, die in Genua AktivistInnen davor warnten, ins Krankenhaus zu gehen, um sie vor der dortigen Verhaftung durch die Polizei zu schützen (vgl. Azzellini 2001/2002), oder die Entscheidung von JournalistInnen, mit unabhängigen Medien wie indymedia zusammenzuarbeiten (vgl. Azzellini/Ressler 2002). Der Einschätzung Roberto Buis ähnlich gibt Francesco Raparelli von den Tute Bianche bzw. Disobbedienti zu bedenken, dass die Gefahr bestehe, mit dem Begriff des sozialen Ungehorsams nur Praktiken zu benennen, die ohnehin schon lange existieren: „Presenting as a linguistic element of unification something that is going to happen anyways does not work".[5] Mit einem weiten Verständnis von zivilem Ungehorsam, wie es z.B. Howard Zinn repräsentiert, sind also Aktionen, die als sozialer Ungehorsam angesehen werden, bereits erfasst. Spätestens hier wird deutlich, dass es sich bei dem Begriff des sozialen Ungehorsams vor allem um politische Rhetorik handelt. Durch die große Popularität der Tute Bianche bzw. Disobbedienti auch über Italien hinaus verbreitete sich der Begriff des sozialen Ungehorsams. Für den 20. und 21. Dezember 2002 wurde beispielsweise zu zwei globalen Aktionstagen des sozialen Ungehorsams in Solidarität mit den Protesten in Argentinien aufgerufen. Letztlich setzte sich der Begriff des sozialen Ungehorsams aber gegen den des zivilen Ungehorsams – zumindest bisher – nicht durch. Deshalb liegt der weitere Fokus dieses Beitrags auf zivilem Ungehorsam.

Ziviler Ungehorsam und globalisierungskritischer Protest

Bei ‚der' globalisierungskritischen Bewegung handelt es sich um ein weltweites, transnationales Netz kapitalismuskritischer, Formen horizontaler Politik favorisierender Assoziationen, die insbesondere durch große transnational bedeutsame Protestereignisse wie in Seattle, Genua, Davos oder den Weltsozialforen bekannt geworden sind. Die Vielfalt der Initiativen und Kampagnen hat verschiedene Versuche zur Folge, die Bewegung(en) auf den Begriff zu bringen: Global Justice Movement, Multitude, Transnationale Guerilla, Protestformationen, um nur einige zu nennen. Diese durchaus notwendigen Begriffsdiskussionen müssen an anderer Stelle geführt werden. In diesem Beitrag geht es um zivilen Ungehorsam innerhalb dieser Bewegung(en). Ich verwende hier die allgemeinere Formulierung ‚globalisierungskritischer Protest', womit die Aktion im Verhältnis zur Organisierungsfrage in den Vordergrund gerückt wird.[6]

Die Proteste gegen den G8-Gipfel in Heiligendamm im Juni 2007 stellten ein bis dato in Deutschland ungekanntes Ausmaß an kollektivem zivilen Ungehorsam dar. Allein an den Blockaden des Gipfelortes vom 6.-8. Juni beteiligten sich über 10 000 Menschen. Sie wandten damit nicht nur ein klassisches Mittel des zivilen Ungehorsams an, sondern widersetzten sich damit auch dem umfassenden Demonstrationsverbot (vgl. Gericke 2008). Die größte Blockade wurde organisiert von ‚BlockG8', einem breiten Bündnis, an dem unter anderen sowohl Post-Autonome als auch die katholische Friedensbewegung Pax Christi beteiligt waren. Angeknüpft wurde damit an das vielfach bei Castortransporten erprobte Blockadekonzept von x-tausend-mal-quer. Bereits Monate im Voraus wurde zu diesem „massenhaften zivilen Ungehorsam" aufgerufen.[7]

Vor dem eigentlichen Beginn des Gipfels gab es rund um Heiligendamm mehrere Aktionstage, so dass eine ganze Woche lang verschiedene Protestaktionen stattfanden. Am Aktionstag Landwirtschaft am 3. Juni wirkte auch die Kampagne ‚Gendreck weg' mit, die öffentlich zu ‚Feldbefreiungen' aufruft, also zum Zerstören von gentechnisch veränderten Pflanzen.[8] Während der Abschlussveranstaltung dieses Aktionstages in Groß Lüsewitz in der Nähe von Rostock hatten PolizistInnen vorsorglich den örtlichen Genacker umzingelt und so nicht zuletzt für mögliche spätere Aktionen markiert. Während der Aktionstage gegen den G8 wurden in Mecklenburg-Vorpommern mehrere Felder mit genmanipuliertem Mais zerstört.

Bereits für den 1. Juni wurde aufgerufen, „in einer Aktion zivilen Ungehorsams das Bombodrom-Gelände in der Kyritz-Ruppiner Heide, ca. 80 km nordwestlich von Berlin im Vorfeld des G8 symbolisch zu besiedeln".[9] Das Bombodrom ist als geplanter Bombenabwurfplatz militärisches Sperrgebiet. Diesem Aufruf folgten ca. 700 Menschen.[10] In einer weiteren anti-militaristischen Aktion zivilen Ungehorsams sollte der Militärflughafen Rostock-Laage blockiert werden, an dem darüber hinaus die G8-Delegationen eintrafen.[11] Ein massives Polizeiaufgebot verhinderte dies weitgehend. Trotz Demonstrationsverbot versammelten sich aber ca. 1000 Menschen.[12]

Die bisher genannten Aktionen folgten ähnlichen Verständnissen von zivilem Ungehorsam: Sowohl die Blockaden von BlockG8 als auch die Demonstrationen am Militärflughafen Rostock-Laage und die Besetzung bzw. Besiedlung des Bombodroms waren zuvor angekündigt worden und erfolgten offen – also nicht klandestin. Auch Feldbefreiungen werden – nicht immer, aber oftmals – vorher öffentlich angekündigt. Dies ist Teil der Öffentlichkeitsarbeit, um möglichst breite Unterstützung für die Aktion zu erlangen. Zu dem Blockadekonzept von BlockG8 gehörte die vorherige Ankündigung von massenhaftem zivilen Ungehorsam, um dem Protest Nachdruck zu verleihen. Das Gebot der Gewaltfreiheit wurde beachtet, was jedoch nicht zwingend einhergeht mit einer Anerkennung des staatlichen Gewaltmonopols. Letzteres als illegitim zu betrachten, zieht nicht unmittelbar die Anwendung gewaltvoller Mittel nach sich, sondern kann auch bedeuten, niemandem – auch nicht sich selbst – ein solches Gewaltmonopol zuzugestehen.

Ziviler Ungehorsam und transnationale Friedensbewegung

Die Friedensbewegung hatte schon lange vor den Protesten gegen die WTO in Seattle 1999, die oftmals, aber keinesfalls unumstritten als Ausgangspunkt globalisierungskritischer Bewegungen verstanden wird, eine transnationale Dimension. Ein Beispiel dafür ist die Pflugscharbewegung, die nicht nur mit ideeller, sondern auch personaler Unterstützung US-amerikanischer PflugschärlerInnen in den 1980ern in West-Deutschland entstanden ist. Anders als die oben genannten Aktionen zivilen Ungehorsams fanden Pflugscharaktionen in den wenigsten Fällen mit vorheriger Ankündigung statt, denn dies hätte ihre Durchführung vermutlich in den meisten Fällen unmöglich gemacht. Die Pflugscharbewegung entstand aus christlicher Motivation, nämlich dem biblischen Aufruf „Schwerter zu Pflugscharen" (Micha 4). Pflugscharaktionen finden zumeist in kleinen Gruppen statt, die insofern offen agieren, als dass sie am Tatort bis zu ihrer Verhaftung warten und zumeist auch den anschließenden Prozess noch als Teil ihrer Aktion, nämlich als notwendige Öffentlichkeitsarbeit verstehen. Die Möglichkeit einer Haftstrafe ist mit einkalkuliert. Der katholische Priester Carl Kabat verbrachte beispielsweise insgesamt mehr als 15 Jahre in US-amerikanischen Gefängnissen für mehrere Pflugscharaktionen (vgl. Philipp 2006: 136). Beteiligt war er auch an der ersten von zwei Pflugscharaktionen in West-Deutschland, die 1983 und 1986 gegen die Stationierung von Pershing-II-Raketen stattfanden. 1983 verursachten Carl Kabat und drei weitere AktivistInnen mit Hämmern einen Schaden in Höhe von 18 000 Mark an einem Raketentransporter, der in der Hardt-Kaserne bei Schwäbisch-Gmünd zur Abfahrt nach Mutlangen bereitstand, und warteten anschließend vor Ort auf ihre Festnahme. „[Die Polizei] kam mit einem Polizeifahrzeug, einem VW-Bully, begrüßte uns mit ‚guten Morgen' und forderte uns höflich auf, einzusteigen" – so der beteiligte Aktivist Wolfgang Sternstein (2005: 362). Sechs Stunden später waren sie wieder auf freiem Fuß; die Anklage lautete Sabotage, Sachbeschädigung und Hausfriedensbruch; die Urteile fielen überraschend mild aus: Sternstein z.B. wurde zu 90 Tagessätzen à 20 Mark verurteilt. Der Richter kommentierte den Urteilsspruch damit, dass die Tat der Verurteilten nicht „Ausdruck krimineller Energie, sondern ihres Gewissens" gewesen sei (Philipp 2006: 121). Die Pflugscharaktion 1986 in der selben Kaserne verlief sehr ähnlich. Diesmal beteiligte sich unter anderen auch Heike Huschauer, SPD-Stadträtin in Neuss (vgl. ebd.: 144).

Als am 31. Juli 2007 in einer anti-militaristischen Aktion versucht wurde, drei Bundeswehrlastwagen in Brand zu setzen, wurden die drei Beschuldigten unter Terrorverdacht gestellt und wie der bereits oben genannte Andrej Holm, der als intellektueller Hintermann galt, verhaftet. Gemeinsam mit drei weiteren der ‚intellektuellen Täterschaft' Beschuldigten, gegen die keine Haftbefehle vorlagen, wurden sie der Mitgliedschaft in der ‚militanten gruppe' angeklagt, die als terroristische Vereinigung behandelt wurde. Eine Anklage bzw. bereits der Verdacht nach dem Terrorparagraphen §129a beinhaltet nicht nur eine Einschätzung der Tat als staatsgefährdend, sondern auch eine weitgehende Entrechtung der Beschuldigten, einschließlich der Möglichkeiten umfangreicher Überwachung, Untersuchungshaft auch ohne Fluchtgefahr bis hin zu Isolationshaft. Der Haftbefehl gegen Andrej Holm wurde Ende Oktober aufgehoben, die drei weiteren Inhaftierten Ende November gegen hohe Kautionen aus der Haft entlassen. Der Bundesgerichtshof hatte erst zu diesem Zeitpunkt entschieden, dass die Anklage nicht mehr auf Mitgliedschaft in einer ‚terroristischen Vereinigung' (§129a), sondern in einer ‚kriminellen Vereinigung' (§129) lautet. Bis dahin wurden die Beschuldigten aber bereits mehr als ein Jahr umfangreich observiert. Verdacht auf Mittäterschaft wurde u.a. auf der Grundlage formuliert, dass Andrej Holm und die drei weiteren nicht verhafteten Personen in ihren wissenschaftlichen Texten Begriffe wie ‚Gentrifizierung' verwandt hatten, die auch in BekennerInnenschreiben der ‚militanten gruppe' auftauchten; Treffen wurden als konspirativ deklariert, weil keine Mobiltelefone mitgenommen wurden.[13]

Die Beschädigung von militärischem Gerät als Akt symbolischer Abrüstung kann also auch in Deutschland auf eine gewisse Geschichte innerhalb der Friedensbewegung zurückblicken. Im Vergleich der Abrüstungsaktionen von 1983 und 1986 mit denjenigen vom Juli 2007 fallen mehrere Aspekte auf. Hinsichtlich der Thematik und der Ausführung ähneln sich die Aktionen stark. Legt man Verständnisse von zivilem Ungehorsam an, so gibt es ein paar Unterschiede: Wie bei Pflugscharaktionen üblich, wurden die Aktionen 1983 und 1986 offen begangen, eine mögliche Haftstrafe wurde bewusst einkalkuliert. Die Offenheit bestand gleichwohl nicht in einer vorherigen Ankündigung und war damit auch nicht für die Polizei kalkulierbar, was Habermas allerdings als Bedingung für zivilen Ungehorsam formuliert (s.o.). Die versuchte Inbrandsetzung der Bundeswehrfahrzeuge im Sommer 2007 fand verdeckt statt. Während erstere christlich motiviert waren, lässt dies zumindest der UnterstützerInnenkreis bei letzterer kaum vermuten. Was aber besonders auffällt, sind die eklatant unterschiedlichen juristischen und politischen Einschätzungen der Aktionen. Die Festnahmen bei den Pflugscharaktionen 1983 und 1986 werden als „freundlich" beschrieben. 2007 gehen sie mit Verletzungen und Erniedrigungen einher und der Terrorverdacht wird auch medial in Szene gesetzt mit dem direkten Hubschrauberflug nach Karlsruhe, um die Beschuldigten beim Bundesgerichtshof dem Haftrichter vorzuführen.[14] Während die PflugschärlerInnen wegen der Aktion 1983 sechs Stunden nach ihrer Festnahme wieder auf freiem Fuß waren, setzte sich der Umgang mit den Beschuldigten 2007 während ihrer Verhaftung in der weiteren Behandlung fort. Der Terrorverdacht bestand im letzteren Fall bis zur Aufhebung durch den Bundesgerichtshof im November 2007 – also erst vier Monate nach der Festnahme (und nach über einem Jahr der terrorverdachtsbedingten umfassenden Überwachung). Während Andrej Holm als vermeintlicher intellektueller Kopf internationale Solidaritätsbekundungen erhielt, fiel die Unterstützung für die drei anderen wegen versuchter Beschädigung von Bundeswehrfahrzeugen Angeklagten wesentlich geringer aus. Wenn überhaupt von einem öffentlichen Diskurs über diesen Tatvorwurf die Rede sein kann, so bewegt er sich in den politisch und juristisch vorgegebenen Mustern des

Terrorverdachts und einer Gewaltdebatte, die implizit Sachbeschädigung und Gewalt gegen Menschen gleichsetzt. Von einer pazifistischen Tat ist außerhalb relativ kleiner UnterstützerInnenkreise nicht die Rede.

Den politischen und juristischen Umgang betreffend ähnelt die antimilitaristische Aktion des Jahres 2007 damit stärker dem massenhaften zivilen Ungehorsam anlässlich der Proteste gegen den G8-Gipfel in Heiligendamm im selben Jahr. Auch letztere Aktionen waren zumindest zum Teil bereits im Vorfeld als terroristisch eingestuft worden: Am 9. Mai, einen knappen Monat vor dem G8-Gipfel, fanden bundesweit ca. 40 Hausdurchsuchungen statt, die mit dem Verdacht auf eine terroristische Vereinigung nach §129a begründet wurden. Noch nach den Protesten, im August 2007, wurde die Wohnung des Inhabers einer Internetseite, auf der auch der Aufruf zu den Massenblockaden von BlockG8 verbreitet wurde, durchsucht und sein Computer beschlagnahmt. Begründet wurde die Hausdurchsuchung damit, dass es sich bei der im Aufruf enthaltenen Formulierung „Wegdrücken von Polizeiabsperrungen" um den Aufruf zu einer Straftat handle.[15]

Während in den 1980ern auf den US-amerikanischen Militärbasen den Soldaten auf ausdrückliche Bitte der baden-württembergischen Landesregierung ihre Schusswaffen genommen worden waren, weil man einen ‚Benno Ohnesorg der Friedensbewegung' fürchtete (vgl. Sternstein 2005: 368), wurde gegen die Proteste rund um Heiligendamm 2007 auch die Bundeswehr eingesetzt (vgl. Euskirchen 2008, Heinecke 2008, Komitee für Grundrechte und Demokratie 2007: 125ff).

Ziviler Ungehorsam revisited

Die genannten Beispiele zeigen, dass die Bezugnahme auf zivilen Ungehorsam trotz dessen Aufkündigung durch die Disobbedienti in Italien für globalisierungskritische Bewegungen nicht obsolet geworden ist. Vielmehr scheint gerade mit den Massenblockaden gegen den G8-Gipfel in Heiligendamm der Begriff des zivilen Ungehorsams neuerliche Verbreitung gefunden zu haben. Auffällig ist aber auch, dass die versuchte Beschädigung der Militärfahrzeuge 2007 anders als 1983 und 1986 und auch im Unterschied zu den vielfältigen Protestaktionen während des G8-Gipfels 2007 von den UnterstützerInnen nicht als ziviler Ungehorsam bezeichnet wird. Die staatsbürgerliche Konnotation des Begriffes ‚ziviler Ungehorsam' scheint ein wesentlicher Grund dafür sein, warum in der anti-kapitalistischen und staatskritischen Linken in Deutschland – wenn überhaupt – nur zögerlich auf ihn rekurriert wird. Am ehesten lässt sich ein positiver Bezug der radikalen Linken auf zivilen Ungehorsam im post-autonomen Spektrum finden, das auch maßgeblich an der Vorbereitung und Durchführung des ‚massenhaften zivilen Ungehorsams' BlockG8 beteiligt war. Am Aufruf zu diesen Blockaden lässt sich jedoch auch sehen, dass Offenheit der Aktion dabei nicht unmittelbar die Bereitschaft oder sogar Intention zur Festnahme bedeutet – ein Charakteristikum, das in manchen Verständnissen zivilen Ungehorsams integraler Bestandteil ist (vgl. Habermas). Umgekehrt ist dabei nicht der Schluss zu ziehen, dass AktivistInnen, die am Tatort auf ihre Festnahme warten und für ihre Tat ins Gefängnis gehen, diese Strafen als legitim akzeptieren. Wie Damian Moran berichtet, der an einer Pflugscharaktion im Flughafen Shannon (Irland) im Februar 2003 beteiligt war, bestand die Entscheidung für die Offenheit der Aktion und das Ausharren bis zur Festnahme nicht in der Anerkennung staatlicher Gewalt, sondern darin, der Legitimität der Aktion Nachdruck zu verleihen sowie ihre Tat in der Öffentlichkeit verteidigen und diskutieren zu können.[16]

Politisch scheint die Verwendung des Begriffs ‚ziviler Ungehorsam' besonders in zweierlei Hinsicht sinnvoll. Zum einen ist es damit möglich, ein großes Spektrum an Beteiligten anzusprechen, wie insbesondere an BlockG8 deutlich wird: Zu den Blockaden hatten sowohl Post-Autonome als auch katholische Friedensbewegte aufgerufen. Zum anderen hätte der Diskurs um die Inbrandsetzung der Bundeswehrlastwagen im Sommer 2007 vermutlich eine andere Richtung eingenommen, andere Beurteilungen und weitere UnterstützerInnenkreise gefunden, wäre sie als Aktion zivilen Ungehorsams deklariert worden. Allerdings hätte dies auch einer umfangreicheren Kommunikation der anti-militaristischen Beweggründe der Tat und damit vermutlich der Offenheit der Aktion bedurft.

Mit dem Begriff des zivilen Ungehorsams – im Sinne eines staatsbürgerlichen Ungehorsams – laufen Proteste jedoch auch Gefahr, die Radikalität ihrer Kritik zu verschleiern. Die Blockaden des G8-Gipfels in Heiligendamm waren eben nicht ein Appell an die dort versammelten RegierungschefInnen, sondern sollten die Delegitimierung dieser Institution zum Ausdruck bringen. Die Zerstörung von Bundeswehrlastwagen richteten sich nicht gegen einen bestimmten, als ungerecht verstandenen Krieg, sondern gegen Krieg allgemein und damit auch gegen Staatlichkeit, die letztlich immer auf militärischer Gewalt aufbaut. Wenn Elke Stevens zudem die Überlegung anstellt, vielleicht gleich besser von ‚zivilem Gehorsam' zu sprechen, da es darum gehe, „auf die Verletzung der Ordnung durch staatliches Handeln aufmerksam zu machen" (2007: 262), scheint die Begrifflichkeit jegliche Attraktivität für AktivistInnen zu verlieren.

Die Verwendung des Begriffes ziviler Ungehorsam bleibt also trotz oder vielleicht gerade aufgrund der Vielzahl an konzeptionellen Definitionsversuchen ähnlich dem Begriff des sozialen Ungehorsams vor allem eine politische Entscheidung, die situativ, nicht allgemein getroffen wird und sich als unterschiedlich sinnvoll erweist. Das Politische besteht dabei nicht zuletzt darin, das von John K. Samson im Eingangszitat als problematisch betrachtete Aufstellen von Regeln des Protests immer wieder zu hinterfragen, was bei den Protesten gegen den G8-Gipfel in Heiligendamm mit der Nichtbeachtung des umfassenden Demonstrationsverbots geschah. Der zivile Ungehorsam lebt eben gerade vom Regelbruch.

Literatur:

Azzellini, Dario (2001/2002): Von den Tute Bianche zu den Ungehorsamen, in: Arranca!, No. 23 (Winter), Berlin, pp. 26-30.
Azzellini, Dario, and Oliver Ressler (2002): Disobbedienti (Film, 54 min).
Ellis, Deb, and Denis Mueller (2004): Howard Zinn. You Can't Be Neutral on a Moving Train (Film, 78 min).

Euskirchen, Markus (2008): Bundeswehreinsatz im Inneren. Besichtigung im Hinterland des globalen zivilen Krieges, in: Republikanischer Anwältinnen- und Anwälteverein and Legal Team (eds.): Feindbild Demonstrant. Polizeigewalt, Militäreinsatz, Medienmanipulation – Der G8-Gipfel aus Sicht des Anwaltlichen Notdienstes, Berlin and Hamburg (Assoziation A), pp. 137-141.

Gericke, Carsten (2008): Von Brokdorf nach Heiligendamm. Das Bundesverfassungsgericht und die Versammlungsverbote und -beschränkungen beim G8-Gipfel 2007, in: Republikanischer Anwältinnen- und Anwälteverein and Legal Team (eds.): Feindbild Demonstrant. Polizeigewalt, Militäreinsatz, Medienmanipulation – Der G8-Gipfel aus Sicht des Anwaltlichen Notdienstes, Berlin and Hamburg (Assoziation A), pp. 53-65.

Habermas, Jürgen (1983): Ziviler Ungehorsam – Testfall für den demokratischen Rechtsstaat. Wider den autoritären Legalismus in der Bundesrepublik, in: Glotz, Peter (ed.): Ziviler Ungehorsam im Rechtsstaat, Frankfurt a. M. (Suhrkamp Verlag), pp. 29-53.

Heinecke, Gabriele (2008): Gegen Demokraten helfen nur Soldaten. Die Verpolizeilichung des Militärischen, in: Republikanischer Anwältinnen- und Anwälteverein and Legal Team (eds.): Feindbild Demonstrant. Polizeigewalt, Militäreinsatz, Medienmanipulation – Der G8-Gipfel aus Sicht des Anwaltlichen Notdienstes, Berlin and Hamburg (Assoziation A), pp. 143-148.

Komitee für Grundrechte und Demokratie (ed.) (2007): Gewaltbereite Politik und der G8-Gipfel. Demonstrationsbeobachtungen vom 2.-8. Juni 2007 rund um Heiligendamm, Köln (Komitee für Grundrechte und Demokratie e. V.).

Laker, Thomas (1986): Ziviler Ungehorsam. Geschichte – Begriff – Rechtfertigung, Baden-Baden (Nomos Verlagsgesellschaft).

Philipp, Ulrich (2006): Politik von unten. Wolfgang Sternstein – Erfahrungen eines Graswurzelpolitikers und Aktionsforschers, Berlin (Nora Verlagsgemeinschaft).

Sternstein, Wolfgang (2005): Mein Weg zwischen Gewalt und Gewaltfreiheit. Autobiographie, Norderstedt (Books on Demand).

Steven, Elke (2007): Ziviler Ungehorsam, in: Brand, Ulrich, Bettina Lösch, and Stefan Thimmel (eds.): ABC der Alternativen. Von „Ästhetik des Widerstands" bis „ziviler Ungehorsam", Hamburg (VSA Verlag), pp. 262-263.

Zinn, Howard (1968). Disobedience and Democracy. Nine Fallacies on Law and Order, New York (Random House).

1 Für hilfreiche kritische Kommentare danke ich André Bank und Daniela Grimm.
2 Zur Dokumentation des Falles siehe https://einstellung.so36.net.
3 Zitiert nach Ellis und Mueller 2004.
4 www.wumingfoundation.com/english/giap/kreuzberg.html, 27.2.2008.
5 Zitiert nach Azzellini und Ressler 2002.
6 Formen von Globalisierungskritik wie Neonazismus oder Islamismus bleiben dabei jedoch unbesehen. Diesen Formen globalisierungskritischen Protests Akte des zivilen Ungehorsams zuzurechnen, würde den Begriff gänzlich sinnentleeren.
7 Vgl. den Aufruf von BlockG8 unter http://www.nadir.org/nadir/initiativ/fels/de/2007/03/358.shtml, 10.3.2008; hier als Aufruf der beteiligten Gruppe FelS ('Für eine Linke Strömung').
8 http://www.gendreck-weg.de/, 10.3.2008.
9 http://www.sichelschmiede.org/Aktion/G8/, 26.2.2008.
10 http://de.indymedia.org/2007/06/179899.shtml, 26.2.2008.
11 vgl. den Aufruf unter http://g8andwar.de/bombodrom/download/aufruf_deutsch.pdf, 26.2.2008.
12 vgl. den Pressespiegel unter http://www.jpberlin.de/badespasz/presse/wp/?cat=39, 26.2.2008.
13 Vgl. http://einstellung.so36.net/de/offenerbrief, 28.2.2008.
14 In der Presserklärung heißt es u.a. „Durch seinen Anwalt wurde bekannt, dass Florian L. angeschnallt sitzend schwer verprügelt wurde und Prellungen und Schwellungen im Gesicht und an den Rippen erlitt. (...) Den Verhafteten wurden Säcke über die Köpfe gezogen, alle drei wurden in dünne, weiße Plastik-Overalls gesteckt und sie mussten gefesselt über einen langen Zeitraum auf der Straße liegen." Vgl. https://einstellung.so36.net/de/pm/134, 28.2.2008.
15 Vgl. den für die Hausdurchsuchung maßgeblichen Text unter http://www.antiatombonn.de/index.php?option=com_content&task=view&id=126&Itemid=16, 28.2.2008.
16 Angesichts des kurz bevorstehenden Irak-Krieges drangen am 3. Februar 2003 fünf AktivistInnen in den Militärflughafen Shannon ein und richteten mit Hämmern an einem Militärflugzeug einen Schaden von 2,5 Millionen Dollar an, warteten dann auf ihre Festnahme und ließen gleichzeitig eine Internetseite freischalten, die über die Motive ihrer Tat informierte. Während der anschließenden fast dreieinhalb Jahre dauernden gerichtlichen Verhandlungen verbrachten sie fast täglich Stunden auf der Straße, um Flugblätter über ihre Aktion zu verteilen und mit PassantInnen zu diskutieren. Den zwölf Geschworenen konnten sie schließlich glaubhaft versichern, dass die Demolierung des Militärflugzeuges darauf abzielte, Menschenleben im Irak zu retten und so erreichten sie einen Freispruch. (Diskussion während der Veranstaltung „Kriegsgerät interessiert uns brennend", 23.2.2008, Berlin)

From Civil to Social Disobedience and Back Again

On the Conceptual Politics of Alter-Globalization Protest[1]

Andrea Pabst

> *"I'm not saying that I would support an armed revolution, necessarily – I'm just saying that I wouldn't rule it out as an option. When you do, you fall into this trap of creating rules of protesting."*
> John K. Samson

Introduction

After the protests against the 2001 G8 summit in Genoa, Luca Casarini, one of the speakers for the Italian tute bianche, declared that the phase of civil disobedience had come to an end and that social disobedience was now the necessary next step (cf. Azzellini 2001/2002). Before anything else, this statement raises questions: what does 'civil disobedience' mean? Why has it been exhausted? What is social, as distinct from civil, disobedience to look like? How is the transition from the one to the other to take place? And for whom, in fact, is Casarini speaking here? For the tute bianche, the activists in white overalls, who rose to prominence especially with their protests against the World Trade Organization (WTO) and the International Monetary Fund (IMF) in Prague in 2000, and renamed themselves the 'disobedient ones' (disobbedienti) in Genoa? Or is he speaking for 'the' alter-globalization movement as a whole? Is this a conclusion drawn from the Genoa protests, or is he diagnosing a global historical shift in forms of protest?

These questions indicate the fundamental issue the present contribution confronts: by engaging civil disobedience and social disobedience and their forms within 'the' alter-globalization movement, it addresses terms the conceptual debates over each of which might—or already do—fill libraries. Consensual definitions of what these terms substantially mean hardly exist, if at all. Moreover, these are terms that are politically contentious in a particular way. Conceptual politics consists in academic debates over adequate definitions on the one hand, and in the associated political-strategic use of these terms by activists on the other hand. The present chapter constitutes an approach to and discussion of the interrelations between the critique of globalization and civil and social disobedience. The first section will introduce the terms 'civil' and 'social disobedience.' As will be seen, however, the term 'social disobedience' has so far failed to become widely accepted. I will therefore in the following refer only to civil disobedience. With respect to alter-globalization protests, the second section will offer an exemplary presentation by drawing on the protests against the 2007 G8 summit at Heiligendamm (Germany). Whereas the latter events primarily represent examples of civil disobedience involving a great number of participants, the third section, on civil disobedience and the transnational peace movement, will focus, in a historical comparison, on actions by smaller groups. Closing, I will discuss the strategic use of the notion of civil disobedience.

From civil to social disobedience?

Since the mid-90s, the academic engagement of civil disobedience has markedly declined, at least in the German and English-speaking parts of the world. Whereas civil disobedience prior to that time represented both a political and a legal problem and was the subject of extensive discussions, the waves seem to have calmed a little since then. Yet to understand this decline as an indication that civil disobedience has, for the time being, lost virtually all of its explosive power might turn out to be a rash and deceptive conclusion. It is quite possible that political urgency might be found today precisely in an engagement with civil disobedience or, to put it differently, such engagements might touch in particular upon political issues that have been declared taboo in the security matrix that emerged after the September 11, 2001 terror attacks. The suspicion of terrorist activities leveled against the sociologist Andrej Holm based on, among other things, his research on gentrification, is not the weakest demonstration of the consequences critical academic work can have.[2]

With respect to the anglo-american academic discourses on civil disobedience since the 1950s, and those in the German-speaking countries since around 15 years later, we can distinguish between narrow and wide definitions. For an exemplary narrow definition, we can cite Jürgen Habermas: "Civil disobedience is a morally motivated protest that must not be based only on privately held convictions or individual interests; it is a public act, usually announced in advance, and its course is predictable to the police; it includes premeditated infractions against individual legal norms without affecting obedience toward the legal order as a whole; it requires willingness to accept the legal consequences of these infractions; the infraction against a rule that is the expression of civil disobedience is purely symbolic in character—from the latter stipulation alone follows that this protest be limited to nonviolent means" (Habermas 1983: 35). Howard Zinn's explanation that civil disobedience is "the deliberate violation of law for a vital social purpose" (Zinn 1968:39), by contrast, can serve here as a wide definition.

Ideas of what civil disobedience is range between these narrow and wide definitions. The same is true of activist conceptions of civil disobedience, to the extent that they are at all distinguishable from academic ones. Howard Zinn, for instance, not only engages civil disobedience in his work as a professor of history, he also publicly defends it. During a demonstration against the Vietnam War in Boston in 1971, he declared: "A lot of people are troubled by civil disobedience. As soon as you talk about committing civil disobedience they get a little upset. But that's exactly the purpose of civil disobedience, to upset people, to trouble them, to disturb them. We who commit civil disobedience are disturbed too and we need to disturb those who are in charge of the war [...]"[3]

The adjective 'civil' deserves special attention. During wartime, a distinction is made between civilians and combatants; that is to say, 'civil' is understood in contrast with 'military.' From this angle, it would seem natural to describe anti-militarist protests—such as discussed especially in the third section of this chapter—as civil disobedience. Citizen or citoyen has meant, since the French Revolution, primarily the male (and by now also the female) citizen of a nation. The characteristics one associates with 'civil,' then, are derived from a status defined by the state. Narrower definitions of civil disobedience, such as Habermas's, hence also include the acceptance of penalties imposed by the state's courts of law for acts of civil disobedience (cf. also Laker 1986: 153ff.). As will be seen, this connotation—that the civil disobedient is seen as the citizen of a nation—often renders the term's application to protests problematic.

Civil disobedience, then, is a concept whose claim to importance is supported by an extensive academic as well as activist discourse. Given the great variety of ways in which the term is understood, the abovementioned declaration by the Italian disobbedienti that civil disobedience has served its purpose is hard to pin down. At the same time, the substance of the second part of this farewell to civil disobedience, the proclamation of social disobedience, remains largely undetermined. Roberto Bui from the authors' collective Wu Ming calls social disobedience "a sort of sleight of hand [...] with which to find one's way in the post-Genoa era."[4] In those contexts where social disobedience was proclaimed by Italy's disobbedienti, this seems to have been primarily an appeal to extend disobedience to all areas of social life. This shift was triggered—thus activists from the tute bianche—by the experience of violence in Genoa, as a consequence of which civil disobedience appeared to be hardly sufficient or adequate anymore (cf. Azzellini / Ressler 2002). This means that actions immediately directed at public audiences such as blockades no longer have an exclusive claim to our attention. The conception of social disobedience includes also support for the doctors in Genoa who warned activists not to go to a hospital in order to protect them from being arrested there (cf. Azzellini 2001/2002), or the decision made by journalists to collaborate with independent media such as indymedia (cf. Azzellini / Ressler 2002). In an assessment similar to Roberto Bui's, Francesco Raparelli from the tute bianche or disobbedienti cautions that the term 'social disobedience' may not do anything but put a name on practices that have long existed: "Presenting as a linguistic element of unification something that is going to happen anyways does not work."[5] That is to say, a wide conception of civil disobedience such as the one represented by Howard Zinn already includes actions that would be regarded as social disobedience. At this point it becomes clear, if it hasn't already, that the term 'social disobedience' is mostly political rhetoric. The great popularity the tute bianche or disobbedienti enjoyed in Italy and beyond led to a proliferation of the concept of social disobedience. For instance, two days of action of global social disobedience were proclaimed for December 20 and 21, 2002, in solidarity with the protests in Argentina. Ultimately, however, the concept of social disobedience as distinct from that of civil disobedience has not —at least not yet—gained wide currency. The present contribution, then, will in the following focus on the concept of civil disobedience.

Civil disobedience and anti-globalization protest

'The' alter-globalization movement is a global transnational network of associations that are critical of capitalism and favor forms of horizontal politics, associations that have gained notoriety primarily by means of large protest events of transnational significance such as those in Seattle, Genoa, and Davos and during the World Social Forums. The variety of these initiatives and campaigns has led to diverse attempts to propose one concept that would unify this movement (or these movements): Global Justice Movement, Multitude, Transnational Guerrilla, Protest Formations, to list only a few. Although I do not wish to deny the need for these conceptual debates, they will have to take place outside of the present contribution, which is concerned with civil disobedience within this movement (or these movements). I here use the more general term 'alter-globalization protest,' foregrounding the subject of action as opposed to the question of organization.[6]

The protests against the G8 summit held at Heiligendamm in July 2007 constituted a display of civil disobedience of an extent heretofore unseen in Germany. The blockades of the site where the summit was held between June 6 and 8 alone involved more than 10,000 participants. The latter thus not only employed a classical instrument of civil disobedience but also defied a comprehensive ban on demonstrations (cf. Gericke 2008). The biggest blockade was organized by 'BlockG8,' a wide confederation that included, among others, both post-Autonom leftist radicals and the Catholic peace movement Pax Christi, and drew on the blockade concept developed by the initiative 'x-tausendmal quer' that was tested during protests against numerous Castor nuclear-waste transports. Calls for participation in this act of 'massive civil disobedience' went out even months before the event.[7]

Before the summit proper began, a number of day-of-action events were held around Heiligendamm such that various protests took place over the course of an entire week. The day of agricultural action, June 3, was co-organized by the anti-genetic-engineering campaign 'Gendreck weg,' which has publicly called for 'field liberations,' that is, for the destruction of genetically modified crops.[8] During the final event of this day of action, held at Groß Lüsewitz near Rostock, policemen had, by way of precaution, taken up station around the local field of genetically modified crops and thus also marked it for possible later actions. During the days of action directed against the G8 summit, a number of fields of genetically modified maize in Mecklenburg-Vorpommern were destroyed.

Appeals called for protesters to arrive as early as June 1 in order to "symbolically settle, in an act of civil disobedience ahead of the G8 summit, the Bombodrom area of the Kyritz-Ruppin heath."[9] As a projected bomb-testing site, the Bombodrom is a military restricted area. Ca. 700 people followed this call to action.[10] In another action of anti-militarist civil disobedience, protesters planned to blockade the military airport at Rostock-Laage, where the G8 delegations also arrived.[11] A massive deployment of police largely prevented this project. Despite a ban on demonstrations, however, ca. 1000 people assembled.[12]

The actions discussed so far followed similar conceptions of civil disobedience: both the blockades of the G8 summit and the demonstrations at the Rostock-Laage military airport as well as the occupation of or settlement on the Bombodrom had been announced publicly and were undertaken in full view of the authorities—that is to say, not clandestinely. Similarly, field liberations are often—though not always—publicly announced beforehand. Such announcements are part of a publicity strategy aimed at maximizing support for an action. Part of the blockade concept developed by BlockG8 was that massive civil disobedience was announced in advance in order to lend weight to the protest. Participants observed the injunction to refrain from violence; that, however, does not necessarily entail that they acknowledged the state's monopoly on the use of force. To regard the latter as illegitimate does not inevitably entrain the use of forcible means but can also mean that protesters do not concede to anyone—nor even to themselves—such a monopoly.

Civil disobedience and the transnational peace movement

There was a transnational dimension to the peace movement long before the protests against the 1999 WTO meeting in Seattle, which is often, though that is by no means an uncontentious claim, taken to be the origin of the alter-globalization movements. One example is the Ploughshare movement that emerged in West Germany during the 1980s and received not only ideational but also personal support from American Ploughshare members. In contradistinction to the abovementioned actions of civil disobedience, Ploughshare actions were in most cases held without prior announcement, as such announcements would most likely have made their execution impossible. The Ploughshare movement arose from a Christian motivation; to be specific, it followed the Biblical call to "beat their swords into ploughshares" (Micah 4). Ploughshare actions are usually performed by small groups that act openly insofar as they wait at the crime scene to be arrested and in most cases understand the subsequent trial to be a part of their action, that is, as the necessarily publicity work. They openly accept the possibility that they will be sentenced to prison terms. The Catholic priest Carl Kabat, for instance, spent altogether more than 15 years in American prisons for his participation in various Ploughshare actions (cf. Philipp 2006: 136). He also participated in the first of two Ploughshare actions held in 1983 and 1986 in West Germany against the deployment of Pershing II missiles. In 1983, Carl Kabat and three other activists took hammers to a missile transporter awaiting departure from the Hardt barracks near Schwäbisch-Gmund for the missile site at Mutlangen, causing 18,000 German Marks in damage, and then waited at the crime scene to be arrested. "[The police] came in a police vehicle, a VW van, offered us a 'good morning,' and politely asked as to get in their car"—thus the participant and activist Wolfang Sternstein (2005:362). Six hours later, they were back on the street; they were tried for sabotage, damage to property, and trespassing, and received surprisingly mild sentences: Sternstein, for instance, was sentenced to pay 1800 Marks over 90 days. In their sentence, the judge noted that the defendants' actions had been "an expression not of criminal energy but of their conscience" (Philipp 2006: 121). The second Ploughshare action, held at the same barracks in 1986, took a very similar course. This time, one participant was Heike Huschauer, a Social-Democratic member of the Neuss city council (cf. ibid.: 144).

When the participants of an anti-militarist action held on July 31, 2007 attempted to set three German army transport vehicles on fire, the three defendants were declared terror suspects and arrested together with the abovementioned Andrej Holm, allegedly the intellectual mastermind. Together with three others who were said to be 'intellectual perpetrators,' against whom no arrest warrants had been issued, they were accused of membership in 'militante gruppe,' a group that was treated as a terrorist association. An accusation and even the mere suspicion of infractions according to section 129 of the German penal code, which deals with terrorism, not only implies that the underlying act is classified as a threat to the state but also entrains a far-reaching loss of defendants' rights, including permission for authorities to keep a defendant under comprehensive surveillance, place him or her in detention on remand even in the absence of a flight risk, and even keep him or her in solitary confinement. The arrest warrant against Andrej Holm was cancelled in late October; the three other imprisoned defendants were released in late November on high bail. At the time, the German Federal Court of Justice had decided that the defendants stood accused of membership no longer in a 'terrorist association' (section 129a) but now in a 'criminal association' (section 129). Yet at this point, the defendants had been subject to extensive observation for more than a year. The suspicion of involvement in a criminal act against Andrej Holm and the three other defendants who were not imprisoned was said to be based, among other things, on the fact that their academic writing had included terms such as 'gentrification' that also appear in letters claiming responsibility by the 'militante gruppe'; their meetings were declared to have been conspiratorial because they had not taken their mobile phones.[13]

So there is a certain amount of history within the peace movement in Germany, too, when it comes to damaging military matériel in an act of symbolic disarmament. In a comparison between the disarmament actions of 1983 and 1986 and those of July 2007, a number of aspects are salient. These actions are very similar regarding the issues they address and the acts performed. From the perspective of a conception of civil disobedience, there are a number of differences: as was standard for Ploughshare actions, the 1983 and 1986 actions were committed publicly and in open acceptance of possible prison sentences. The perpetrator's frankness, however, did not extend to an advance announcement of their act, making it impossible for the police to expect it—a condition Habermas stipulates as necessary for civil disobedience to be present (see above). The attempt in the summer of 2007 to set the army transporters on fire was undertaken covertly. Whereas the former actions were motivated by Christian convictions, the latter gives little cause to suspect similar motivations, or so it would seem from the milieu that supported them. Yet what is especially striking are the diverging legal and political assessments of the actions. The arrests after the Ploughshare actions of 1983 and 1986 are described as "amicable". Those of 2007 were accompanied by physical injuries and humiliation; the suspicion of terrorism was also staged for the media by having the defendants immediately flown by helicopter to Karlsruhe in order to present them to the Federal custodial judge.[14] Whereas the Ploughshare activists of the 1983 action were back on the street within six hours of their arrest, the way the defendants of 2007 were treated during their arrest presaged the following months. In the latter case, the suspicion of terrorism was maintained until the Federal Court of Justice abrogated it in November 2007—a full four months, that is, after the arrest (and after more than a year of comprehensive surveillance based on the suspicion of terrorism). While Andrej Holm, as the alleged intellectual mastermind, received international expressions of solidarity, support for the three other defendants accused of attempting to damage army vehicles was much scantier. The public discourse on these accusations, to the extent such a discourse can be said to exist at all, proceeds within the politically and legally prescribed patterns of the suspicion of terrorism and a debate on violence that implicitly equates violence against objects with violence against human beings. Outside of relatively small circles of supporters, no one speaks of a pacifist act.

With respect to the political and legal response, then, the anti-militarist action of 2007 has more in common with the mass acts of civil disobedience during the protests against the G8 summit at Heiligendamm of the same year. The latter actions, too, had at least in part been classified as terrorist in advance: on May 9, almost a month before the G8 summit, ca. 40 residences were searched across Germany; the search warrants were based on the suspicion that a terrorist association according to section 129a had been formed. Even after the protests, in August 2007, the apartment of the owner of a website that had also served to distribute the call to action for the mass blockades organized by BlockG8 was searched; his computer was seized. The search was justified with the phrase "pushing police barricades out of the way" contained in the call to action, which, thus the authorities, constituted incitement to commit a crime.[15]

Whereas in the 1980s, the soldiers on the American bases had been disarmed at the explicit request of the government of the state of Baden-Württemberg, which feared that the peace movement would get its own martyr comparable to the 1968 student revolt's Benno Ohnesorg (cf. Sternstein 2005: 368), army troops were among the security forces deployed against the protests around Heiligendamm in 2007 (cf. Euskirchen 2008, Heinecke 2008, Komitee für Grundrechte und Demokratie 2007: 125ff.).

Civil disobedience revisited

The examples discussed here show that reference to the tradition of civil disobedience has not become obsolete for alter-globalization movements, despite the Italian disobbedienti's declared break from that tradition. To the contrary, the mass blockades against the G8 summit in Heiligendamm seem to me to have led to a renewed rise in the use of the term 'civil disobedience.' Just as conspicuous, however, is the fact that the 2007 attempt to damage military vehicles, in contrast with those of 1983 and 1986 as well as the variety of protest actions during the 2007 G8 summit, is not described, by the supporters of such actions, as civil disobedience. The overtone of nation-state citizenship in the concept of 'civil disobedience' seems to be one central reason why the German left, insofar as it is anti-capitalist and critical of the nation-state, is hesitant to take recourse to the term. Expressly positive views of civil disobedience within the radical left can be found, if at all, in the post-Autonom spectrum, which also played a leading role in preparing and executing the 'mass civil disobedience' represented by BlockG8. The calls to action for such blockades, however, also show that openness of the actions involved does not immediately include the willingness, let alone the intention, to be arrested—a feature that, according to some conceptions, is an integral part of civil disobedience (cf. Habermas). Conversely, there is no basis for the conclusion that activists who wait to be arrested at the crime scene and go to prison for their actions accept these sentences as legitimate. As Damian Moran, who was involved in a Ploughshare action at the Shannon airport (Ireland) in February 2003, reports, the decision to perform this action openly and to wait to be arrested did not constitute recognition of state force but was intended to emphasize the action's legitimacy and to create the ability to defend and discuss this action publicly.[16]

From a political perspective, using the term 'civil disobedience' seems to make sense primarily for two reasons. On the one hand, it enables activists to appeal to a broad spectrum of participants, an aspect exemplarily demonstrated by BlockG8: calls to action for these blockades were supported both by post-Autonom leftists and the Catholic peace movement. On the other hand, the discourse surrounding the arson directed against the army transporters in the summer of 2007 would probably have taken a different course and would have led to different assessments and found wider support had that act been declared one of civil disobedience. Yet to do so would have required more extensive communication of the act's anti-militarist motivation and probably would have necessitated that the act be performed openly.

Still, by using the concept of civil disobedience—in the sense of citizens' disobedience—protests also risk obscuring the radicality of their critique. The blockades against the G8 summit in Heiligendamm were precisely not an appeal to the heads of government who had congregated there but intended to express a delegitimation of that institution. The destruction of army trucks was directed not against a specific war understood to be unjust but against war in general and hence also against the nation-state as such, which is ultimately always based on military force. Elke Stevens's consideration that it might be better to speak of 'civil obedience' in the first place, since such actions seek precisely "to point out the injury to order inflicted by the state's actions" (2007: 262), would seem to render the concept perfectly unattractive to activists.

Despite or perhaps precisely because of the multiplicity of conceptual attempts at definition, then, to use the term 'civil disobedience'—or else that of 'social disobedience'—remains a largely political decision, one that is made not in general but in a particular situation and proves to be now more, now less helpful. This decision is political not least because it involves an ongoing reexamination of what John K. Samson, quoted in my epigraph, has stressed as problematic: "creating rules of protesting". A reexamination of this sort took place when the participants of the protests against the G8 summit at Heiligendamm disregarded the comprehensive ban on demonstrations. Civil disobedience, after all, is alive when rules are being broken.

Translated from the German by Gerrit Jackson.

Literature:

Azzellini, Dario (2001/2002): Von den Tute Bianche zu den Ungehorsamen, in: Arranca!, No. 23 (Winter), Berlin, pp. 26-30.
Azzellini, Dario, and Oliver Ressler (2002): Disobbedienti (Film, 54 min).
Ellis, Deb, and Denis Mueller (2004): Howard Zinn. You Can't Be Neutral on a Moving Train (Film, 78 min).
Euskirchen, Markus (2008): Bundeswehreinsatz im Inneren. Besichtigung im Hinterland des globalen zivilen Krieges, in: Republikanischer Anwältinnen- und Anwälteverein und Legal Team (eds.): Feindbild Demonstrant. Polizeigewalt, Militäreinsatz, Medienmanipulation – Der G8-Gipfel aus Sicht des Anwaltlichen Notdienstes, Berlin und Hamburg (Assoziation A), pp. 137-141.
Gericke, Carsten (2008): Von Brokdorf nach Heiligendamm. Das Bundesverfassungsgericht und die Versammlungsverbote und -beschränkungen beim G8-Gipfel 2007, in: Republikanischer Anwältinnen- und Anwälte-

verein and Legal Team (eds.): Feindbild Demonstrant. Polizeigewalt, Militäreinsatz, Medienmanipulation – Der G8-Gipfel aus Sicht des Anwaltlichen Notdienstes, Berlin and Hamburg (Assoziation A), pp. 53-65.

Habermas, Jürgen (1983): Ziviler Ungehorsam – Testfall für den demokratischen Rechtsstaat. Wider den autoritären Legalismus in der Bundesrepublik, in: Glotz, Peter (ed.): Ziviler Ungehorsam im Rechtsstaat, Frankfurt a. M. (Suhrkamp Verlag), pp. 29-53.

Heinecke, Gabriele (2008): Gegen Demokraten helfen nur Soldaten. Die Verpolizeilichung des Militärischen, in: Republikanischer Anwältinnen- und Anwälteverein and Legal Team (eds.): Feindbild Demonstrant. Polizeigewalt, Militäreinsatz, Medienmanipulation – Der G8-Gipfel aus Sicht des Anwaltlichen Notdienstes, Berlin and Hamburg (Assoziation A), pp. 143-148.

Komitee für Grundrechte und Demokratie (ed.) (2007): Gewaltbereite Politik und der G8-Gipfel. Demonstrationsbeobachtungen vom 2.-8. Juni 2007 rund um Heiligendamm, Köln (Komitee für Grundrechte und Demokratie e. V.).

Laker, Thomas (1986): Ziviler Ungehorsam. Geschichte – Begriff – Rechtfertigung, Baden-Baden (Nomos Verlagsgesellschaft).

Philipp, Ulrich (2006): Politik von unten. Wolfgang Sternstein – Erfahrungen eines Graswurzelpolitikers und Aktionsforschers, Berlin (Nora Verlagsgemeinschaft).

Sternstein, Wolfgang (2005): Mein Weg zwischen Gewalt und Gewaltfreiheit. Autobiographie, Norderstedt (Books on Demand).

Steven, Elke (2007): Ziviler Ungehorsam, in: Brand, Ulrich, Bettina Lösch, and Stefan Thimmel (eds.): ABC der Alternativen. Von „Ästhetik des Widerstands" bis „ziviler Ungehorsam", Hamburg (VSA Verlag), pp. 262-263.

Zinn, Howard (1968). Disobedience and Democracy. Nine Fallacies on Law and Order, New York (Random House).

1 I am grateful to André Bank and Daniela Grimm for their critical support.
2 For documentation of his case, see https://einstellung.so36.net/en.
3 Quoted from Ellis / Mueller 2004.
4 www.wumingfoundation.com/english/giap/kreuzberg.html, 2/27/2008.
5 Quoted from Azzellini / Ressler 2002.
6 I will disregard forms of the critique of globalization such as neo-Nazism or Islamism. To ascribe civil disobedience to these forms of anti-globalization protest would render the concept in question perfectly meaningless.
7 Cf. the call to action by BlockG8 at http://www.nadir.org/nadir/initiativ/fels/de/2007/03/358.shtml, 3/10/2008; there as the call to action by the participating group FelS ('Für eine linke Strömung,' 'For a leftist current').
8 http://www.gendreck-weg.de/, 3/10/2008.
9 http://www.sichelschmiede.org/Aktion/G8/, 2/26/2008
10 http://de.indymedia.org/2007/06/179899.shtml, 2/26/2008
11 Cf. the call to action at http://www.g8andwar.de/archiv/rostocklaage/rl2.php, 2/26/2008.
12 Cf. the press review at http://www.jpberlin.de/badespasz/presse/wp/?cat=39, 2/26/2008.
13 Cf. http://einstellung.so36.net/en/openletter, 2/28/2008.
14 The press release includes the following: "Florian L.'s lawyer has stated that he was severely beaten whilst still sitting in the car with his seatbelt on. His face and rib injuries had to be treated in hospital. Sacks were pulled over the heads of the arrested men and all three were forced to put on thin white plastic overalls." Cf. https://einstellung.so36.net/en/pm/187,, 2/28/2008.
15 For the decisive piece of writing used to justify the search, see http://www.antiatombonn.de/index.php?option=com_content&task=view&id=126&Itemid=16, 2/28/2008.
16 In view of the impending Iraq war, three activists entered the Shannon military airport on February 3, 2003 and caused $2.5 million damage to a military plane using hammers; they then waited for their arrest and simultaneously had an Internet page released that contained information regarding the motivation of their action. During the subsequent court trial, which took almost three and a half years, they spent hours on the street almost every day, passing out flyers about their action and debating with pas

Die Windungen der Schlange

Minoritäre Taktiken im Zeitalter der Transparenz

Inke Arns

„*Gideon, Mendelsohn, Corbusier machen den Aufenthaltsraum von Menschen vor allem zum Durchgangsraum aller erdenklichen Kräfte und Wellen von Licht und Luft. Was kommt, steht im Zeitalter der Transparenz.*"
Walter Benjamin (1980 [1929]: 169 f.)

„*Die Windungen einer Schlange sind noch viel komplizierter als die Gänge eines Maulwurfbaus.*"
Gilles Deleuze (1993 [1990]: 262)

Mit Deleuze in die Sümpfe von Louisiana

Jim Jarmusch ist mit seinem Film „Down by Law" 1986 ein überaus präzises Bild des Paradigmenwechsels gelungen, der heute Wirklichkeit wird: der Wechsel von den Einschließungsmilieus der Disziplinargesellschaft (Michel Foucault) zu den geschmeidigen Modulationen der Kontrollgesellschaft (Gilles Deleuze).

In „Down by Law" sitzen drei Kleinkriminelle – Jack, Zack und Bob – zufällig gemeinsam in einer Gefängniszelle in New Orleans. Zack (Tom Waits) ist ein arbeitsloser DJ, Jack (John Lurie) ein Gelegenheitszuhälter und Bob (Roberto Benigni) ein ehrlicher, gutmütiger aber auch etwas naiver Italiener, der wegen Totschlags einsitzt. Zusammen gelingt ihnen die Flucht aus dem Gefängnis durch die Sümpfe von Louisiana und von dort in ein neues Leben. Neben der Flucht durch die Sümpfe ist vor allem die „Fenster-Szene" für unseren Zusammenhang wichtig: als der nur rudimentär Englisch sprechende Roberto „Bob" Benigni mit Kreide ein Fenster auf die Zellenwand malt und Jack fragt, ob man auf Englisch „I look at the window" oder „I look out of the window" sagt. Jack amüsiert sich über die Frage des Italieners, antwortet dann aber angesichts der ausweglosen Situation zynisch: „Well, in this case I guess you would say ‚I look at the window'". Diese Szene kann heute als unheimliche Vorwegnahme aktueller Entwicklungen gelesen werden.

Der Begriff der Transparenz (Durchsichtigkeit) spielt in diesem Dispositiv eine wichtige Rolle. In Jarmuschs trostloser Gefängnissituation, die Michel Foucaults System der Einschließungen der Disziplinargesellschaft entspricht, wird das Fenster (oder Interface), das normalerweise transparent – durchsichtig und unsichtbar – ist, plötzlich als Fenster bzw. als Grenze oder Begrenzung selbst sichtbar – und zwar durch die simple Tatsache, dass es mit Kreide auf eine Gefängniswand gemalt und so in seiner Materialität und Faktizität erfahrbar wird. Das Kreidefenster kann als eine Metapher für Software oder programmierte Umgebungen und ihre Interfaces gelesen werden, die zu den neuen ‚post-materiellen' Grundlagen der zeitgenössischen Informationsgesellschaften geworden sind.

Während die von Foucault beschriebenen Disziplinargesellschaften sich durch gebaute Einschließungen (das Gefängnis, die Schule, die Fabrik, die Klinik) auszeichnen, sind diese harten Strukturen in den heutigen Kontrollgesellschaften kontinuierlichen Modulationen gewichen. Diese ‚weichen' Modulationen gleichen einer „sich selbst verformenden Gussform, die sich von einem Moment zum anderen verändert (...)." (Deleuze 1993: 256) Diese geschmeidige Gussform, die in Down by Law von dem Bild der Sümpfe Louisianas repräsentiert wird, zeichnet sich durch drei Eigenschaften aus:

1. Transparenz (Durchsichtigkeit oder Unsichtbarkeit, die sich der unmittelbaren sinnlichen Wahrnehmung entzieht),
2. Immaterialität (als Verbindung zwischen einzelnen Materialitäten) und
3. Performativität („Code is Law"[1] – Computercode wird zum Gesetz).

Im Gegensatz zu den opaken Gefängniswänden ist der Sumpf ‚transparent' (dies ist metaphorisch zu verstehen, denn natürlich ist sumpfiges Brackwasser in den meisten Fällen nicht wirklich klar). Der Sumpf ist im Gegensatz zu festem Material flüssig – was ihn gefährlich macht – und kann sich aufgrund dieser Eigenschaft in jedem Moment verformen, er kann entstehende Hohlräume ausfüllen und Körper und Objekte jederzeit umschließen. Eine solch perfekte Umschließung verhindert – hier kommt nun das Performative ins Spiel – die Fortbewegung mindestens ebenso stark, vielleicht aber noch stärker, als gebaute Einfriedungen – aber das wird noch zu argumentieren sein.

Transparenz

Das Zeitalter der Transparenz (vgl. Arns 2008), das Walter Benjamin in der Glasarchitektur seiner Zeitgenossen hoffnungsvoll heraufdämmern sah, erscheint heute ambivalent. Zum einen durchqueren nicht nur sichtbare Lichtwellen die transparenten Architekturen, sondern eine ganze Menge anderer, aus unterschiedlichsten technischen Quellen stammender, elektromagnetischer Wellen.[2] Zum anderen erweist sich der Begriff der Transparenz in seiner Doppeldeutigkeit von Sichtbarkeit und Unsichtbarkeit bzw. in der Ambivalenz des Panoptischen und des Postoptischen[3] als überaus geeignet für die Charakterisierung gegenwärtiger performativer (Informations-)Architekturen und Räume. Der Begriff von Foucault (1994) geprägte Begriff des Panoptismus leitet sich von Jeremy Benthams „Panopticon" her – dem Entwurf des perfekten Gefängnisses, das die Gefangenen in einem kreisrunden Gefängnisbau der permanenten Sichtbarkeit durch einen in der Mitte platzierten Aufseher aussetzt. Der von mir verwendete Begriff des Postoptischen bezeichnet dagegen all die digitalen Datenströme und (programmierten) Kommunikationsstrukturen und -architekturen, die mindestens ebenso gut zu überwachen sind, aber nur zu einem kleinen Teil aus visuellen Informationen bestehen (Stichwort „Dataveillance").

Während „Transparenz" im alltäglichen Verständnis für Übersichtlichkeit, Klarheit und für Kontrollierbarkeit durch Einsehbarkeit steht (so z.B. im Namen von Transparency International, einer Organisation, die weltweit Korruption bekämpft[4], oder im Namen von Prozrachnyj Mir[5] (Transparente Welt), einer russischen Firma, die hochauflösende Satellitenbilder der Erde für privatwirtschaftliche Zwecke zur Verfügung stellt), bedeutet der Begriff in der Informatik das genaue Gegenteil, nämlich Durchsichtigkeit, Unsichtbarkeit und Information Hiding. Ist ein Interface „transparent", so bedeutet das, dass es für den Benutzer nicht erkenn- oder wahrnehmbar ist. Während dieses Verstecken von (überschüssigen, exzessiven) Informationen im Sinne einer Komplexitätsreduktion in vielen Fällen sinnvoll ist, kann es den Benutzer jedoch zugleich in einer falschen Sicherheit wiegen, denn es suggeriert durch seine Unsichtbarkeit eine direkte Sicht auf etwas, eine durch nichts gestörte Transparenz, an die zu glauben natürlich Unsinn wäre. Lev Manovich schreibt daher in The Language of New Media: „Far from being a transparent window into the data inside a computer, the interface brings with it strong messages of its own." (Manovich 2001:65) Um diese »message« sichtbar zu machen, gilt es, die Aufmerksamkeit auf die transparente »Fensterscheibe« selbst zu lenken. So, wie sich durchsichtige Glasfronten von Gebäuden auf Knopfdruck in transluzide, also halbtransparente Flächen verwandeln lassen und damit sichtbar gemacht werden können,[6] gilt es auch informationstechnische, postoptische Strukturen der Transparenz zu entreißen. In den Kommunikationsnetzen ginge es analog dazu darum, transparente Strukturen ökonomischer, politischer, gesellschaftlicher Machtverteilungen opak werden zu lassen und so wahrnehmbar zu machen. Letztendlich geht es um die Rückführung des informatisch geprägten Begriffs der Transparenz in seine ursprüngliche Bedeutung von Übersichtlichkeit, Klarheit und Kontrollierbarkeit durch Einsehbarkeit.

Immaterialität

Je mehr Dinge des täglichen Lebens durch Software reguliert werden, desto weniger sinnlich wahrnehmbar sind sie im alltäglichen Umgang. Dass sie aus der direkten Anschauung verschwinden, bedeutet jedoch nicht, dass sie nicht da sind. Ganz im Gegenteil: Dass die uns umgebende Welt zunehmend programmiert ist, heißt, dass Regeln, Konventionen und Beziehungen, die grundsätzlich veränder- und verhandelbar sind, in Software übersetzt und festgeschrieben werden. Immaterielle, in Software festgeschriebene Strukturen sind – und das ist das Paradox – mindestens ebenso beständig, wenn nicht sogar wirkungsvoller als materielle Strukturen und Architekturen. Das (un-)heimliche Zum-Verschwinden-Bringen von Welt mittels des Einsatzes von Software hat dabei nicht nur einen Entzug aus der Sicht- und Wahrnehmbarkeit zur Folge, sondern bedeutet auch eine Immaterialisierung von Strukturen. ‚Immateriell' heißt dabei jedoch nicht, dass diese Strukturen weniger wirksam wären als ihre materiellen Gegenstücke. Den Begriff ‚immateriell' als Gegensatz zu ‚materiell' zu verstehen, hieße, ihn gänzlich misszuverstehen. (Vgl. Terranova 2006: 31) Vielmehr muss man das Immaterielle als etwas begreifen lernen, das „qualitative, intensive Differenzen in quantitative Tausch- und Äquivalenzbeziehungen umwandelt" (ebd.). Es stellt Beziehungen zwischen einzelnen Materialitäten – Dingen und Menschen, Waren und Individuen, Objekten und Subjekten – her und kann so mit hoher Geschwindigkeit z.B. Konsumenten- oder Bewegungsprofile errechnen.[7] Das Immaterielle ist in jedem Augenblick irgendwo (und nicht nirgendwo), zwischen den Dingen. Es umschließt die Materialitäten, verformt sich elastisch, folgt den Objekten und Körpern geschmeidig und stellt immerzu Verbindungen her. Zwar ist das Immaterielle nicht das, „was die Welt im Innersten zusammenhält", aber es schmiedet die Dinge in der Welt zusammen indem es sie miteinander in Beziehung setzt und macht dies auf effektivere Weise, als starre Strukturen das jemals vermocht haben. Software erweist sich somit als sehr harter Werkstoff und Immaterialität als quasi faktische Materialität – die sich jedoch unserer (visuellen, taktilen) Sinneswahrnehmung entzieht.

Performativität

Programmierte Strukturen bestehen aus zwei Arten von ‚Texten': aus einem sichtbaren ‚front end' (dem „Fenster") und einem unsichtbaren, transparenten ‚back end' (der Software bzw. dem Programmcode). Sie verhalten sich zueinander wie Phäno- und Genotext in der Biologie. Die Oberflächeneffekte des Phänotextes (das „Fenster") werden durch unter den Oberflächen liegende effektive Texte, den Programmcodes oder Quelltexten, hervorgerufen und gesteuert. Programmcode zeichnet sich dadurch aus, dass in ihm Sagen und Tun (Handlung/Aktion) zusammenfallen, Code als handlungsmächtiger Sprechakt also keine Beschreibung oder Repräsentation von etwas ist, sondern direkt affiziert, in Bewegung setzt, Effekte zeitigt. Code macht das, was er sagt.

Code wirkt sich jedoch nicht nur auf die Phänotexte, also die grafischen Benutzeroberflächen aus. »Codierte Performativität« (Grether 2001) hat genauso unmittelbare, auch politische Auswirkungen auf die (virtuellen) Räume, in denen wir uns bewegen: „Programmcode", so der amerikanische Jurist Lawrence Lessig (2000), „tendiert immer mehr dazu, zum Gesetz zu werden." Heute werden Kontrollfunktionen direkt in die Architektur des Netzes, also seinen Code, eingebaut. Diese These stellt Lessig in „Code and other Laws of Cyberspace" (1999) auf. Am Beispiel des Online-Dienstes AOL macht Lessig eindringlich klar, wie die AOL-Architektur mit Hilfe des sie bestimmenden Codes zum Beispiel jegliche Form von virtueller ›Zusammenrottung‹ verhindert und eine weitgehende Kontrolle der Nutzer erlaubt. Graham Harwood bezeichnet daher diese transparente Welt auch als „invisible shadow world of process" (Harwood 2001: 47). Diese „unsichtbare Schattenwelt des Prozessierens" hat unmittelbare, auch politische Konsequenzen für die virtuellen und realen Räume, in denen wir uns heute bewegen: Indem sie festlegt, was in diesen Räumen möglich ist und was nicht, mobilisiert bzw. immobilisiert sie ihre Benutzer. Die Frage nach der Durchlässigkeit – wann und für wen? – ist zentral für gegenwärtige Räume und ist eng mit dem Begriff der Performativität[8] verknüpft. „Man braucht keine Science-Fiction," schreibt Deleuze, „um sich einen Kontrollmechanismus vorzustellen, der in jedem Moment die Position eines Elements in einem offenen Milieu angibt, Tier in einem Reservat, Mensch in einem Unternehmen (elektronisches Halsband). Félix Guattari malte sich eine Stadt aus, in der jeder seine Wohnung, seine Straße, sein Viertel dank seiner elektronischen (dividuellen) Karte verlassen kann, durch die diese oder jene Schranke sich öffnet; aber die Karte könnte auch an einem bestimmten Tag oder für bestimmte Stunden ungültig sein; was zählt, ist nicht die Barriere, sondern der Computer, der die – erlaubte oder unerlaubte – Position jedes einzelnen erfaßt und eine universelle Modulation durchführt." (Deleuze 1993: 261)

Eine Technologie, die genau dies ermöglicht, ist zum Beispiel die so genannte Radio Frequency Identification (RFID) Technologie[9]. RFID Tags sind kleine Funk-Etiketten, passive Radiosender, die drahtlos Informationen übertragen und abspeichern können und den Barcode ersetzen sollen. Sie werden bereits heute in der Warenlogistik, Personenüberwachung und Diebstahlsicherung eingesetzt. RFID Tags senden auf einen schwachen, drahtlosen Energieimpuls hin die auf ihnen gespeicherten Informationen an ein Lesegerät zurück. Dies kann heute schon auf eine Entfernung von bis zu mehreren hundert Metern geschehen – ohne dass der/die TrägerIn dies bemerkt. Außerdem ermöglicht diese Technologie eine weltweit eindeutige Identifizierung von Objekten – neben dem unbemerkten Auslesen von Informationen ein weiteres signifikantes Merkmal, das RFID vom herkömmlichen Barcode unterscheidet. RFID erlaubt eine lückenlose Rückverfolgung von Warenströmen und damit ganz neue Dimensionen des Dataminings (zum Beispiel durch die Erstellung von Konsumentenprofilen). Zieht man den potentiellen Einsatz von RFID-Technologie an und in Menschen in Betracht – z.B. durch Reisepässe oder Krankenkassenkarten, die mit RFID Chips versehen sind, auf denen biometrische Daten gespeichert sind, oder mit biometrischen Daten versehene RFID Tags, die unter die Haut implantiert werden[10] –, werden neue Formen ubiquitärer Kontrolle denkbar. Der britische Künstler Chris Oakley hat dies in seinem Video „The Catalogue" (2004, 5:30 Min.) anschaulich dargestellt.[11]

Das Zeitalter der Transparenz ist durch eine Doppelstruktur des Panoptischen und des Postoptischen gekennzeichnet. Einerseits sind wir mit einem Dispositiv der totalen, panoptischen Sichtbarkeit konfrontiert, das spätestens mit dem Aufbau von Videoüberwachungssystemen in den 1980er Jahren einsetzt und heute in staatliche und privatwirtschaftliche Strukturen von Überwachungssatelliten[12] mündet. Bruce Sterling hat 2001 mit seiner fiktiven, angeblich im Jahr 2067 verfassten Zeitungsmeldung „Anna Kournikova Deleted by Memeright Trusted System"[13] das sich bereits heute abzeichnende Dispositiv der Transparenz – gekoppelt mit einer zunehmend strikten Verfolgung von Urheberrechtsverstößen – konsequent zu Ende gedacht. Clevere Aktivisten, Werbeagenturen oder religiöse Fundamentalisten machen bereits heute gezielt Werbung für Google Earth: Es entstehen gigantische Land Art-Projekte, die nur von Flugzeugen aus oder für die Kameras von Satelliten sichtbar sind. (Vgl. Waldt 2008: 7)

Parallel zu dieser panoptischen Sichtbarkeit haben sich die technischen Strukturen, die beobachten und performativ handeln, zunehmend in die Unsichtbarkeit zurückgezogen. Performative Strukturen – ob unvorstellbar klein, unvorstellbar immateriell oder unvorstellbar weit weg – sind in vielen Fällen nur noch in ihren Effekten erkennbar – aber nicht mehr zwangsläufig sichtbar. So sind zum Beispiel Satelliten aufgrund ihrer Entfernung von der Erdoberfläche für das unbewaffnete menschliche Auge fast nicht erkennbar, miniaturisierte Nanomaschinen sind zu klein und Software entzieht sich der menschlichen Wahrnehmung, da es sich hierbei meist um ‚unscheinbare' performative (Geno-)Texte handelt, die hinter den sichtbaren Oberflächen (Phänotexten) liegen, welche sie generieren. Wir haben es im Zeitalter der Transparenz mit einer fundamentalen Entkopplung von Sichtbarkeit und Performativität/Effektivität zu tun. Während alles andere dem Paradigma ständiger Sichtbarkeit unterworfen wird, entziehen sich die wirklich handelnden, performativen Strukturen eben dieser Sichtbarkeit und unserer direkten Kontrolle – sie sind transparent geworden. Unsichtbarkeit wird gleichermaßen zum Privileg handelnder, performativer Strukturen. In diesem Sinne spreche ich von der Gegenwart als von einem postoptischen Zeitalter, in dem der Programmcode – den man in Anlehnung an Walter Benjamin auch als Postoptisch-Unbewusstes[14] bezeichnen könnte – als performativer Text zum „Gesetz" wird.

Minoritäre Taktiken im Zeitalter der Transparenz

„(T)he vocation of an art of the kind that reflects on electronic crowds and networks is not the representation of the visible world but the visualisation of what is otherwise inaccessible to perception and is difficult to imagine because of its cosmic or microscopic scale, its discontinuity in space and time, or its impenetrability – from the insides of the body, the atom, or the black box to the outside of our galaxy and our universe."

Margaret Morse (1998: 192)

Wie kann sich nun in solch unwahrnehmbar gewordenen, der direkten Anschauung entzogenen Räumen politisches und/oder künstlerisches Handeln artikulieren? Wo und wie können angesichts eines solchen softwaregestützten Verschwindens von Welt potentielle Räume des Politischen (neu) entstehen? Verschiedene medien- und netzkünstlerische Projekte sowie Projekte aus dem Bereich der Softwarekunst[15] haben in den letzten Jahren Ansätze entwickelt, die die Strukturen ökonomischer, politischer und gesellschaftlicher Machtverteilungen in Kommunikationsnetzen opak (= sichtbar) werden lassen. Immer geht es darum, informationstechnische Strukturen aus einem Zustand der Transparenz in einen der Sicht- oder Wahrnehmbarkeit zu überführen. Allein dieser erste Schritt ist im Zeitalter der softwaregestützen Implosion des Politischen ein eminent politischer. Gilles Deleuze jedenfalls konstatierte bereits vor fast 20 Jahren: „Weder zur Furcht noch zur Hoffnung besteht Grund, sondern nur dazu, neue Waffen zu suchen." (Deleuze 1993: 256)

Sind widerständige Taktiken[16] in dieser durchsichtigen Welt überhaupt möglich? Und wenn ja, wie sehen diese aus? Zwei taktische Richtungen sollen hier beschrieben werden: a) die des Sichtens, Kartografierens und Intervenierens, d.h. der Sichtbarmachung von Strukturen der Überwachungs- und/oder Informationslandschaft und b) die des Verschwindens und Unsichtbarwerdens durch maximale Sichtbarkeit (Überidentifizierung mit dem, und Bedienen des panoptischen Regime).

Sichten, Kartografieren, Intervenieren

In diese Kategorie gehören Projekte, die auf die Existenz verborgener Strukturen der Überwachungs- und/oder Informationslandschaft hinweisen. Die medienkünstlerische und -aktivistische Auseinandersetzung mit dem Thema Videoüberwachung ist in der Medienkunst ein gängiger Topos[17] – z.B. führten Yann Beauvais (F) und die Surveillance Camera Players[18] (US) in den 1990er Jahren Stücke für die Betreiber von Überwachungskameras auf und machten so auf die im Stadtraum verstreuten Videokameras aufmerksam. Die Arbeiten des französischen Künstlers Renaud Auguste-Dormeuil wären hier zu nennen, ebenso wie das 2003 von der Schweizer Künstlerin Annina Rüst entwickelte Systen track-the-trackers—-, das die Standorte von Überwachungskameras im öffentlichen Raum per GPS lokalisiert, in eine Datenbank einträgt und die Kamerastandorte während der Bewegung durch den Stadtraum sonifiziert.

Darüber hinaus gibt es jedoch auch Projekte, die nicht nur auf die Existenz von Videokameras im Stadtraum aufmerksam machen wollen, sondern die auf die Sichtbarmachung der dahinter liegenden transparenten (Macht-)Strukturen selbst abzielen. Dazu gehört z.B. die kanadische Künstlerin Michelle Teran[19], die 2005 mit einem seltsamen Rollkoffer durch die Straßen von Berlin zog. „Life: A User's Manual"[20] war eine Performance, die die Footage von Überwachungskameras, die in öffentlichen und privaten Räumen installiert sind, auf einem Fernseher sichtbar machte. Dazu setzte die Künstlerin einen handelsüblichen Videoscanner ein, der

Funksigale von Kameras einfangen kann, die auf dem 2.4 Ghz Frequenzband senden. Ein Spaziergang durch die Stadt wurde so zu einer „shared experience in visualizing the invisible" (Michelle Teran).

Einen Schritt weiter als Yann Beauvais und die Surveillance Camera Players geht Manu Luksch in „Faceless" (2007, 50 min.). Für dieses Video produzierte die österreichische Künstlerin sich in London vor zahllosen CCTV-Kameras und forderte dann die Bilder, die die Kameras von ihr gemacht hatten, unter Berufung auf das britische Datenschutzgesetz (das das Recht auf das eigene Bild garantiert) bei den Betreibern dieser Videoüberwachungsanlagen an. Aus diesem Material, auf dem die Gesichter aller Menschen – außer dem der Künstlerin – aus Datenschutzgründen unkenntlich gemacht worden waren, baute Luksch eine beklemmende Science Fiction Geschichte, „die in ihrer durch das Überwachungsmaterial bedingten Single-Frame-Ästhetik an Chris Markers Geschichte-machenden Film-Comic La Jetée (1962) denken lässt."[21]

Die französische Gruppe Bureau d'Etudes (dt. Studienbüro) produziert seit mehreren Jahren Kartografierungen gegenwärtiger politischer, sozialer und ökonomischer Systeme. Diese großformatigen visuellen Analysen des transnationalen Kapitalismus, die auf aufwändigen Recherchen basieren, werden meist in Form großformatiger Wandbilder präsentiert. Auf der 2003 entstandenen Karte „Governing by Networks" werden die wechselseitigen Beteiligungen und transnationalen Verflechtungen globaler Medienkonglomerate visualisiert. Indem sie darstellen, was normalerweise unsichtbar bleibt, und auf sinnvolle Weise zu einem Großen Ganzen verbinden, was normalerweise singulär und ohne Zusammenhang bleibt, funktionieren diese Visualisierungen von Besitzverhältnissen wie „Resymbolisierungsmaschinen". Damit bezeichnet das Bureau d'Etudes den widerständigen Prozess des Zusammenfügens und der Repräsentation dessen, was aufgrund seiner feinsten Verästelungen und Kapillarstrukturen – nämlich der globale Kapitalismus – nicht mehr als ganzes wahrnehmbar ist. Bureau d'Etudes, zu deren konzeptuellen Vorläufern die Künstler Öyvind Fahlström (1928-1976) und Mark Lombardi (1951-2000) gehören, gelingt in ihrer visuellen Analyse gegenwärtiger Wirtschaftskonglomerate eine scharfe Diagnose der Gegenwart.

Dass durch simple Beobachtung transparente Strukturen aufgedeckt werden können, haben uns in den letzten Jahren die sogenannten ‚Plane Spotter' eindringlich vor Augen geführt. Durch genaue Beobachtung von Flugzeugstarts und -landungen an verschiedenen Orten der Welt und einen fortwährenden Abgleich mit zivilen Flugplänen konnten Flugzeugenthusiasten die sogenannten „Guantanamo-Flüge" der CIA aufdecken. Der amerikanische Geheimdienst bringt des Terrorismus verdächtige Menschen in Zivilflugzeugen in Gefangenenlager wie Guantanamo. Da diese Flüge jedoch in keinem Flugplan der zivilen Luftfahrt verzeichnet sind, fiel diese geheime Aktivität irgendwann auf. Der amerikanische Experimentalgeograf Trevor Paglen[22] und das Institute for Applied Autonomy[23] haben mit „Terminal Air" (2007) ein System (Software und Datenbank) entwickelt, das diese illegalen Flüge der CIA in annähernder Echtzeit darstellen kann. Paglens Hauptinteresse gilt der

Erforschung und Dokumentation so genannter ‚militärischer Landschaften' – so beispielsweise tief in der amerikanischen Wüste versteckter militärischer Einrichtungen. Um diese vollkommen den Blicken entzogenen entfernten Orte zu fotografieren und so gleichsam das „Optisch-Unbewusste"[24] sichtbar zu machen, bedient sich Paglen in Limit Telephotography der Methoden der Weltraumfotografie, in der Teleobjektive mit Brennweiten zwischen 1300 mm und 7000 mm eingesetzt werden. Bei dieser Vergrößerung werden für das menschliche Auge unsichtbare Aspekte der Landschaft erkennbar. Missing Persons (2006) wiederum beschäftigt sich mit der durchschaubaren Oberfläche der (Briefkasten-)Firmen, in deren Besitz die Flugzeuge sind, die die Guantanamo-Flüge durchführen und stellt die Unterschriften der Fake-CEOs aus.[25]

Marko Peljhan und Mario Purkathofer untersuchen mit ihren Arbeiten die materiellen Strukturen, auf denen das Regime der Transparenz beruht. Während Marko Peljhans als mobiles und autonomes Forschungslabor konzipiertes makrolab (1997-2007) sich von unterschiedlichen Standorten auf verschiedenen Kontinenten in die Kommunikationsströme einklinkte und so das Territorium der Signale über einem bestimmten geografischen Punkt kartografierte,[26] bietet Mario Purkathofers Reisebüro sofatrips.com „Reisen in die Informationslandschaft" an. Die von dem Schweizer Künstler seit 2006 durchgeführten „Sofatrips"[27] sind Bewegungen in virtuellen und physischen Räumen, wie z. B. die Verfolgung und Erwanderung des Weges, den eine SMS im Stadtraum von Zürich nimmt, Busreisen in das Europäische Forschungszentrum CERN in Genf (am CERN wurde in den frühen 1990er Jahren das World Wide Web und der erste grafische Browser Mosaic entwickelt) und Stadtwanderungen bzw. menschliche Datenprozessionen durch die Informationslandschaft – bis zur Netzgrenze von Zürich. Dabei geht es immer vorbei an öffentlichen Telefonzellen, Providern, Rechenzentren, Webcams, WLAN Hotspots, kurz: mitten durch neue und alte Kommunikationsinfrastrukturen. Sofatrips lenken unsere Aufmerksamkeit auf die materielle Basis unserer ansonsten zunehmend virtuellen Welt.

Ein gutes Beispiel für aktivistisches Intervenieren in die unsichtbaren, geschmeidigen Modulationen der Kontrollgesellschaft – den Code – stellt das Projekt „insert_coin"[28] von Dragan Espenschied und Alvar Freude dar. Unter dem Motto »Zwei Personen kontrollieren 250 Personen« installierten die beiden Studenten im Rahmen ihrer Diplomarbeit 2000/2001 an der Merz-Akademie in Stuttgart unbemerkt einen Web-Proxyserver, der mittels eines Perl-Skripts den gesamten Web-Datenverkehr von Studierenden und Lehrenden im Computer-Netzwerk der Akademie manipulierte. Ziel war es, so Espenschied/Freude, die „Kompetenz und Kritikfähigkeit der Anwender bezüglich des Alltags-Mediums Internet zu überprüfen".[29] Der manipulierte Proxy-Server leitete eingegebene URLs auf andere Seiten um, modifizierte HTML-Formatierungscode, veränderte mittels einer simplen Suche-und-Ersetze-Funktion sowohl aktuelle Meldungen auf Nachrichten-Sites (zum Beispiel durch Austausch von Politikernamen) als auch den Inhalt privater Emails, die über Web-Interfaces wie Hotmail, gmx oder Yahoo! abgerufen wurden.

Vier Wochen lang lief der solchermaßen manipulierte Web-Zugang unbemerkt von den Studierenden und Lehrenden der Merz-Akademie. Als Espenschied und Freude das Experiment bekannt machten, interessierte sich jedoch so gut wie niemand dafür. Obwohl die beiden eine simpel zu befolgende Anleitung veröffentlichten, mit der jeder selbstständig den Filter ausschalten konnte, nahm sich nur ein verschwindend geringer Teil der Betroffenen Zeit, um eine einfache Einstellung und so wieder an ungefilterte Daten heranzukommen.[30]

Verschwinden und Unsichtbarwerden durch maximale Sichtbarkeit

Räume der Unerreichbarkeit und der Unsichtbarkeit gibt es heute bis auf wenige Ausnahmen nicht mehr. Ein Verschwinden aus der Aufzeichnung ist utopisch, wenn nicht sogar potentiell verdächtig. Zur zweiten Kategorie gehören daher Projekte, die eine Überidentifizierung mit dem System favorisieren und das panoptische Regime in seinem Verlangen nach permanenter Sichtbarkeit bedienen und bestätigen. Das Motto dieser Kategorie heißt: Unsichtbarkeit durch maximale Sichtbarkeit; Überlastung des Systems durch Dissimulation.

Eine sehr frühe und dezidierte Position hat in diesem Bereich der Lüneburger Künstler Andreas Peschka entwickelt. Anlässlich der Ausstellung „un.frieden. sabotage von wirklichkeiten"[31] (1996) ließ er einen Stempel mit dem Fingerabdruck seines rechten Zeigefingers produzieren (Stempelset für Attentäter), den er zusammen mit einer Dose Vaseline vertrieb. Peschka forderte die Käufer des Stempels qua Kaufvertrag dazu auf, seinen Fingerabdruck so weit wie möglich zu verbreiten. Indem der Fingerabdruck des Künstlers zeitgleich an verschiedenen (Tat-)Orten der Welt auftauchte, sprich durch absurde Selbstvervielfältigung, sollte das System lahm gelegt werden. Nach einem ähnlichen Prinzip funktionierte übrigens der im September 2001 ausgeschriebene Wettbewerb „Metamute Meets Echelon – A Literary Competition". Für diesen Wettbewerb wurden literarische Werke gesucht, die das gesamte Wörterbuch des Echelon-Systems verwendeten. Durch die Überschwemmung der Netze mit Echelon-Suchwörtern sollte das amerikanische Überwachungs- und Spionagesystem überlastet werden.[32]

Auch Annina Rüst widmet sich – als Einzelkünstlerin aber auch als Mitglied der Gruppe Local Area Network (LAN) – seit 2001 dem Thema Überwachung im Internet und im öffentlichen Raum. Die Gruppe LAN hat mit „TraceNoizer – Disinformation on Demand" (2001/2002) ein Arbeitsinstrument geschaffen, das helfen soll, die eigene Online-Identität zu schützen. Die Arbeit verwischt die Online-Spuren im Internet durch algorithmische Erzeugung einer geklonten Homepage mit irreführenden persönlichen Informationen, die automatisch online gestellt wird. In Anbetracht der bereits zugänglichen Vielzahl an ‚authentischen' Personen-Informationen im Internet scheint der Bedarf nach einem solchen Werkzeug durchaus gegeben. 2002 haben Annina Rüst und LAN den Verschwörungsgenerator „SuperVillainizer"[33] ins Netz gestellt, um gegen die Paranoia und die Rhetorik zu protestieren, mit der Politiker die Überwachungen des E-Mail-Verkehrs und des Internets zunehmend legitimieren. Mit dem „SuperVillainizer" kann jeder Internetnutzer auf

Knopfdruck Bösewichte schaffen, die sich gegenseitig subversive (automatisch generierte und mit verdächtigen Schlüsselwörtern gespickte) Mails zusenden und die die von Geheimdiensten weltweit genutzten Überwachungssysteme Carnivore, Echelon und Onyx verwirren sollen. Seit 2002 haben die Nutzer von SuperVillainizer 1.345 Bösewichte geschaffen, die 1.137 Verschwörungen in insgesamt 205.146 Mails kommuniziert haben.

Das italienische Netzkunst-Duo 0100101110101101.org arbeitet seit Anfang 2001 an der Realisierung seines bislang umfangreichsten und aufwändigsten Projektes, das unter dem Titel „Glasnost" (Transparenz) firmiert. Hierbei handelt es sich um ein Selbstüberwachungssystem, das unablässig Daten über das Leben der beiden Mitglieder von 0100101110101101.org sammelt und diese Informationen unzensiert öffentlich macht. Der erste Schritt zur Realisierung von Glasnost war das Projekt „life_sharing" (2001).[34] life_sharing, ein Anagramm des Begriffs „file sharing", ermöglicht Internet-NutzerInnen den direkten Online-Zugang zum Computer der Künstler. Alle auf der Festplatte befindlichen Daten – Texte, Bilder, Software, privater Mailverkehr, etc. – unterliegen der Gnu Public License (GPL) und sind frei zugänglich und kopier- und manipulierbar: "life_sharing is a brand new concept of net architecture turning a website into a hardcore personal media for complete digital transparency." Seit dem Beginn des Projektes VOPOS[35] im Januar 2002 trägt das Duo GPS-Transmitter (Global Positioning System), die in regelmäßigen Abständen die Koordinaten der Künstler an deren Website senden, auf die die Öffentlichkeit jederzeit zugreifen kann. Die Daten werden auf Stadtkarten übertragen und visualisieren somit ständig den aktuellen Aufenthaltsort der Künstler.

Heute erscheint das Projekt der beiden Italiener fast wie eine prophetische und vielleicht auch frivole Vorwegnahme dessen, was Hasan Elahi[36], Assistant Professor des Department of Visual Art der Rutgers University, kurz nach dem 11. September 2001 zustieß. Nachdem er von einem Unbekannten wegen Sprengstoff-Besitzes angezeigt wurde, begann das FBI, den aus Bangladesh stammenden Amerikaner zu beobachten. 2002 wurde er, aus den Niederlanden kommend, auf dem Detroiter Flughafen von FBI-Beamten festgenommen, die ihm erklären, dass er unter Terrorverdacht stehe (seine mehr als 100.000 Flugmeilen pro Jahr machten ihn zusätzlich verdächtig). Es folgten sechs Monate permanenter Verhöre. Nach einem halben Jahr gab sich das FBI schließlich mit den detaillierten Auskünften von Elahi zufrieden. Aus Angst, irgendwann doch noch nach Guantanamo verbracht zu werden, ging Elahi jedoch in die Offensive: Seit Dezember 2003 ist seine Website Tracking Transience online, auf der er sein gesamtes Leben im Netz dokumentiert.[37] Dank eines GPS-Peilsenders kann man genau verfolgen, wo auf der Welt Elahi sich gerade aufhält. Außerdem dokumentieren Fotos minutiös seinen Tagesablauf: Mahlzeiten, Einkäufe, Treffen mit Freunden, Bankbewegungen und sogar Toilettenbesuche.

Die Windungen der Schlange

Entdeckt haben die drei Protagonisten in „Down by Law" jenseits der Gefängnismauern in den Sümpfen Louisianas nichts anderes als die „sich selbst verformenden Gussformen" der Kontrollgesellschaft. Diese unheimlichen Räume zeichnen sich durch Transparenz, Immaterialität und Performativität aus und umschließen die sich in ihnen bewegenden Körper und Objekte zu jeder Zeit wie ein feines Netz oder Sieb, dessen Maschen sich von einem Moment zum anderen verändern. Diese geschmeidigen, sich jederzeit selbst adaptierenden Modulationen sind unsichtbar, transparent. Sie entziehen sich der menschlichen Wahrnehmung – und sind doch, da sie an jedem Ort zugleich sind, härter als alle gebauten Einschließungen zuvor. Die Windungen einer Schlange sind in der Tat noch viel komplizierter als die Gänge eines Maulwurfsbaus.

Das Zeitalter der Transparenz zeichnet sich durch eine Entkopplung von (panoptischer) Sichtbarkeit und (postoptischer) Performativität aus. Die wirklich handelnden, performativen Strukturen sind heute transparent geworden – und entziehen sich so unserer direkten Kontrolle. In diesem Sinne ist das von Roberto „Bob" Benigni auf die Zellenwand gezeichnete Kreidefenster als eine Metapher für „Windows" (bzw. für alle – nicht nur proprietären – Betriebssysteme und ihre Interfaces) zu verstehen und der diese Interfaces hervorbringende Programmcode als die neue, post-materielle' Grundlage der zeitgenössischen Informations- und Kontrollgesellschaften – ihr unsichtbares, immaterielles Gesetz. Diese komplizierten Windungen der Schlange gilt es zu beobachten – und ihnen, gegebenenfalls, das Privileg der Transparenz streitig zu machen.

Literatur:

Arns Inke (2004): Texte, die (sich) bewegen: Zur Performativität von Programmiercodes in Netzkunst und Software Art, in: Arns, Inke, Mirjam Goller, Susanne Strätling und Georg Witte (Hg.): Kinetographien, Bielefeld (Aisthesis Verlag), S. 57-78. http://www.inkearns.de/Texts/0kineto-arns-publ.pdf (19.03.2008)

Arns, Inke (2005a): Netzkulturen im postoptischen Zeitalter, in: Schade, Sigrid, Thomas Sieber und Georg Christoph Tholen (Hg.): SchnittStellen, Basler Beiträge zur Medienwissenschaft BBM, Basel (Institut für Medienwissenschaften/Universität Basel).

Arns, Inke (2005b): Read_me, run_me, execute_me. Code als ausführbarer Text: Softwarekunst und ihr Fokus auf Programmcodes als performative Texte, in: Frieling, Rudolf und Dieter Daniels (Hg.): Medien Kunst Netz 2: Thematische Schwerpunkte, Wien/New York (Springer Verlag), S. 177-193.

Arns, Inke (2005c): Faktur und Interface: Chlebnikov, Tesla und der himmlische Datenverkehr in Marko Peljhans makrolab (1997-2007), in: Kwastek, Katja (Hg.): „Ohne Schnur...." Kunst und drahtlose Kommunikation. Kommunikationskunst im Spannungsfeld von Kunst, Technologie und Gesellschaft, Frankfurt a. M. (Revolver Verlag), S. 62-79.

Arns, Inke (2008): Transparency and Politics. On Spaces of the Political beyond the Visible, or: How transparency came to be the lead paradigm of the 21st century, Vortrag auf der Konferenz The Aesthetic Interface, University of Aarhus, Denmark, 2007, Rotterdam (NAI Publishers), i. E.

Benjamin, Walter (1977): Kleine Geschichte der Photographie [1931], in: ders.: Das Kunstwerk im Zeitalter seiner technischen Reproduzierbarkeit, Frankfurt a. M. (Suhrkamp Verlag), S. 45–63.

Benjamin, Walter (1980): Die Wiederkehr des Flaneurs [1929], in: ders.: Gesammelte Schriften, Bd. III, Frankfurt a. M. (Suhrkamp Verlag).

Certeau, Michel de (1988): Die Kunst des Handelns, Berlin (Merve Verlag).

Deleuze, Gilles (1993): Postskriptum über die Kontrollgesellschaften [1990], in: ders.: Unterhandlungen 1972-1990, Frankfurt a. M. (Suhrkamp Verlag), S. 254-262.

Foucault, Michel (1994): Überwachen und Strafen. Die Geburt des Gefängnisses, Frankfurt a. M. (Suhrkamp Verlag).

Frohne, Ursula, Thomas Y. Levin und Peter Weibel (Hg.) (2002): Ctrl_Space. Rhetorics of Surveillance from Betham to Big Brother, ZKM Karlsruhe, Cambridge, MA (MIT Press).
Grether, Reinhold 2001: The Performing Arts in a New Era, in: Rohrpost, 26.7.2001, http://www.nettime.org/Lists-Archives/rohrpost-0107/msg00205.html
Harwood, Graham (2001): Speculative Software, in: Broeckmann, Andreas und Susanne Jaschko (Hg.): DIY Media – Art and Digital Media, Software – Participation – Distribution. Transmediale.01, Berlin, S. 47–49.
Lessig, Lawrence (1999): Code and other Laws of Cyberspace, New York (Basic Books), sowie http://code-is-law.org/
Lessig, Lawrence (2000): futurezone.orf.at: Stalin & Disney – Copyright killt das Internet, in: Rohrpost, 30.5.2000, http://www.nettime.org/Lists-Archives/rohrpost-0005/msg00190.html
Manovich, Lev (2001): The Language of New Media, Cambridge, Massachusetts/London, England (MIT Press).
Morse, Margaret (1998): Virtualities. Television, Media art and Cyberculture, Indiana (University Press).
David Rice (2001): Anna Kournikova Deleted by Memeright Trusted System (December 6, 2067), in: Future Feed Forward, 18. März 2001, http://futurefeedforward.com/front.php?fid=33
Terranova, Tiziana (2006): Of Sense and Sensibility: Immaterial Labour in Open Systems, in: Krysa, Joasia (Hg.): Curating Immateriality, New York (Autonomedia).
Waldt, Anton (2008): Graffiti für Gott, in: De:Bug, Nr. 118, Januar 2008, S. 7. http://www.de-bug.de/texte/5306.html (19.03.2008).

1 „Code is Law" stammt von Lawrence Lessig (1999).
2 Vgl. dazu die von Armin Medosch konzipierte Ausstellung Waves - the Art of the Electromagnetic Society, Hartware MedienKunstVerein Dortmund 2008 (sowie Waves, RIXC Riga 2006, http://rixc.lv/06/).
3 Zum Postoptischen vgl. ausführlich Arns 2005a.
4 http://www.transparency.org/ (last accessed March 19, 2008).
5 http://www.transparentworld.ru/ (last accessed March 19, 2008).
6 Transparenz - *lat. trans - parere, „durch - scheinen". Es handelt sich um Transparenz, wenn dahinter Liegendes relativ klar erkennbar ist; um Transluzenz (Lichtdurchlässigkeit), wenn nur diffuses Licht durchscheint (z.B. Milchglas) und um Opazität (Lichtundurchlässigkeit), wenn Materialien undurchsichtig sind (z.B. Holz).
7 „Die numerische Sprache der Kontrolle besteht aus Chiffren, die den Zugang zur Information kennzeichnen bzw. die Abweisung. Die Individuen sind »dividuell« geworden, und die Massen Stichproben, Daten, Märkte oder »Banken«." (Deleuze 1993: 258)
8 Zum Begriff der Performativität vgl. ausführlich Arns 2004 und Arns 2005b.
9 Radio Frequency Identification Technology (RFID), vgl. Wikipedia, http://de.wikipedia.org/wiki/RFID (19.03.2008); vgl. zu RFID auch die Veranstaltung Wie ich lernte, RFID zu lieben / How I learned to love RFID, HMKV in der PHOENIX Halle Dortmund, 2006, http://www.hmkv.de/dyn/d_programm_veranstaltungen/detail.php?nr=1046&rubric=veranstaltungen& (19.03.2008).
10 Vgl. „Wo gibt es RFID?", http://www.foebud.org/rfid/wo-gibt-es-rfid/ (21.03.2008).
11 Vgl. http://www.chrisoakley.com/the_catalogue.html (19.03.2008).
12 Vgl. Lisa Parks: Cultures in Orbit: Satellites and the Televisual, Durham and London: Duke Univesity Press 2005; sowie die von Francis Hunger konzipierte Veranstaltung Satellitenvoyeurismus, HMKV in der PHOENIX Halle Dortmund, 2007, http://www.hmkv.de/dyn/d_programm_veranstaltungen/detail.php?nr=2338&rubric=veranstaltungen& (last accessed March 19, 2008).
13 David Rice: Anna Kournikova Deleted by Memeright Trusted System (December 6, 2067), in: Future Feed Forward, 18. März 2001, http://futurefeedforward.com/front.php?fid=33 (26.03.2008).
14 Vgl. http://www.sofatrips.com (19.03.2008).
15 Vgl. Vgl. „Wo gibt es RFID?", http://www.foebud.org/rfid/wo-gibt-es-rfid/ (21.03.2008).
16 Eine Taktik agiert nicht von einem eigenen (Macht-)Ort, von einer eigenen Basis aus, wie die Strategie, sondern immer im Blickfeld des Feindes. Strategien und Taktiken unterscheiden sich durch Typen des Handelns: Während die Strategie ihre eigenen Räume produzieren und aufzwingen kann, können Taktiken diese Räume lediglich gebrauchen, manipulieren, umfunktionieren. Die Taktik muss „Coups landen" und „günstige Gelegenheiten nutzen". (Vgl. de Certeau 1988: 22-31 und 77-97).
17 Viele dieser Projekte sind im Ausstellungskatalog von Ctrl_Space dokumentiert (Vgl. Frohne/Levin/Weibel 2002).
18 http://www.notbored.org/the-scp.html (19.03.2008).
19 http://www.ubermatic.org/misha/ (19.03.2008).
20 http://www.ubermatic.org/life/ (19.03.2008).
21 Markus Keuschnigg über Faceless (2007), http://www.sixpackfilm.com/catalogue.php?oid=1631&lang=de (last accessed March 19, 2008).
22 http://www.paglen.com/ (last accessed March 19, 2008).
23 http://www.appliedautonomy.com/ (19.03.2008).

24 Walter Benjamin definierte das »Optisch-Unbewusste« in seiner Kleinen Geschichte der Photographie als eine unbewusste visuelle Dimension der materiellen Welt, die normalerweise vom gesellschaftlichen Bewusstsein des Menschen herausgefiltert wird und somit unsichtbar bleibt, die aber durch den Einsatz mechanischer Aufnahmetechniken (Fotografie und Film: Zeitlupen, Vergrößerungen) sichtbar gemacht werden kann: „Es ist ja eine andere Natur, welche zur Kamera als welche zum Auge spricht; anders vor allem so, dass an die Stelle eines vom Menschen mit Bewusstsein durchwirkten Raums ein unbewusst durchwirkter tritt. Ist es schon üblich, dass einer, beispielsweise, vom Gang der Leute, sei es auch nur im groben, sich Rechenschaft gibt, so weiß er bestimmt nichts mehr von ihrer Haltung im Sekundenbruchteil des ›Ausschreitens‹. Die Photographie mit ihren Hilfsmitteln: Zeitlupen, Vergrößerungen erschließt sie ihm. Von diesem Optisch-Unbewussten erfährt er erst durch sie, wie von dem Triebhaft-Unbewussten durch die Psychoanalyse." (Benjamin 1977: 50).
25 http://www.paglen.com/pages/projects/CIA/missing_persons.html (19.03.2008).
26 Vgl. ausführlich zu Marko Peljhan: Arns 2005c.
27 http://www.sofatrips.com (19.03.2008).
28 Vgl. http://www.odem.org/insert_coin/ (22.03.2008).
29 Vgl. den Text von Dragan Espenschied und Alvar Freude zum Internationalen Medienkunstpreis 2001.
30 Noch mehrere Monate nach dem Ende des Experiments war der Web-Zugriff von den meisten Computern der Akademie aus gefiltert.
31 http://www.inkearns.de/Archiv/Discord/index.html (19.03.2008).
32 „Metamute Meets Echelon - A Literary Competition", http://www.metamute.org/node/6961 (19.03.2008).
33 http://www.supervillainizer.ch (19.03.2008).
34 http://0100101110101101.org/home/life_sharing/ (19.03.2008).
35 http://0100101110101101.org/home/vopos/ (19.03.2008).
36 http://elahi.rutgers.edu/ (19.03.2008).
37 http://www.trackingtransience.com/ (19.03.2008).

The Serpent's Coils

Minoritarian Tactics in the Age of Transparency

Inke Arns

"Giedion, Mendelsohn, Corbusier turned the abiding places of man into a transit area for every conceivable kind of energy and for waves of light and air. The time that is coming will be dominated by transparency."
Walter Benjamin (1977 [1929])

"The coils of a serpent are even more complex that the burrows of a molehill."
Gilles Deleuze (1992 [1990])

With Deleuze into the Louisiana swamps

With his film "Down by Law" (1986), Jim Jarmusch created a highly accurate image of the paradigm shift that is now becoming reality – the shift from the milieus of confinement in a disciplinary society (as described by Michel Foucault) to the smooth modulations of the society of control (as described by Gilles Deleuze).

In "Down by Law", three small-time criminals – Jack, Zack and Bob – happen to end up in the same New Orleans prison cell. Zack (Tom Waits) is an out-of-work DJ, Jack (John Lurie) is a casual labourer, and Bob (Roberto Benigni) is an honest, good-natured, but rather naïve Italian who has been jailed for manslaughter. Together, they succeed in escaping into the swamps of Louisiana and from there to new lives. Apart from this flight through the swamps, the crucial scene for us here is the "window scene" in which Roberto "Bob" Benigni, whose command of

English is rudimentary at best, draws a window on the cell wall with chalk and asks Jack if, in English, one says "I look at the window" or "I look out of the window". Jack is amused by the Italian's questions, but, in view of their hopeless situation, gives a cynical answer: "Well, in this case I guess you'd say 'I look at the window'". Today, this scene can be read as an uncannily clairvoyant anticipation of current developments.

In this context, the concept of transparency plays an important role. In Jarmusch's dreary prison situation, which corresponds with Michel Foucault's system of confinement in a disciplinary society, the window (or interface), which is normally transparent and invisible, suddenly becomes visible itself, as a window and as a border or boundary, due to the simple fact that it is drawn with chalk on a prison wall, rendering it accessible to experience on account of its materiality and facticity. The chalk window can be read as a metaphor for software and programmed environments and their interfaces, which have become the new "postmaterial" foundations of today's information society.

While the disciplinary societies described by Foucault are characterized by built enclosures (the prison, the school, the factory, the hospital), in today's societies of control, these hard structures have given way to continuous modulations. These "soft" structures are like "a self-deforming cast that will continuously change from one moment to the other (...)." This flexible cast, represented in Down by Law by the image of the Louisiana swamps, has three characteristic properties:

1. Transparency (or invisibility, eluding direct sensory perception)
2. Immateriality (as a link between separate materialities)
3. Performativity ("code is law")[1].

In contrast to the opaque prison walls, the swamp is "transparent" (in metaphorical terms, of course, as stagnant swamp water is usually not clear). Unlike solid matter, the swamp is liquid (and thus dangerous), a property that allows it to change shape instantaneously, to fill voids as they appear, and to enclose bodies and objects at any time. Such a perfect enclosure – and this is the performative part – prevents forward movement at least as effectively, if not more effectively, than any building. But this point still needs to be argued.

Transparency

The age of transparency (cf. Arns 2008), whose dawn Walter Benjamin optimistically identified in the glass architecture of his contemporaries, now seems ambivalent. For one thing, the transparent architectures are passed through not only by visible light waves, but also by a whole host of other electromagnetic waves from a vast range of technical sources.[2] And for another, with its double meaning of visibility and invisibility and the ambivalence of the panoptical and the post-optical,[3] the concept of transparency seems well suited to characterise today's performative (information) architectures and spaces. The notion of "panopticism" coined by Foucault (1979) is derived from Jeremy Bentham's "panopticon" – his design for a perfect prison whose inmates are housed in a circular structure and exposed to permanent visibility from a central watchtower. My concept of the post-optical, on the other hand, refers to all the digital data flows and (programmed) communications structures and architectures which are just as exposed to monitoring, if not more so, but which consist chiefly of non-visual information (cf. "dataveillance").

Whereas in everyday usage, "transparency" stands for clarity and accountability by visibility (as in the names of Transparency International, an organisation that combats corruption worldwide,[4] or Prozrachnyj Mir[5] (Transparent World), a Russian company supplying high-resolution satellite images of the Earth for commercial purposes), in computer science, it means the exact opposite, i.e. invisibility and information hiding. If an interface is "transparent," this means the user cannot identify or perceive it. While this hiding of (superfluous, excessive) data makes sense in many cases in the name of reduced complexity, it can also lull the user into a false sense of security, as this invisibility suggests a direct view of something, an undisturbed transparency – even if it would be nonsense to believe such a thing. In The Language of New Media, Lev Manovich writes: "Far from being a transparent window into the data inside a computer, the interface brings with it strong messages of its own." (Manovich 2001:65) To make this "message" visible, it is necessary to direct attention towards the transparent "windowpane" itself. In the same way that transparent glass facades on buildings can be turned at the press of a button into translucent, semi-transparent surfaces, making them visible,[6] post-optical IT structures also need to be dragged out of their transparency. In communications networks, this would involve rendering transparent structures that channel economic, political and social power opaque and thus perceivable. Finally, it's a matter of reclaiming the concept of transparency from information technology and returning it to its original meaning of clarity and accountability via visibility.

Immateriality

The more the things of everyday life are regulated by software, the more they withdraw from sensory perception in daily usage. But their disappearance from direct contemplation does not mean they are not there. On the contrary: the fact that the world around us is increasingly programmed means that rules, conventions and relationships, which are usually subject to change and negotiation, are translated into software, where they become fixed. Immaterial structures fixed in software are – and this is the paradox – at least as stable and effective as material structures and architectures, if not more so. As well as this withdrawal beyond the reach of vision and perception, the way the world is secretly and eerily made to vanish by means of software also entails a dematerialisation of structures. Here, however, "immaterial" does not mean that these structures are less effective than their material counterparts. To understand the concept of "immaterial" as the opposite of "material" would be to entirely misunderstand it. (cf. Terranova

2006: 31) Instead, one must learn to understand the immaterial as something "which turns qualitative, intensive differences into quantitative relations of exchange and equivalence" (ibid.). It creates links between separate materialities – things and people, commodities and individuals, objects and subjects – allowing, for example, swift calculation of consumer or movement profiles.[7] At any given moment, the immaterial is somewhere (and not nowhere), between things. It encloses materialities elastically, smoothly pursuing objects and bodies, constantly making connections. The immaterial is not "what holds the world together", but it welds the things in the world together by relating them to each other, and it does so far more effectively than rigid structures ever could. In this light, software appears as a very hard material and immateriality as a quasi factual materiality – but one which evades our (visual, tactile) sensory perception.

Performativity

Programmed structures consist of two kinds of "texts": a visible "front end" (the "window") and an invisible, transparent "back end" (the software or program code). They are to one another as phenotext is to genotext in biology. The surface effects of the phenotext (the "window") are called up and controlled by the underlying active texts, the program codes or source texts. It is a characteristic property of program code that in it, saying and doing coincide; as a speech act with the power to actually act, code is not a description or representation of something, but an active agent, setting things in motion, triggering effects. Code does what it says.

The impact of code, however, is not limited to the phenotexts, i.e. the graphical user interfaces. "Coded performativity" (Grether 2001) has equally direct, sometimes political effects on the (virtual) spaces in which we move: "Program code," writes American law professor Lawrence Lessig, "increasingly tends towards becoming law." Today, control functions are being built directly into the architecture of the network, into its code. This theory is proposed by Lessig in "Code and other Laws of Cyberspace" (1999). Using the example of America Online, Lessig powerfully demonstrates how the code that shapes the AOL architecture prevents any form of virtual "gathering" and permits extensive monitoring of users. Graham Harwood also refers to this transparent world as an "invisible shadow world of process" (Harwood 2001: 47). This shadow world has direct and political consequences for the virtual and real spaces in which we move today; by fixing what is and is not possible in these spaces, it mobilises or immobilises their users. The question of free movement – when and for whom? – is a central one for today's spaces and it is closely related to the concept of performativity.[8] "The conception of a control mechanism", writes Deleuze, "giving the position of any element within an open environment at any given instant (whether animal in a reserve or human in a corporation, as with an electronic collar), is not necessarily one of science fiction. Felix Guattari has imagined a city where one would be able to leave one's apartment, one's street, one's neighbourhood, thanks to one's (dividual) electronic card that raises a given barrier; but the card could just as easily be rejected on a given day or between certain hours; what counts is not the barrier but the computer that tracks each person's position – licit or illicit – and effects a universal modulation." (Deleuze 1992)

One example of a technology that enables precisely this is Radio Frequency Identification (RFID).[9] RFID tags are passive wireless broadcasters capable of sending and storing information. Destined to replace barcodes, they are already being used in commodity logistics, the surveillance of individuals, and protection against theft. Prompted by a weak, wireless energy impulse, RFID tags send the data stored on them to a remote reading device. Today, this can already be achieved over a distance of up to several hundred metres – without the bearer noticing. This technology also allows objects to be unambiguously identified worldwide – another significant feature (besides unnoticed remote reading) that sets RFID apart from the conventional barcode. RFID allows seamless tracing of commodity flows and therefore an entirely new dimension of data mining (e.g. for the creation of consumer profiles). If one considers the potential use of RFID technology on and in human individuals – e.g. passports or health insurance cards equipped with RFID chips storing biometric data, or RFID tags with biometric data that are implanted under the skin[10] – new forms of ubiquitous control become conceivable. The British artist Chris Oakley has created a striking illustration of this with his video "The Catalogue" (2004, 5:30 min.).[11]

The age of transparency is characterized by a double structure of the panoptical and the post-optical. On the one hand, we are confronted with a situation of total, panoptical visibility which began with the development of video surveillance systems in the 1980s, if not before, and which is culminating today in state- and privately-owned networks of surveillance satellites.[12] In 2001, Bruce Sterling thought the emerging surveillance situation, coupled with increasingly strict prosecution of copyright infringements, through to its logical conclusion in his fictitious newspaper report, allegedly written in 2067, under the title "Anna Kournikova Deleted by Memeright Trusted System".[13] Clever activists, advertising agencies and religious fundamentalists are already using Google Earth for carefully orchestrated campaigns: the results are gigantic Land Art projects that can only be seen from aeroplanes or by satellite cameras. (cf. Waldt 2008: 7)

The rise of this panoptical visibility has been accompanied by an increasing withdrawal into invisibility of the technical structures responsible for observation and performative action. Performative structures, whether inconceivably small, inconceivably immaterial or inconceivably far away, are often identifiable via their effects only, no longer necessarily visible themselves: satellites are almost impossible to identify with the naked human eye on account of their distance from Earth's surface; miniaturised nano-machines are too small; and software eludes human perception because it usually consists of "discrete" performative (geno-)texts that lie behind the visible interfaces (phenotexts) which they generate. In the age of transparency, we are faced with a fundamental severing of the link between visibility and performativity/effectiveness. While everything else is subjected to the paradigm of constant visibility, the actual active, performative structures elude visibility and our direct control – they have become transparent. Invisibility, then, becomes the privilege of active, performative structures. In this sense, I speak of the present as a post-optical age in which the performative text of programming code – which one could refer to, by analogy with Walter Benjamin, as the post-optical unconscious[14] – becomes "law".

Minoritarian tactics in the age of transparency

"(T)he vocation of an art of the kind that reflects on electronic crowds and networks is not the representation of the visible world but the visualisation of what is otherwise inaccessible to perception and is difficult to imagine because of its cosmic or microscopic scale, its discontinuity in space and time, or its impenetrability – from the insides of the body, the atom, or the black box to the outside of our galaxy and our universe."

Margaret Morse (1998: 192)

How, in spaces that have become imperceptible, inaccessible to direct perception, can political and/or artistic acts be articulated? In the face of such software-assisted vanishing of the world, where and how can potential spaces of the political be (re-)created? In recent years, various media, net and software art projects[15] have developed approaches that render the economic, political and social power structures in communications networks opaque (i.e. visible). The aim is always to push IT structures from a state of transparency into one of visibility or perceptibility. In an age of the software-assisted implosion of the political, this first step alone is already eminently political. As Gilles Deleuze noted almost twenty years ago, "There is no need to fear or hope, but only to look for new weapons." (Deleuze 1993)

Are tactics of resistance[16] even possible in this transparent world? And if they are, what form do they take? In the following, I describe two tactical approaches: a) that of viewing, mapping and intervening, i.e. making visible structures of the surveillance and/or information landscape and b) that of disappearing and becoming invisible via maximum visibility (over-identification with and active playing to the panoptical regime).

Viewing, mapping, intervening

This category includes projects that highlight the existence of hidden structures of the surveillance and/or information landscape. Artistic and activist engagement with the theme of video surveillance is a common topos in media art:[17] during the 1990s, Yann Beauvais (F) and the Surveillance Camera Players[18] (US) performed plays for the operators of surveillance cameras, thus drawing attention to the widespread presence of cameras in the urban environment. The works of French artist Renaud Auguste-Dormeuil fit into this category, as well as the track-the-trackers system developed in 2003 by the Swiss artist Annina Rüst, which uses

GPS to pinpoint the positions of surveillance cameras in public space, enters them in a database, and "sonifies" them, translating them into soundscapes generated by movement through the city.

There are also projects directed not just at drawing attention to the existence of video cameras in the urban space, but at making visible the transparent (power) structures on which they are based. In 2005, Canadian artist Michelle Teran[19] walked the streets of Berlin with a peculiar suitcase on wheels. "Life: A User's Manual"[20] was a performance that showed footage from surveillance cameras installed in public and private spaces on a television set. To achieve this, she used a commercially available video scanner capable of capturing radio signals from cameras broadcasting on the 2.4 Ghz wavelength. In this way, a walk through the city became, in the artist's own words, a "shared experience in visualizing the invisible."

In "Faceless" (2007, 50 min.), Austrian artist Manu Luksch goes one step further than Yann Beauvais and the Surveillance Camera Players. For this video, she performed in front of CCTV cameras and then requested the footage featuring her from the operators of the surveillance equipment under the terms of Britain's Data Protection Act (which guarantees the right to one's own image). Using this material, in which all faces except that of the artist herself had been erased for data protection reasons, Luksch created an oppressive science-fiction story "in which the single-frame aesthetic resulting from the surveillance camera material recalls Chris Marker's epoch-making film comic "La Jetée" (1962)."[21]

For some years, the French group Bureau d'études has been mapping current political, social and economic systems. These visual analyses of transnational capitalism based on in-depth research are usually presented in the form of large-format charts. "Governing by Networks" (2003) visualizes the mutual holdings and transnational connections of global media conglomerates. By showing something that usually remains invisible, and by bringing something together as a coherent, meaningful whole which usually remains separate and unconnected, these visualisations of relations of ownership act as "resymbolisation machines" – the term used by Bureau d'études to describe the process of assembling and representing something whose fine branching and capillary structures prevent it from being perceived as a whole, i.e. global capitalism. In their visual analysis of current business conglomerates, Bureau d'études, whose conceptual precursors include the artists Öyvind Fahlström (1928-1976) and Mark Lombardi (1951-2000), achieve a trenchant diagnosis of the present.

The possibility of uncovering transparent structures by means of simple observation has been strikingly demonstrated in recent years by "plane-spotters". By carefully monitoring take-offs and landings around the world and checking them against civilian flight schedules, aviation enthusiasts revealed the CIA's practice of "extraordinary rendition", using civilian aircraft to transfer suspected terrorists to prisons like Guantanamo Bay. As such flights did not feature in civilian timetables, these secret activities were eventually noticed. With "Terminal Air" (2007), American experimental geographer Trevor Paglen[22] and the Institute for Applied Autonomy[23] developed a system (software and database) capable of displaying these illegal CIA flights almost in real time. Paglen's main interest is in researching and documenting "military landscapes" – such as facilities concealed deep in American desert territories. To take pictures of these remote locations totally hidden from view, thus making the "optical unconscious"[24] visible, Paglen's work entitled Limit Telephotography deployed the methods of photography from space, using telephoto lenses with focal lengths between 1300 and 7000 mm. The resulting enlargement reveals aspects of the landscape not visible with the naked eye. Missing Persons (2006) deals with the transparent surface of the (front) companies that own the aircraft used for extraordinary rendition, displaying the signatures of the fake CEOs.[25]

Marko Peljhan and Mario Purkathofer use their works to examine the material structures on which the regime of transparency is based. Whereas *makrolab* (1997-2007), a mobile and autonomous research laboratory designed by Marko Peljhan, engaged with communications flows at different locations on different continents, mapping the territory of signals at a given geographical point,[26] Swiss artist Mario Purkathofer's travel agency sofatrips.com[27] offers "journeys into the information landscape". The "sofa trips" carried out by the artist since 2006 are movements in virtual and physical spaces: tracking and walking the path taken by an SMS text message inside Zurich; bus trips to CERN, the European research centre in Geneva (where the World Wide Web and Mosaic, the first graphic browser, were developed in the early 1990s); and city walks as human data processions through the information landscape – to the outer limit of Zurich's network; past public phone boxes, providers, computer centres, webcams, WLAN hotspots; through communications infrastructures both old and new. Sofatrips direct attention towards the material basis of our otherwise increasingly virtual world.

A good example of activist intervention in the invisible, smooth modulations of the society of control – the code – is the "insert_coin"[28] project by Dragan Espenschied and Alvar Freude. As part of their diploma show at Stuttgart's Merz Academy in 2000/2001, with the motto "two people monitor 250 people", they surreptitiously installed a web proxy server that used a Perl script to manipulate the entire web data traffic of all students and teaching staff in the academy's computer network. The aim, according to Espenschied and Freude, was to "test the competency and critical faculties of the users with respect to the everyday medium of the Internet."[29] The manipulated proxy server redirected URLs entered by users to other pages, modified HTML formatting code, used a simple search and replace function to alter both current reports on news websites (e.g. by changing the names of politicians) and the content of private emails being read via web interfaces such as Hotmail, gmx or Yahoo! For four weeks, the Academy's teaching staff and students didn't notice that their web access was being manipulated in this way. And when Espenschied and Freude revealed the details of the experiment, hardly anyone was interested. Though they published a simple set of instructions with which anyone could switch off the filters, very few took the time to make this change and thus regain access to unfiltered data.[30]

Disappearing and becoming invisible by means of maximum visibility

Today, with very few exceptions, spaces of inaccessibility and invisibility no longer exist. The idea of vanishing from the records is utopian, even potentially suspicious. This second category, then, includes projects that favour over-identification with the system, confirming and playing to the panoptic regime in its demand for permanent visibility. The watchwords here are invisibility via maximum visibility, and overloading the system via dissimulation.

A very early and determined position in the field was developed by Lüneburg artist Andreas Peschka. As his contribution to the exhibition "discord. sabotage of realities"[31] (1996), he had a rubberstamp made of the fingerprint of his right index finger (entitled Stempelset für Attentäter, stamp kit for assassins), which he distributed with a pot of Vaseline. In the contract of sale, Peschka called on buyers to spread his fingerprint as widely as possible. The idea was to jam the system by making the artist's fingerprint appear simultaneously at (crime) scenes around the world – a process of absurd self-duplication. The competition "Metamute Meets Echelon – A Literary Competition" launched in September 2001 was based on a similar principle: entrants were invited to submit literary words using the entire contents of the Echelon dictionary. By flooding the networks with Echelon-blacklisted words, the American surveillance and espionage system was to be overloaded.[32]

Since 2001, Annina Rüst – in her solo projects and as part of the group Local Area Network (LAN) – has been focusing on surveillance on the Internet and in public spaces. With " TraceNoizer – Disinformation on Demand" (2001/2002), LAN created a tool designed to help protect one's own online identity. To erase online traces, it uses an algorithm to generate a cloned homepage with misleading personal information that is automatically put online. In view of the huge quantity of existing "authentic" personal details available online, there really does seem to be a need for such a tool. In 2002, Annina Rüst and LAN put the conspiracy generator SuperVillainizer[34] online to protest against the paranoia and the rhetoric with which politicians increasingly seek to legitimate the surveillance of email traffic and the Internet. At the press of a button, the "SuperVillainizer"[33] allows any Internet user to generate villains who send each other subversive emails (automatically generated and full of suspect keywords) and who are designed to confuse the Carnivore, Echelon and Onyx surveillance systems used by secret services worldwide. Since 2002, the users of "SuperVillainizer" have created 1,345 villains who have communicated about 1,137 conspiracies in a total of 205,146 emails.

Since early 2001, the Italian net art duo 0100101110101101.org has been working on its most extensive and elaborate project to date under the title "Glasnost" (transparency). It is a self-surveillance system that constantly collects data concerning the life of the two members of 0100101110101101.org and publishes this information in uncensored form. The first step towards realizing Glasnost was the project "life_sharing" (2001).[34] life_sharing, an anagram of "file sharing", gives Internet users direct online access to artists' computers. All data on the hard drives (texts, images, software, private mail traffic, etc.) are subject to the Gnu Public License (GPL) and can be freely accessed, copied and manipulated: "life_sharing is a brand new concept of net architecture turning a website into a hardcore personal media for complete digital transparency." Since the start of the VOPOS[35] project in January 2002, the two artists have been wearing GPS transmitters that regularly send coordinates to their publicly accessible website. The data are transferred onto city maps, thus constantly visualizing their current location.

Today, this project appears as a quasi prophetic and perhaps frivolous anticipation of what happened to Hasan Elahi,[36] assistant professor at the Department of Visual Art at Rutgers University, shortly after 11 September 2001. Elahi, an American of Bangladeshi origin, was anonymously reported to the authorities for possession of explosives, and the FBI began observing him. Returning from the Netherlands in 2002, he was arrested at Detroit airport by FBI agents who told him he was suspected of terrorism (a suspicion nourished by the 100,000 miles he travelled by air every year). There followed six months of non-stop interrogation, after which the FBI finally accepted Elahi's detailed accounts. But fears that he might end up in Guantanamo nonetheless prompted him to take an offensive approach: his website Tracking Transience, online since December 2003, documents his entire life online.[37] Thanks to a GPS tracking device, it is possible to see exactly where Elahi is at any time. In addition, photographs document his daily routine in minute detail: meals, shopping, meetings with friends, bank transactions, even visits to the toilet.

The Serpent's Coils

What the three protagonists in "Down by Law" discover outside the prison walls in the Louisiana swamps is nothing other than the "self-deforming cast" of the society of control. This eerie space is characterized by transparency, immateriality and performativity, and it encloses the bodies and objects that move within it at all times like a fine net or sieve whose mesh changes from one moment to the next. Such flexible, constantly self-adapting modulations are invisible, transparent. They elude human perception – but because they are everywhere at once, they are harder than any built enclosure has ever been. The coils of a serpent are indeed more complex than the burrows of a molehill.

The age of transparency is characterized by a severing of the link between (panoptical) visibility and (post-optical) performativity. The actual active, performative structures have become transparent – thus eluding our direct control. In this sense, the chalk window drawn on the prison wall by Roberto "Bob" Benigni can be understood as a metaphor for "Windows" (and for all other operating systems and their interfaces, whether proprietary or not), and the program code that brings forth these interfaces can be understood as the new "post-material" basis of the contemporary information and control societies – their invisible, immaterial law. These complicated coils of the serpent need to be watched – and where necessary, their privilege of transparency must be contested.

Translated from the German by Nicolas Grindell

Literature:

Arns, Inke (2004): Texte, die (sich) bewegen: Zur Performativität von Programmiercodes in Netzkunst und Software Art, in: Arns, Inke, Mirjam Goller, Susanne Strätling, and Georg Witte (eds.): Kinetographien, Bielefeld (Aisthesis Verlag) pp. 57-78.
http://www.inkearns.de/Texts/0kineto-arns-publ.pdf (accessed 19.03.2008)
Arns, Inke (2005a): Netzkulturen im postoptischen Zeitalter, in: Schade, Sigrid, Thomas Sieber, and Georg Christoph Tholen (eds.): SchnittStellen, Basler Beiträge zur Medienwissenschaft BBM, Basel (Institute of Media Studies / Basel University).
Arns, Inke (2005b): Read_me, run_me, execute_me. Code als ausführbarer Text: Softwarekunst und ihr Fokus auf Programmcodes als performative Texte, in: Frieling, Rudolf, and Dieter Daniels (eds.): Medien Kunst Netz 2: Thematische Schwerpunkte, Vienna/New York (Springer Verlag), pp. 197-207.
Arns, Inke (2005c): Faktur und Interface: Chlebnikov, Tesla und der himmlische Datenverkehr in Marko Peljhans makrolab (1997-2007), in: Kwastek, Katja (ed.): "Ohne Schnur...." Kunst und drahtlose Kommunikation. Kommunikationskunst im Spannungsfeld von Kunst, Technologie und Gesellschaft, Frankfurt a. M. (Revolver Verlag), pp. 62-79.
Arns, Inke (2008): Transparency and Politics. On Spaces of the Political beyond the Visible, or: How transparency came to be the lead paradigm of the 21st century, paper given at the conference "The Aesthetic Interface", University of Aarhus, Denmark, 2007. (forthcoming from NAI Publishers, Rotterdam).
Benjamin, Walter (1977): A Short History of Photography [1931], Artforum 15:6 (February 1977), pp. 46-51.
Benjamin, Walter (1999): The Return of the Flâneur [1929], in: Benjamin, Walter: Selected Writings, Volume 2, 1927-1934, Harvard (Harvard University Press), 1999.
Certeau, Michel de (1984): The Practice of Everyday Life [1980], Berkeley (University of California Press).
Deleuze, Gilles (1992): Postscript on the Societies of Control [1990], in: OCTOBER 59, Winter 1992, MIT Press, Cambridge, MA, pp. 3-7.
Foucault, Michel (1979): Discipline and Punish. The Birth of the Prison [1975], New York (Vintage Books).
Frohne, Ursula, Thomas Y. Levin, and Peter Weibel (eds.) (2002): Ctrl_Space. Rhetorics of Surveillance from Betham to Big Brother, ZKM Karlsruhe, Cambridge, MA (MIT Press).
Grether, Reinhold (2001): The Performing Arts in a New Era, in: Rohrpost, 26.7.2001,
http://www.nettime.org/Lists-Archives/rohrpost-0107/msg00205.html
Harwood, Graham (2001): Speculative Software, in: Broeckmann, Andreas, and Susanne Jaschko (eds.): DIY Media – Art and Digital Media, Software – Participation – Distribution. Transmediale.01, Berlin, pp. 47–49.
Lessig, Lawrence (1999): Code and other Laws of Cyberspace, New York (Basic Books), http://code-is-law.org/
Manovich, Lev (2001): The Language of New Media, Cambridge, Massachusetts/London, England (MIT Press).
Morse, Margaret (1998): Virtualities. Television, Media art and Cyberculture, Indiana (University Press).
Rice, David (2001): Anna Kournikova Deleted by Memeright Trusted System (December 6, 2067), in: Future Feed Forward, 18 March 2001, http://futurefeedforward.com/front.php?fid=33
Terranova, Tiziana (2006): Of Sense and Sensibility: Immaterial Labour in Open Systems, in: Krysa, Joasia (ed.): Curating Immateriality, New York (Autonomedia).
Waldt, Anton (2008): Graffiti für Gott, in: De:Bug, No. 118, January 2008, p. 7. http://www.de-bug.de/texte/5306.html (accessed 19.03.2008).

1   "Code is Law" is from Lawrence Lessig (2000).
2   Cf. the exhibition devised by Armin Medosch "Waves - the Art of the Electromagnetic Society", Hartware MedienKunstVerein Dortmund 2008 (also "Waves" , RIXC Riga 2006, http://rixc.lv/06/).
3   For more detail on the concept of the post-optical, see Arns 2005a.
4   http://www.transparency.org/ (accessed 19.03.2008).
5   http://www.transparentworld.ru/ (accessed 19.03.2008).
6   Transparency - *lat. trans - parere, "through - appear". Something is transparent when what is behind it can be identified relatively clearly, translucent when only diffuse light shines through (e.g. frosted glass), opaque when it cannot be seen through (e.g. wood).
7   "The numerical language of control is made of codes that mark access to information, or reject it. Individuals have become 'dividuals', and masses, samples, data, markets, or 'banks'." (Deleuze 1992)

8   For more detail on the concept of performativity, see Arns 2004 and Arns 2005b.
9   Radio Frequency Identification Technology (RFID), cf. Wikipedia, http://en.wikipedia.org/wiki/Radio-frequency_identification (accessed 19.03.2008); see also the event How I learned to love RFID, HMKV at PHOENIX Halle Dortmund, 2006, http://www.hmkv.de/dyn/d_programm_veranstaltungen/detail.php?nr=1046&rubric=veranstaltungen& (accessed 19.03.2008).
10 Cf. "Where do I find RFID?", http://www.foebud.org/rfid/en/where-find (accessed 21.03.2008).
11 Cf. http://www.chrisoakley.com/the_catalogue.html (accessed 19.03.2008).
12 Cf. Lisa Parks: Cultures in Orbit: Satellites and the Televisual, Durham and London: Duke University Press 2005; and the Satellitenvoyeurismus event organized by Francis Hunger, HMKV at PHOENIX Halle Dortmund, 2007, http://www.hmkv.de/dyn/d_programm_veranstaltungen/detail.php?nr=2338&rubric=veranstaltungen& (accessed 19.03.2008).
13 David Rice: "Anna Kournikova Deleted by Memeright Trusted System (December 6, 2067)", in: Future Feed Forward, 18 March 2001, http://futurefeedforward.com/front.php?fid=33 (accessed 26.03.2008).
14 Cf. http://www.sofatrips.com (accessed 19.03.2008).
15 Cf. "Where do I find RFID?", http://www.foebud.org/rfid/en/where-find (accessed 21.03.2008).
16 Unlike a strategy, a tactic does not operate from a position (of power) or base of its own, but always in view of the enemy. Strategies and tactics differ in their modes of action: while a strategy can produce and impose its own spaces, tactics can only use, manipulate and repurpose such spaces. Tactics must "land coups" and "use opportunities". (Cf. de Certeau 1984).
17 Many of these projects are documented in the "Ctrl_Space" exhibition catalogue (cf. Frohne/Levin/Weibel 2002).
18 http://www.notbored.org/the-scp.html (accessed 19.03.2008).
19 http://www.ubermatic.org/misha/ (accessed 19.03.2008).
20 http://www.ubermatic.org/life/ (accessed 19.03.2008).
21 Markus Keuschnigg on Faceless (2007), http://www.sixpackfilm.com/catalogue.php?oid=1631&lang=de (accessed 19.03.2008).
22 http://www.paglen.com/ (accessed 19.03.2008).
23 http://www.appliedautonomy.com/ (accessed 19.03.2008).
24 In A Short History of Photography, Walter Benjamin defined the "optical unconscious" as an unconscious visual dimension of the material world that is usually filtered out of human social consciousness and thus remains invisible, but which can be rendered visible by the use of mechanical recording technology (photography and film, slow motion and zoom): "A different nature speaks to the camera than speaks to the eye; most different in that in place of a space interwoven by a person with consciousness is formed a space interwoven by the unconscious. It is already quite common that someone, for example, can give a rough account of how a person walks. But he would not be able to describe their position at the fracture of a moment of stepping out. Photographic aids like time lapse and enlargements unlocks this for him. It is photography that gives access to the optical-unconscious, just as the drive-unconscious is discovered through psychoanalysis." (Benjamin 1977: 50).
25 http://www.paglen.com/pages/projects/CIA/missing_persons.html (accessed 19.03.2008).
26 For more detail on Marko Peljhan, see Arns 2005c.
27 http://www.sofatrips.com (accessed 19.03.2008).
28 Vgl. http://www.odem.org/insert_coin/ (accessed 22.03.2008).
29 See the text by Dragan Espenschied and Alvar Freude on the International Media Art Prize 2001.
30 Several months after the end of the experiment, the web access of most of the Academy's computers was still being filtered.
31 http://www.inkearns.de/Archiv/Discord/index.html (accessed 19.03.2008).
32 "Metamute Meets Echelon - A Literary Competition", http://www.metamute.org/node/6961 (accessed 19.03.2008).
33 http://www.supervillainizer.ch (accessed 19.03.2008).
34 http://0100101110101101.org/home/life_sharing/ (accessed 19.03.2008).
35 http://0100101110101101.org/home/vopos/ (accessed 19.03.2008).
36 http://elahi.rutgers.edu/ (accessed 19.03.2008).
37 http://www.trackingtransience

Offensive Flucht statt Gesetzesbruch

Zum Ungehorsam angesichts des Thoreau'schen Imperativs

Jens Kastner und Gerald Raunig

„*Der ‚zivile Ungehorsam' stellt vielleicht die grundlegendste Form des politischen Handelns der Multitude dar, vorausgesetzt, man befreit ihn aus der liberalen Tradition, in der er noch verfangen ist. Es geht nicht darum, ein bestimmtes Gesetz zu missachten, weil es inkohärent ist oder im Widerspruch zu anderen Grundnormen steht, zum Beispiel mit der Verfassung eines Landes. In der Tat steht das Aufbegehren in einem solchen Fall bloß eine tiefer gehende Loyalität gegenüber der Staatsgewalt unter Beweis. Im Gegensatz dazu zieht der radikale Ungehorsam, der uns hier interessiert, das Vermögen der Befehlsgewalt des Staates selbst infrage.*"
Paolo Virno, Grammatik der Multitude (2005a: 96)

Wenn das Recht strukturell so beschaffen ist, dass es aus seinen Subjekten Erfüllungsgehilfen des Unrechts an anderen macht, dann, so der Thoreau'sche Imperativ, „... brich das Gesetz!". Soweit, so scheinbar klar. Bei genauerem Hinsehen ergrauen dieses Bild und seine Vorbedingungen jedoch in vollendeter Opazität. Die gleichermaßen große wie scheinbar klare Losung Henry David Thoreaus (1817-1862) für die Vergangenheit des zivilen Ungehorsams ist keine Lösung für dessen Aktualisierung.

Henry David Thoreaus berühmtes Pamphlet gegen die „bürgerliche Regierung" war eine Rechtfertigungsschrift. Im Juli 1846 war er in Concord, Massachusetts, verhaftet und ins Gefängnis gesperrt worden (welches er am nächsten Tag allerdings wieder verließ, nachdem seine Tante gegen seinen Willen die Kaution bezahlt hatte). Der Grund für seine Verhaftung waren nicht gezahlte Steuern. Um zu verdeutlichen, dass diese Unterlassungshandlung keineswegs einer Laune oder Nachlässigkeit, sondern im Gegenteil tiefster Überzeugung geschuldet war, verfasste Thoreau die Schrift, die 1849 erstmals unter dem Titel „Resistance to Civil Government" erschien und die für die sozialen Bewegungen der kommenden hundertfünfzig Jahre so wichtig werden sollte. Darin entwickelt Thoreau seine radikal individualistische Konzeption von ungehorsamem Verhalten in Auflehnung gegen zwei konkrete Formen des Unrechts, die staatlich legitimiert und/oder betrieben werden. Zum einen ist dies die Sklaverei, die in den USA zu Lebzeiten Thoreaus noch gesetzlich erlaubt war. Und zum anderen der Krieg, speziell jener, den die USA in den Jahren 1846 bis 1848 gegen Mexiko als Eroberungskrieg geführt haben: „(W)enn ein Sechstel der Bevölkerung einer Nation, die sich selbst zu einer Zuflucht der Freiheit gemacht hat, versklavt ist, und wenn ein ganzes Land widerrechtlich überrannt, von einer fremden Armee erobert und dem Kriegsrecht unterworfen wird, dann, meine ich, ist es nicht zu früh für ehrliche Leute, aufzustehen und zu rebellieren." (Thoreau 1973: 11)

Auch wenn Thoreau sich bei seiner Darlegung auf die konkrete Situation berief, die er vorfand, handelt es sich bei beiden Gründen für seine Entscheidung doch um zwei strukturelle Phänomene staatlich organisierter Gesellschaften: die Entrechtung bzw. Entmenschlichung von Individuen und der Krieg. Indem er diese strukturellen Bedingungen zu Motiven und Motivationen für ungehorsames Verhalten erklärt, knüpft er zudem die Frage, welches Gesetz der/die Einzelne mit trägt, nicht mehr allein an die direkte Betroffenheit von diesem Gesetz. Nicht nur ein Gesetz zu machen oder zu befolgen, sondern auch, nicht gegen es vorzugehen, kann Einzelne mitverantwortlich machen an dem gegenüber Vielen begangenen Unrecht. Thoreau denkt hier, auch wenn er von Gründen für die Rebellion spricht, in moralischen Begriffen. Es geht ihm um die Gewissensentscheidungen Einzelner. Diese Dimension wurde später von so unterschiedlichen AkteurInnen wie Leo Tolstoi oder der englischen Suffragettenbewegung erweitert und durch das Konzept des „passiven Widerstands" zum Mittel des gesellschaftlichen und politischen Kampfes gemacht.

Dass Thoreaus Konzeption aus dem 19. Jahrhundert streng von der Position des Individuums ausgeht und damit in Kontrast zu kollektiven Vorstellungen des Ungehorsams geraten würde, steht nicht im Mittelpunkt unserer Kritik. Eine zeitgenössische Problematisierung des zivilen Ungehorsams wird genau jene Subjektivierungsweisen beleuchten, die den scheinbaren Gegensatz von individuellen Gewissensfragen und kollektiver Politisierung zu durchkreuzen suchen. Uns geht es im Folgenden darüber hinaus um vier Aspekte des produktiven Weiterdenkens von Thoreaus Imperativ des Gesetzesbruchs, die wir theoretisch wie praktisch als zentrale Komponenten jeder zeitgemäßen Vorstellung von Ungehorsam verstehen.

1. Zunächst ist für eine kritische Aktualisierung dieses Imperativs festzuhalten, dass er sich an einer Struktur abzuarbeiten scheint, welche nicht mehr das alleinige Zentrum von Herrschaft ausmacht – oder es vielleicht niemals ausgemacht hat. Die Fixierung auf das juridische Dispositiv homogenisiert die Relation von Machtverhältnissen und nicht zuletzt damit auch die strategischen Möglichkeiten von Widerstand. (Vgl. Foucault 1983: 102, Lorey 1996: 49-70)[1] Recht und Gesetz (und ihr ständiger Bezug zur Staatsform) sind nicht erst in der Entwicklung des neoliberalen Kapitalismus als Funktionen eines breiteren Machtgefüges zu verstehen, das Foucault trefflich als Gouvernementalität bezeichnete. Schon im 18. und 19. Jahrhundert hatte sich eine Regierungsform durchgesetzt, die nicht einfach über Repression und Souveränität des Herrschers funktioniert: Diese Regierung implementiert über die Logik von Autonomie und Eigentum ein Selbstverhältnis der Einzelnen, welches gesamte Bevölkerungen zu „biopolitischen" Subjekten macht. (Vgl. Foucault 2004, Lemke 1997: 126ff., Bröckling/Krasmann/Lemke 2000, Pieper/Gutiérrez Rodríguez 2003, Lorey 2007: 125f.) Das heißt, neben den juridisch-politischen Strukturen und dem Rechtsstatus des Subjekts (als gleichzeitig souverän und unterworfen) entwickelt sich eine maschinische Form der Selbst-Indienstnahme, die Lebens- und Arbeitsbedingungen der Subjekte durchzieht und diese umso regierungsfähiger macht (vgl. Raunig 2008, Lazzarato 2008). Im Setting neoliberaler Gouvernementalität ist diese verwobene Qualität von sozialer Unterwerfung und maschinischer Selbst-Indienstnahme gleichermaßen als mehrfache Komplizität wie auch als Quelle neuer Formen dessen zu verstehen, was Foucault nun statt Widerstand als Gegen-Verhalten bezeichnet (vgl. Kastner 2008). In diesem Zusammenhang wird auch der Begriff des Ungehorsams erneut fruchtbar – darauf wird später zurückzukommen sein. An dieser Stelle sei jedoch zunächst festgehalten, dass eine reduzierte Fokussierung auf Gesetz, Recht und Staat weder theoretisch ausreichend noch für aktuelle Praxen des Ungehorsams relevant zu sein scheint.

2. Aber legen wir die Begriffe „des Gesetzes" und „des Rechts" doch einmal grundlegender aus denn als juridische Verfasstheit eines Staates. Versuchen wir, das juridische Dispositiv Foucaults aufzubrechen, so weit, dass es jenen Bereich berührt, der für Foucault den strategisch-produktiven Aspekt der Macht umfasst. Verstehen wir „das Gesetz" also als eine Grammatik, die allen sozialen und sprachlichen, diskursiven wie nicht-diskursiven Beziehungen zugrunde liegt. Wenn wir einer derartigen Erweiterung des juridischen Dispositivs nachgehen, stoßen wir zunächst auf das Problem der Metapher des Gesetzesbruchs, den Thoreau als Lösung vorschlägt.

   Eine Grammatik lässt sich nicht „brechen". Wie Paolo Virno bereits in der Grammatik der Multitude (2005a) ausführt, findet sich der Ausweg nicht im Bruch als Negation oder einer dialektischen Form von Widerstand, sondern gerade in einer Kombination aus radikalem Ungehorsam und Exodus, also offensiver, kollektiver Flucht. In seinem jüngsten Buch über Witz und Innovation setzt Virno

(2005b)[2] diese Figur des Exodus analog mit den sprachlich-kommunikativen Strategien des plötzlichen Themenwechsels in einem Gespräch, das in wohl strukturierten Bahnen verläuft, sowie vor allem des Witzes, der sich einer sprachlichen Doppeldeutigkeit bedient. Auf dem Feld des Politischen aktualisiert sich diese Abweichung als kollektives Abfallen vom Staat als Sezession, als Exodus. Hier dreht es sich also um eine nicht-dialektische Form der Negation und des Widerstands, oder besser: des Abfallens und Fliehens. Es geht nicht allein um den Entwurf neuer Spielzüge, von Taktiken, um den Gegner auszuspielen, sondern um einen Angriff auf die Regeln, auf den Glauben an das Spiel selbst.[3] Oder, nochmals in den Worten Virnos (2005a: 98), um Erfindungen, „die die Regeln des Spiels abändern und die Kompassnadel des Gegners zum Rotieren bringt."

Die postoperaistische Linie des Begriffs Exodus, wenn sie auch nicht mehr vom ganz anderen Außen träumen lässt, ist keineswegs als harmlos, individualistisch oder eskapistisch-esoterisch zu verstehen. Es geht in dieser exodischen Form des Widerstands um eine positive, eine offensive, eine gefährliche Form des Abfallens (vgl. Virno 2007).[4] Anstatt Herrschaftsverhältnisse als unverrückbaren Horizont vorauszusetzen und dennoch gegen sie anzukämpfen, verändert diese Flucht die Bedingungen, unter denen die Voraussetzung stattfindet. Der Exodus, so heißt es in der Grammatik der Multitude, verwandelt den Zusammenhang, in dem ein Problem aufgetaucht ist, anstatt das Problem über eine Entscheidung zwischen vorgegebenen Alternativen zu behandeln. Er eröffnet als die nicht-passive, nichtdialektische, nichtindividualistische Form des Abfallens einen Ausweg, der auf den Karten der juridischen Dispositive nicht ausgewiesen ist und „verändert genau jene ‚Grammatik', die die Auswahl aller Wahlmöglichkeiten bestimmt". In der Flucht, die zugleich etwas Neues konstituiert, ereignet sich eine Modifizierung der Grammatik. Nicht Gesetz also, sondern Grammatik, nicht Gesetzesbruch, sondern Flucht „vor dem Gesetz".

3. Vor diesem Hintergrund lässt sich schließlich auch das Problem neu stellen, das als dichotome Figur von Gewalt und Gewaltlosigkeit viele historische wie aktuelle Diskussionen zu Aktivismus und sozialen Bewegungen unproduktiv beherrscht.

Thoreau selber stellt sich die Frage nach der Gewalt nicht, denn er denkt den zivilen Ungehorsam nicht als kollektive und/oder politische Strategie. Die Revolution habe gesiegt, wenn die Untertanen den Gehorsam verweigerten und wenn die Beamten ihre Ämter niederlegen würden. „Doch nehmt ruhig an", schreibt Thoreau (1973: 21) dann, „daß dabei auch Blut vergossen werden müßte. Wird denn nicht gewissermaßen Blut vergossen, wenn das Gewissen verletzt ist?" Offenbar scheint es ihm hier durchaus möglich, für die Durchsetzung des Handelns auf Gewissensbasis auch in das Dilemma zu geraten, Gewalt anzuwenden. Dass aber jene Bewegungen, die sich später auf Thoreau bezogen haben (vgl. Komitee für Grundrechte und Demokratie 1992), meist gewaltfreie Aktionsgruppen waren, ist dennoch kein Zufall und steht durchaus in Einklang mit den Grundgedanken seiner Schrift. In der Auseinandersetzung mit einer gewaltigen Übermacht sehe er nicht nur die rohe Gewalt, sondern auch die menschliche Macht und halte daher daran fest, „daß ein Appell möglich ist" (Thoreau 1973: 30). Die Steuerverweigerung und die Verweigerung im Allgemeinen sind insgesamt wohl eher als friedliche Reaktionen denn als militante Aktionen zu begreifen. Thoreaus Text durchzieht ein geradezu fröhlich philanthropischer Ton, so beispielsweise wenn er betont, er habe die Steuer verweigert, „denn ich will so gerne ein guter Nachbar sein wie ein schlechter Untertan." (Thoreau 1973: 29)

Thoreau ist in diesem Zusammenhang vor allem genealogischer Bezugspunkt für den einen Pol, für den Diskurs gewaltloser Aktion, wie er etwa das Denken von M. K. Ghandi oder Martin Luther King durchzieht. Nichts steht uns weiter fern, als den anderen Pol, jenen des Terrors, zu verherrlichen. Und dennoch scheint uns eine immanent-involvierte, und dennoch distanzierte Haltung zu diesem dichotomen Gefüge erstrebenswert; nicht nur auf Basis der Erfahrung in den – meist medialen – Ritualen der Abgrenzung „gewaltloser" AktivistInnen von solchen, die sie als gewalttätig verstehen, etwa Black Blocks, sondern auch, weil es die theoretische Unzulänglichkeit einer dichotomen Abgrenzung von Gewaltlosigkeit und Terrorismus nahe legt.

Theoretisch unzulänglich ist diese Dichotomie deswegen, weil die gewaltfreie Aktion erstens nicht selten ihre Kraft – Motivation und Wirksamkeit – aus einer Politik der Viktimisierung zieht, die höchst ambivalent ist: Die Selbstdarstellung der AktivistInnen als Opfer bestimmter Strukturen oder, schlimmer noch, die aktivistische Stellvertretung anderer Opfer, die der moralischen Legitimierung dient, ist vielen gewaltfreien Aktionen immanent. Zweitens folgt aus dieser moralischen Positionierung häufig eine grundsätzliche Gleichsetzung von Gewaltfreiheit und Gerechtigkeit. Selbst aus der Perspektive von Positionen, die das Moralische als eine Dimension des Politischen verstehen, ist keineswegs per se die gewaltfreie Position die gerechtere. VertreterInnen der gewaltfreien Aktion aber agieren häufig aus einer Position moralischer Überlegenheit, die auf nichts gründet. Auf nichts deshalb, weil es den Standpunkt außerhalb der Gewalt, der dafür vorausgesetzt werden muss, nicht gibt.[5]

4. Von Virno ausgehend, muss daran anschließend über ihn hinaus argumentiert werden: Jener Ungehorsam, der ein radikaler wird, „vorausgesetzt, man befreit ihn aus der liberalen Tradition, in der er noch verfangen ist", der „das Vermögen der Befehlsgewalt des Staates selbst infrage" stellt, jener radikale Ungehorsam muss als sozialer Ungehorsam begriffen werden, und das in zweierlei Hinsicht. Erstens geht es darum, soziale Verhältnisse für Motive und Motivationslagen in Anschlag zu bringen. Der soziale Ungehorsam kann unabhängig von den anthropologischen Konstanten konzipiert werden, auf die Virno ihn meint zurückzuführen zu müssen. Denn die zentralen Momente seiner Gegenwartsdiagnose kommen auch ohne die anthropologische Einbettung aus: Virno konstatiert neben der gegenwärtigen Krise der Unterteilung menschlicher Erfahrung in Arbeit, politisches Handeln und Intellekt eine Krise „substanzieller Gemeinschaften". Vor dem Hintergrund dieser mehrfachen Krise seien die Menschen notwendiger Weise auf ihre Basiskompetenzen angewiesen, auf die sprachlich-kognitiven Fähigkeiten. (Vgl. Virno 2005a: 54) In dieser gesteigerten Bedeutung dessen, was er „den öffentlichen Intellekt" oder, nach Marx, General Intellect nennt, sieht Virno eines der Hauptcharakteristika der gegenwärtigen Multitude. Das ist überhaupt der ambivalente Hintergrund, vor dem Virno für zivilen Ungehorsam und Exodus plädiert: die neue Rolle der Intellektualität innerhalb der sozialen Kämpfe. In den postfordistischen sozialen Konflikten wird auch die Rationalisierung des Staates durch eine „Staatswerdung des Intellekts" (Virno 2005a: 93)[6] abgelöst. Dieser gilt es zu widerstehen – oder eben zu (ent)fliehen. Die positive Wendung, die Virno der theoretisch diagnostizierten, neuen gesellschaftlichen Bedeutung des General Intellect gibt, ist zugleich aktivistische Perspektive.

Zweitens ist es darum zu tun, in der Konzeption sozialen Ungehorsams seine implizite Klassendimension aufzubrechen und ihn nicht mehr als nur zivilen, im Sinne von bürgerlichem Ungehorsam (civil disobedience) zu verstehen, der sich auf die Gesetzeskraft und Grammatik des bürgerlichen Staates und damit auf die durch ihn garantierten Eigentums- und heteronormativen Herrschaftsverhältnisse bezieht. Das ist kein abstrakter Einwand, der sich allein gegen den Begriff richtet, sondern er bezieht sich auch auf einen Teil der historischen Praktiken, die in seinem Kontext vollzogen wurden. Denn obwohl im Kontext Entrechteter angewandt – ursprünglich gegen Sklaverei, später in der Schwarzen US-Bürgerrechtsbewegung – ist dem zivilen als bürgerlichem Ungehorsam doch eine exkludierende Dimension immanent: Viele der Aktionen aus der Geschichte zivilen Ungehorsams hatten einen ungebrochen legalistischen Charakter. Nicht selten zielten sie auf die Einhaltung bestehender oder die Durchsetzung noch nicht verankerter Gesetze. Um die ethische ebenso wie die juristische Legitimität ihres Ungehorsams zu demonstrieren, ließen sich AktivistInnen im Anschluss an ihre Aktion häufig verhaften – ein sowohl in der indischen Unabhängigkeitsbewegung als auch in der transnationalen Pflugscharbewegung gängiges Vorgehen.

Von den Konsequenzen allerdings sind die verschiedenen potenziellen TeilnehmerInnen immer unterschiedlich betroffen: Was heute für bürgerliche Mittelstandssubjekte eine Gewissenstat mit heroischem Ausgang sein kann, würde für Menschen ohne legalen Aufenthaltsstatus in eine lebensbedrohliche Situation münden. Ungehorsam wird so mitunter zu einem Privileg. Auch hier zeigt sich, wie unbedingt relational Aktionen zivilen/sozialen Ungehorsams nicht nur anzusetzen, sondern auch zu reflektieren sind. Unterschiedliche soziale Lagen der AkteurInnen und damit die verschiedenen Ausgangspositionen sind in beiderlei Hinsicht entscheidend.

Ein sozialer Ungehorsam, der den gegenwärtigen Verhältnissen gouvernementaler Führung angepasst ist bzw. ihnen sich gerade nicht anpasst und sie fliehen kann, ist letztlich immer konkret, situativ und relational. Was einmal ungehorsam war, kann in einer anderen Situation und innerhalb anderer sozialer Beziehungen auch konformistisch sein und umgekehrt. Und warum soll es gegenwärtig flüchtigen Formen prinzipiell anders ergehen als den ehemals dissidenten Verhaltensweise der 1960er und 1970er Jahre, deren „Selbst-Prekarisierung" (Lorey 2007) heute zu beobachten ist? Selbst der „Überfluss an Wissensformen, Kommunikation, virtuosem gemeinsamen Handeln" (Virno 2005a: 98), für Virno Grundlage des Exodus, ist vor seiner manageriellen Einpassung und/oder maschinischen (Selbst-) Indienstnahmen nicht gefeit.

Literatur:

Bourdieu, Pierre (2001): Die Regeln der Kunst. Genese und Struktur des literarischen Feldes, Frankfurt a. M. (Suhrkamp Verlag).
Bröckling, Ulrich, Susanne Krasmann und Thomas Lemke (Hg.) (2000): Gouvernementalität der Gegenwart. Studien zur Ökonomisierung des Sozialen. Frankfurt a. M. (Suhrkamp Verlag).
Foucault, Michel (1983): Der Wille zum Wissen. Sexualität und Wahrheit I, Franfurt a. M. (Suhrkamp Verlag).
Foucault, Michel (2004): Geschichte der Gouvernementalität I. Sicherheit, Territorium, Bevölkerung, Frankfurt a. M. (Suhrkamp Verlag).
Kastner, Jens (2008): (Was heißt) Gegen-Verhalten im Neoliberalismus?, in: Hechler, Daniel und Axel Philipps (Hg.): Widerstand denken. Michel Foucault und die Grenzen der Macht, Bielefeld (transcript Verlag), S. 39-56.
Komitee für Grundrechte und Demokratie (Hg.) (1992): Ziviler Ungehorsam. Traditionen, Konzepte, Erfahrungen, Perspektiven, Sensbachtal (Komitee für Grundrechte und Demokratie e. V.).
Lazzarato, Maurizio (2008): Nachwort, in: Raunig, Gerald: Tausend Maschinen. Eine kleine Philosophie der Maschine als sozialer Bewegung, Wien (Verlag Turia+Kant), S. 111-125.
Lemke, Thomas (1997): Eine Kritik der politischen Vernunft. Foucaults Analyse der modernen Gouvernementalität. Berlin/ Hamburg (Argument Verlag).
Lorey, Isabell (1996): Immer Ärger mit dem Subjekt. Theoretische und politische Konsequenzen eines juridischen Machtmodells: Judith Butler, Tübingen (edition diskord), S. 49-70.
Lorey, Isabell (2007): „Vom immanenten Widerspruch zur hegemonialen Funktion. Biopolitische Gouvernementalität und Selbst-Prekarisierung von KulturproduzentInnen", in: Gerald Raunig und Ulf Wuggenig (Hg.), Kritik der Kreativität, Wien (Verlag Turia+Kant), S. 121-136.
Negri, Antonio und Michael Hardt (1997): Die Arbeit des Dionysos. Materialistische Staatskritik in der Postmoderne, Berlin und Amsterdam (Edition ID Archiv).
Pieper, Marianne und Encarnación Gutiérrez Rodriguez (Hg.) (2003): Gouvernementalität. Ein sozialwissenschaftliches Konzept im Anschluss an Foucault, Frankfurt a. M. (Campus Verlag).
Raunig, Gerald (2008): Tausend Maschinen. Eine kleine Philosophie der Maschine als sozialer Bewegung, Wien (Verlag Turia+Kant).
Thoreau, Henry David (1973): Über die Pflicht zum Ungehorsam gegen den Staat, in: ders.: Über die Pflicht zum Ungehorsam gegen den Staat und andere Essays, Zürich (Diogenes Verlag), S. 7-35.
Virno, Paolo (2005a): Grammatik der Multitude. Öffentlichkeit, Intellekt und Arbeit als Lebensform, Wien (Verlag Turia und Kant).
Virno, Paolo (2005b): Motto di spirito e azione innovativa. Per una logica del cambiamento, Torino (Bollati Boringhieri).
Virno, Paolo (2007): „Anthropologie und Theorie der Institutionen", http://eipcp.net/transversal/0407/virno/de

1   Lorey diskutiert in einer kritischen Analyse der frühen Theorie Judith Butlers deren juridisch verkürztes Machtmodell.
2   Der Essay ist 2008 auch auf Englisch erschienen in: Multitude between Innovation and Negation, Los Angeles/New York (Semiotext(e)).
3   Vgl. zu einer ähnlichen Figur auch Pierre Bourdieu (2001: 68): Nach Bourdieu funktionieren gesellschaftliche Felder nur dadurch, dass der Glauben an ihre Funktionsweise in den Habitus der Akteurinnen und Akteure eingeschrieben ist. Diesen Glauben an das Spiel nennt Bourdieu die illusio. Die Verweigerung der illusio gesellschaftlicher Felder ist demnach ein Angriff auf den Glauben an das Spiel.
4   „Was unsere Art gefährlich macht, ist auch das, was es ihr ermöglicht, innovative Handlungen zu vollbringen, die dazu dienen, gefestigte Normen und Gewohnheiten zu verändern."

5   „(U)nsere Komplizenschaft", schreiben Antonio Negri und Michael Hardt, „ist eine Bedingung unserer gesellschaftlichen Existenz." (Negri/Hardt 1997: 156) Im Anschluss an Foucaults Idee einer „Anarchäologie", die keine Macht als notwendiger Weise akzeptabel oder inakzeptabel ansieht, und in Anlehnung an Walter Benjamins Vorstellung einer reinen oder revolutionären Gewalt, die in ihren Wirkungen auf nichts ihr Äußerliches zielt, also keinen Repräsentationsanspruch hat (und auch die Macht nicht übernehmen will), entwickeln Negri/Hardt ihr Konzept der „konstituierenden Macht". Diese enthält keine Botschaft, keine Darstellung, keine Stellvertretung: Für den sozialen Ungehorsam ist sie eine Möglichkeit, denn sie ist, laut Negri/Hardt, beseelt von produktiver Kooperation und der immateriellen und affektiven Arbeit, die ein „Netzwerk der Selbstverwertung" (Negri/Hardt 1997: 159) schafft.
6   Hier, stellt Virno fest, erhielte der alte Ausdruck der Staatsräson erstmals eine nicht-metaphorische Bedeutung.

Offensive Flight instead of Breaking the Law

On Civil Disobedience in View of the Thoreauvian Imperative

Jens Kastner and Gerald Raunig

> "Civil disobedience" represents, perhaps, the fundamental form of political action of the multitude, provided that the multitude is emancipated from the liberal tradition within which it is encapsulated. It is not a matter of ignoring a specific law because it appears incoherent or contradictory to other fundamental norms, for example to the constitutional charter. In such case, in fact, reluctance would signal only a deeper loyalty to state control. Conversely, the radical disobedience which concerns us here casts doubt on the State's actual ability to control.
> Paolo Virno, A Grammar of the Multitude (2004: 69)

If the law is structured in such a way that it turns its subjects into accomplices to injustice toward others, then the Thoreauvian imperative is "break the law." So far, so good, apparently. On closer inspection, however, this picture and its conditions become gray to the point of complete opacity. The both great and apparently clear motto of Henry David Thoreau (1817–62) for the civil disobedience of the past is no solution for the present.

Henry David Thoreau's famous pamphlet against "civil government" was written as a justification. In July 1846 he was arrested and jailed in Concord, Massachusetts (he was, however, released the following day when, against his will, his aunt paid his bail). The reason for his arrest was unpaid taxes. In order to make it clear that this act of omission was by no means due to a whim or negligence but on the contrary to profound conviction, Thoreau wrote the text known as "Civil Disobedience," though first published under the title "Resistance to Civil Government" in 1849, which would become so important for social movements of the next hundred and fifty years. In it Thoreau developed his radically individualistic conception of disobedience in resistance to two specific forms that were legitimated and/or practiced by the state. The first was slavery, which in Thoreau's lifetime was still legal in the United States. The second was war, specifically the one that the United States was fighting against Mexico between 1846 and 1848 as a war of conquest: "[W]hen a sixth of the population of a nation which has undertaken to be the refuge of liberty are slaves, and a whole country is unjustly overrun and conquered by a foreign army, and subjected to military law, I think that it is not too soon for honest men to rebel and revolutionize." (Thoreau 1986: 389)

Although Thoreau's explanation referred to the specific situation in which he found himself, both reasons for his decisions represent structural phenomena of societies organized as states: the deprivation of rights or dehumanization of individuals and war. When he explained these structural conditions as motives and motivations for disobedient behavior, he also ceased to link the question which law is affirmed by the individual no longer the direct affection by this law. Not only making or obeying a law but also not taking action against it can make individuals responsible for the injustice done to many. Even though he is speaking of the reasons for a rebellion, Thoreau is thinking here in moral terms. He is concerned with the moral decisions of individuals. This dimension was later expanded by figures as different as Leo Tolstoy and the English Suffragette movement and turned into a means of social and political struggle by introducing the concept of "passive resistance."

The fact that Thoreau's conception from the nineteenth century is very much derived from the position of the individual, and hence contrasts with collective ideas of disobedience, is not the focus of our critique. A contemporary discussion of the problems of civil disobedience will shed light on precisely the kinds of subjectivation that try to thwart the apparent contradiction between individual moral problems and collective politicizing. What follows beyond that are four aspects of taking Thoreau's imperative to break the law further in productive ways, all of which we see, both theoretically and practically, as central components of any contemporary idea of disobedience.

1. First, any critical updating of this imperative must recognize that it appears to work on a structure that is no longer the sole center of power—or perhaps never was. Its fixation on the legal apparatus homogenizes power relationships and hence in no small measure the strategic possibilities of resistance. (Cf. Foucault 1990: 102; Lorey 1996: 49–70.)[1] Justice and law (and their constant connection to the form of the state) should be understood, and not only in the evolution of neoliberal capitalism, as functions of a broader power structure that Foucault has aptly labeled "governmentality." Already in the eighteenth and nineteenth centuries, a form of government had gained acceptance that did not function solely by means of the ruler's repression and sovereignty. This government used the logic of autonomy and property to implement a relationship of individuals vis-à-vis themselves that turns entire populations into "biopolitical" subjects. (Cf. Foucault 2004; Lemke 1997: 126ff.; Bröckling, Krasmann, and Lemke 2000; Pieper and Gutiérrez Rodríguez 2003; Lorey 2007: 125–26.) That means that in addition to legal and political structures and the legal status of the subject (as at once sovereign and subjugated), a machinic form of self-exploitation evolved that permeates the living and working conditions of the subjects and makes them all the more governable (cf. Raunig 2008, Lazzarato 2008). Within the setting of neoliberal governmentality, this interwoven quality of social subjugation and machinic self-exploitation should be understood equally as a multiple complicity and as a source of new forms for what Foucault labeled counter-conduct rather than resistance (cf. Kastner 2008). In this context, the concept of disobedience becomes fruitful again—and we will return to this later. Here, however, it should first be noted that a reduced focus on the law, justice, and the state appears to be neither theoretically sufficient nor relevant to current practices of disobedience.

2. But first let's interpret the terms "the law" and "justice" more fundamentally than as the legal constitution of a state. Let's attempt to break open Foucault's juridical dispositive to the point where it touches on the field that for Foucault embraces the strategic and productive aspect of power. Let's view "the law" as a grammar, on which all social and linguistic, discursive and nondiscursive relationships are based. If we pursue such an expansion of the legal apparatus, we first run into the problem of the metaphor of breaking the law, which Thoreau proposed as a solution.

A grammar cannot be "broken." As Paolo Virno has shown in A Grammar of the Multitude (2004), the way out lies not in breaking as a negation or a dialectical form of resistance but precisely in a combination of radical disobedience and exodus—that is, as offensive, collective flight. In his most recent text on jokes and innovation, Virno (2005)[2] makes an analogy between this figure of the exodus and the linguistic-communicative strategies of the sudden change of subject in a conversation that follows well-structured paths such as, above all, the joke that makes use of a linguistic ambiguity. In the political field, this deviation is manifested as a collective defection from the state, as secession, as exodus. Hence it is matter of a nondialectical form of negation and resistance, or better: of defection and fleeing. It is not only about designing new moves, tactics to outplay the opponent, but about an attack on the rules, on faith in the game itself.[3] Or, as Virno puts it, about an invention that "alters the rules of the game and throws the adversary completely off balance" (2004: 70).

The postworkerist line of the concept of exodus, even though it does no longer dream of an entirely other outside, should by no means be understood as harmless, individualistic, or escapist and esoteric. This exodic form of resistance is a positive, offensive, dangerous form of defection (cf. Virno 2007).[4] Rather than presuming that power relationships represent an unshakable horizon and nevertheless struggling against them, flight alters the conditions underwhich the presumption is made. The exodus, as A Grammar of the Multitude explains, transforms the context in which a problem emerged rather than addressing the problem by choosing between predetermined alternatives. As the nonpassive, nondialectical, nonindividualist form of defection, it opens up a way out not shown on the maps of the legal apparatus that can "modify the very 'grammar' which determines the selection of all possible choices" (Virno 2008). In flight, which also constitutes something new, a modification of the grammar results. Not law but grammar, not breaking the law but flight "from the law."

3. Against this backdrop, after all, it is possible to reformulate the problem that, as a dichotomous figure of violence and nonviolence has unproductively dominated many historical and current discussions of activism and social movements.

Thoreau himself did not raise the question of violence because he did not think of civil disobedience as a collective and/or political strategy. The revolution will have won, in his view, if the subjects refuse to obey and the civil servants resign their offices. "But even suppose," Thoreau wrote, "blood should flow. Is there not a sort of blood shed when the conscience is wounded?" (Thoreau 1986: 399). Apparently it seemed to him here quite possible to get caught up in the dilemma of using violence to achieve an action on a moral basis. It is, however, no coincidence that most of the action groups that later referred to Thoreau (cf. Komitee für Grundrechte und Demokratie 1992) were nonviolent, and nonviolence certainly accords with the basic ideas of his text. In the conflict with a violent superior power, he saw only raw violence but also human power and therefore noted that "appeal is possible" (Thoreau 1986: 408). Refusal to pay taxes and refusal in general can more easily be understood as peaceful reactions than as militant actions. There is an almost cheerfully philanthropic tone running through Thoreau's text—for example, when he emphasizes that he refused to pay taxes because "I am as desirous of being a good neighbor as I am of being a bad subject" (Thoreau 1986: 407).

In this context Thoreau represents above all a genealogical point of reference for one pole, for the discourse on nonviolent action that runs, though for example, the thought of M. K. Ghandi or Martin Luther King. The last thing we wish to do is glorify the opposite pole, that of terror. And yet it seems to us that an immanent, involved, and yet distanced attitude to this dichotomous structure is desirable; not only on the basis of the experience of the rituals—usually in the media—of distinguishing "nonviolent" activists from those who see themselves as violent, such as Black Blocks, but also because it is suggested by the theoretical inadequacy of a dichotomous distinction between nonviolence and terrorism.

This dichotomy is theoretically inadequate, first, because nonviolent action not infrequently derives its power—its motivation and effectiveness—from a politics of victimization that is highly ambivalent: the self-depiction of activists as victims of certain structures or, even worse, as activist representatives of other victims who serve as moral legitimation, is immanent in many nonviolent actions. Second, from this moral position follows a fundamental equation of nonviolence and justice. Even from the perspective of positions that understand the moral as a dimension of the political, the nonviolent position is by no means per se the most just. However, representatives of nonviolent action often operate from a position of moral superiority that has no basis. It has no basis because the standpoint outside of violence that it necessarily presupposes does not exist.[5]

4. Setting out from Virno, however, it becomes necessary to argue beyond him: every civil disobedience that becomes radical, "provided that [it] is emancipated from the liberal tradition within which it is encapsulated," casts doubt "on the State's actual ability to control"; this sort of radical disobedience has to be understood as social disobedience, and in two respects. First, the point is to take aim at social relationships for motives and motivation. Social disobedience can be conceived of independently of the anthropological constants to which Virno believes he has to trace them back. For the central aspects of his diagnosis of the present can get by without embedding them in anthropology as he does: in addition to the present crisis of the division of human experience into labor, political action, and intellect, Virno sees a crisis of "substantial communities." Against the backdrop of this multiple crisis, people are necessarily thrown back on their basic competence, on their linguistic and cognitive abilities. (Cf. Virno 2004: 41.) Virno sees one of the main characteristics of today's multitude in this increased significance of what he calls "public intellect" or, following Marx, general intellect. That is the ambivalent background against which Virno argues for civil disobedience and exodus: the new role of the intellectualism in social struggles. In post-Fordist social conflicts, the rationalization of the state is replaced by a "statization [statizzazione] of the Intellect" (Virno 2004: 67).[6] The latter has to be resisted—or fled. The positive turn that Virno gives to the theoretically diagnosed, new social significance of the general intellect is also an activist perspective.

Second, it is necessary to break open the class dimension implicit in the conception of social disobedience and not longer understand it as civil in the sense of bourgeois disobedience, which refers to the legal force and grammar of the civil society and hence to the power relationships based on property and heteronormativity that it guarantees. That is not an abstract objection directed only at the concept; rather, it also refers to one aspect of the historical practices that have come to pass in that context. For although it was originally applied in the context of deprivation of rights—specifically, against slavery and later in the civil rights movement for black in the United States—there is an exclusive dimension inherent in civil disobedience: many of the actions in the history of civil disobedience had an undiminished legalist character. Not infrequently, they were aimed at preserving existing laws or putting through new ones. In order to demonstrate the ethical and legal legitimacy of their disobedience, the activists often allowed themselves to be arrested following their action—a common occurrence both in the independence movement in India and in the transnational Ploughshare movement.

The various potential participants are, however, affected differently by the consequences of this: something that for middle-class participants can represent an act of conscience with a heroic ending can lead to a life-threatening situation for people who are not legal residents. Disobedience thus becomes a privilege. Once again this demonstrates how definitely relational actions of civil or social disobedience should not simply be set but also reflected on. The different social statuses of the participants and hence their different starting positions are crucial in both respects.

A social disobedience that is not adapted to the current relationships of governmentalist rule or does not adapt to it and is able to flee it is ultimately always concrete, situational, and relational. What was once disobedient can in another situation and within other social relationships be conformist, and vice versa. And why should it be fundamentally different for present, ephemeral forms than for the once dissident conducts of the 1960s and 1970s whose "self-precarization" (Lorey 2007) is obvious today? Even "the surplus of knowledge, communication, virtuosic acting in concert" (Virno 2004: 71), which for Virno is the basis for exodus, is not immune to managerial conformity and/or machinic (self-)exploitation.

Translated from the German by Steven Lindberg

Literature:

Bourdieu, Pierre (1996): The rules of art: Genesis and structure of the literary field, Palo Alto, CA (Stanford Univ. Press).
Bröckling, Ulrich, Susanne Krasmann, and Thomas Lemke (eds.) (2000): Gouvernementalität der Gegenwart: Studien zur Ökonomisierung des Sozialen, Frankfurt a. M. (Suhrkamp Verlag).
Foucault, Michel (1990): The will to knowledge, London (Penguin Books).
Foucault, Michel (2004): Sécurité, territoire, population: Cours au Collège de France, 1977–1978. Paris (Seuil).
Kastner, Jens (2008): (Was heißt) Gegen-Verhalten im Neoliberalismus? in: Hechler Daniel, and Axel Philipps (eds.): Widerstand denken: Michel Foucault und die Grenzen der Macht, Bielefeld (transcript Verlag), pp. 39–56.
Komitee für Grundrechte und Demokratie (ed.) (1992): Ziviler Ungehorsam: Traditionen, Konzepte, Erfahrungen, Perspektiven, Sensbachtal (Komitee für Grundrechte und Demokratie e. V.).
Lazzarato, Maurizio (2008): Nachwort, in: Raunig, Gerald: Tausend Maschinen: Eine kleine Philosophie der Maschine als sozialer Bewegung, Vienna (Verlag Turia+Kant), pp. 111-25.
Lemke, Thomas (1997): Eine Kritik der politischen Vernunft: Foucaults Analyse der modernen Gouvernementalität, Berlin (Argument Verlag).
Lorey, Isabell (1996): Immer Ärger mit dem Subjekt: Theoretische und politische Konsequenzen eines juridischen Machtmodells: Judith Butler, Tübingen (edition diskord), pp. 49-70.
Lorey, Isabell (2007): Vom immanenten Widerspruch zur hegemonialen Funktion: Biopolitische Gouvernementalität und Selbst-Prekarisierung von KulturproduzentInnen, in: Raunig, Gerald, and Ulf Wuggenig (eds.): Kritik der Kreativität, Vienna (Verlag Turia+Kant), pp. 121-136.
Negri, Antonio, and Michael Hardt (1994): Labor of Dionysus: A critique of the state-form. Minneapolis (Univ. of Minnesota Press).
Pieper, Marianne, and Encarnación Gutíerrez Rodriguez (eds.) (2003): Gouvernementalität: Ein sozialwissenschaftliches Konzept im Anschluss an Foucault, Frankfurt a. M. (Campus Verlag).

Zanny Begg

Lebt und arbeitet / lives and works in Sydney

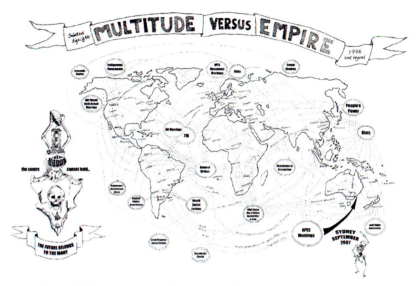

„The Agitators" (2007), Bilderserie in Öl auf Pappe mit Papprahmen

In der Bilderserie „The Agitators" (2007) hat Zanny Begg politische AktivistInnen porträtiert. Die Gemälde lehnen sich stilistisch deutlich an die Bildnisse des Renaissance-Malers Hans Holbein an, gemalt sind sie auf einem recht gegenwärtigen Material, das weniger Zeichen von Hoch- als von Alltagskultur ist: Pappe. Schon in „Glass Half Full" (2006) hatte Zanny Begg in Öl gemalte Porträts an handliche Dachlatten montiert, und auf diese Weise ein klassisches Demo-Utensil mit einem nicht weniger klassischen künstlerischen Medium kombiniert. Diese Verknüpfung der Medien und Methoden zeichnet das gesamte Werk der Künstlerin aus. Dabei entsteht mehr als die (heute so oft gepriesene) Vielfalt künstlerischer Mittel: In den Arbeiten Beggs kommt es zu außergewöhnlichen ästhetisch-politischen Überlappungen. In deren Zeichen steht auch das Aufgreifen der im italienischen Operaismus praktizierten Methode der „militanten Untersuchung", um die kunstimmanente Frage nach der Einbeziehung der BetrachterInnen zu beantworten. Gemeinsam mit AktivistInnen hat Begg auch verschiedene Formate wie Poster, Buttons und Aufkleber entwickelt und dabei gängige Muster von Protestgrafik praktisch hinterfragt. Mit Oliver Ressler hat sie einen Film zu den globalisierungskritischen Bewegungen von Heiligendamm 2007 gemacht und bereits 2005 war sie als Kuratorin (mit David McNeill) einer Ausstellung mit dem Titel „Disobedience" (Sydney, 2005) tätig. JK

http://www.zannybegg.com

KünstlerInnen/Artists

Raunig, Gerald (2008): Tausend Maschinen: Eine kleine Philosophie der Maschine als sozialer Bewegung, Vienna (Verlag Turia+Kant).
Thoreau, Henry David (1986): Walden and Civil disobedience, New York (Penguin).
Virno, Paolo (2004): A grammar of the multitude: For an analysis of contemporary forms of life, Los Angeles (Semiotext(e)).
Virno, Paolo (2007): "Anthropology and Theory of Institutions," http://eipcp.net/transversal/0407/virno/en (May 4, 2008).
Virno, Paolo (2008): Multitude between Innovation and Negation, Los Angeles (Semiotext(e)).

1   In a critical analysis of Judith Butler's early theory, Lorey discusses her reductively juridical model of power.
2   "Wit and Innovative Action," published in Virno 2008.
3   On a similar figure, see also Pierre Bourdieu (1996: 68): According to Bourdieu, social fields function because faith in their functioning is inscribed in the behavior of their participants. Bourdieu calls this faith in the game the illusio. Refusing the illusio of social fields is thus an attack on the faith in the game.
4   "The dangerousness of our species is coextensive with its capacity to accomplish innovative actions, that is actions which are capable of modifying established habits and norms."
5   "[O]ur complicity," write Antonio Negri and Michael Hardt, "is a condition of our social existence" (Negri and Hardt 1994: 291). Taking up Foucault's idea of an "anarchaeology," which does not consider any power as necessarily acceptable or unacceptable, and Benjamin's idea of a pure or revolutionary violence whose effects are not aimed at anything outside itself, and hence has not claim to representation (and also has no desire to take over power), Negri and Hardt developed their concept of "constitutive power." It has no message, no depiction, no representation. It represents an opportunity for social disobedience because it is, according to Negri and Hardt, brought to life by productive cooperation and immaterial and affective work that creates a "network of self-valorization" (Negri and Hardt 1994: 294).
6   Virno notes that the old expression of raison d'état acquires here for the first time a nonmetaphorical meaning.

"The Agitators" (2007), series of paintings, oil on cardboard, cardboard frames

Zanny Begg's series of paintings entitled "The Agitators" (2007) consists of portraits of political activists. In stylistic terms, the paintings clearly emulate the works of the Renaissance painter Hans Holbein; yet they are executed on a fairly contemporary material, one that gestures toward everyday life rather than high culture: cardboard. In "Glass Half Full" (2006), Zanny Begg had already mounted portraits in oil on handy laths, combining a classical street-protest utensil with a no less classical artistic medium. Such conjunctions of media and methods are characteristic of the artist's entire oeuvre. What results is more than the variety of artistic means so often praised these days: Begg's works present moments of extraordinary overlap between aesthetics and politics. The latter returns in her adoption of the method of "militant examination" practiced in Italian Operaism, deployed to resolve the art-immanent question of the involvement of the beholder. In collaboration with activists, Begg also developed various formats such as posters, buttons, and stickers, critically interrogating established patterns in protest graphic design. Together with Oliver Ressler, she made a film about the anti-globalization movements at Heiligendamm in 2007; already in 2005, she was curator (with David McNeill) of an exhibition entitled "Disobedience" (Sydney, 2005). *JK*

http://www.zannybegg.com

Heath Bunting

Lebt und arbeitet / lives and works in Bristol (GB)

„BorderXing Guide" (2001)

Heath Bunting gilt als einer der Pioniere netzbasierter Kunst. Von 1994 bis1997 hat er fast ausschließlich für und mit dem Medium Internet gearbeitet. Sein Interesse gilt offenen, demokratischen Kommunikationssystemen und sozialen Kontexten. In seinen Arbeiten setzt er sich häufig mit Bereichen der Information und Kommunikation auseinander, die entweder als privat oder als kontrolliert gelten und die er durch seine Interventionen in den öffentlichen Bereich überführt.

    Heath Buntings Werke sind geprägt von einer widerständigen Haltung, die als individuelle Form zivilen Ungehorsams gelesen werden kann. Mit seinen Arbeiten bewegt er sich oft im Grenzbereich der Legalität und verstößt mitunter bewusst gegen (unsinnige) Gesetze.

    „BorderXing Guide" (2001) ist eine netzbasierte Arbeit, die die Thematik der Migration aufgreift und sich gleichzeitig gegen die biopolitische Kontrolle durch Nationalstaaten richtet. „BorderXing Guide" besteht aus Plänen von Grenzverläufen und enthält Empfehlungen, an welchen Stellen diese Grenzen am besten unbemerkt überschritten werden können. Das Besondere an dieser „Netzkunstarbeit" liegt in ihrem hybriden Charakter: Die Informationen können nicht einfach aus dem Internet heruntergeladen werden, sondern nur bei von Bunting autorisierten Distributionsstellen wie Internetcafés oder Ausstellungsräumen. Dieser physische Aspekt ist bei aller Widersprüchlichkeit charakteristisch für Bunting, der nicht nur der Begründer zahlreicher Netzkunst-Bewegungen, sondern auch vieler, wie er es nennt, Sport-Kunst-Bewegungen ist.

    Wie eine Reihe anderer Künstler, die sich früh mit Netzkunst und den künstlerischen Handlungsmöglichkeiten im Cyberspace auseinandergesetzt haben, hat er sich in letzter Zeit vermehrt biopolitischen Themen und Genetik zugewandt, die er als das „neue Medium" bezeichnet.

    Bunting ist unter anderem Mitbegründer von „irrational.org" und dem „cybercafe" in London und hat an der Documenta X (1997), auf der erstmals Netzkunst präsentiert wurde, teilgenommen. *EBS*

http://www.irrational.org

„BorderXing Guide" (2001)

Heath Bunting is considered one of the pioneers of net-based art. Between 1994 and 1997, he worked almost exclusively with the medium Internet. His main interest is in open and democratic systems of communication and social contexts. His works often engage areas of information and communication that are regarded as either private or controlled; through his interventions, he transposes them into the public sphere.

Heath Bunting's works are characterized by a refractory attitude that can be read as an individual form of civil disobedience. They often work on the margins of legality and occasionally commit deliberate infractions against (nonsensical) laws.

"BorderXing Guide" (2001) is a net-based work that takes up the issue of migration and at the same time protests against the biopolitical control exercised by nation-states. "BorderXing Guide" consists of maps of international borders and contains recommendations as to where these borders can most easily be crossed without drawing attention. What is particular about this "work of net art" is its hybrid character: the information cannot be simply downloaded from the Internet; it is available only through clients authorized by Bunting, including Internet cafés and exhibition spaces. Contradictory as it seems, this physical aspect is characteristic of Bunting's work, who is the founder not only of numerous net art movements but also of many, as he calls it, sport-art movements.

Like a number of other artists who engaged net art and the possibilities of artistic action in cyberspace early on, he has in recent years increasingly turned toward issues of biopolitics and genetics, which he calls the "new medium."

Among other things, Bunting is a co-founder of "irrational.org" and "cybercafe" (London) and participated in Documenta X (1997), the first Documenta to present net art. *EBS*

http://www.irrational.org

Bureau of Inverse Technology

Das Bureau of Inverse Technology definiert sich selbst ironisch-parodistisch als „information agency servicing the Information Age". Das 1991 von Natalie Jeremijenko, Kate Rich und Daniela Tigani gegründete Techno-Art-Kollektiv bedient sich moderner, handelsüblicher Kommunikations- und Informationstechnologien sowie Guerilla-Taktiken, um auf die wirtschaftlichen wie militärischen Interessen, die technologische Entwicklungen vorantreiben, hinzuweisen.

Die zunächst jahrelang von BIT aufrecht erhaltene Anonymität war Teil einer Strategie, um auf die Anonymität der technischen Produktion aufmerksam zu machen. Die bewusste Referenz auf „bureau" (Büro) reproduziert und parodiert gleichzeitig bürokratische, kommerzielle Strukturen. Diese Taktik wird von BIT zur Verschleierung und kalkulierten Irreführung in Bezug auf die Frage, was das Bureau of Inverse Technology eigentlich ist und macht, eingesetzt.

Durch einfache Umbauten und technische Adaptionen führen sie bestehende Technologien und häufig auch Überwachungssysteme einem neuen, oft subversiven und von den Erzeugerfirmen nicht erwünschten Verwendungszweck zu. „Bit Plane" zum Beispiel ist ein mit einer Spionagekamera ausgerüstetes ferngesteuertes Modellflugzeug. Bei einem Flug über das Silicon Valley, in dem absolutes Film- und Fotoverbot herrscht, hat das Flugzeug ein illegales Spionagevideo aufgezeichnet. „Bit Rocket" wiederum adaptiert am Markt erhältliche Hobbyraketen zu drahtlosen Mikro-Überwachungssystemen und kann zum Beispiel bei Demonstrationen eingesetzt werden, um die TeilnehmerInnenzahl zu erheben.

Neben einer Vielzahl weiterer Produkte, die die aktivistische Praxis erleichtern und unterstützen, umfasst das „Angebot" des Bureau of Inverse Technology auch Wirtschaftsindizes wie den „despondency index" (Verzweiflungsindex): eine Verknüpfung der Selbstmordrate mit der Entwicklung des Dow Jones als zynische Parallele zum Kursmesser der Börse. *EBS*

http://www.bureauit.org

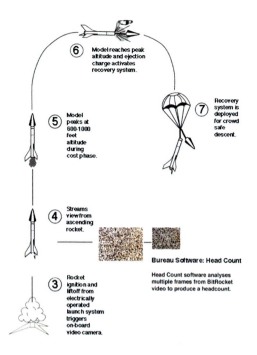

The Bureau of Inverse Technology defines itself, with much irony and parody, as an "information agency servicing the Information Age." Founded by Natalie Jeremijenko, Kate Rich, and Daniela Tigani, this techno-art collective uses commercially available modern communication and information technology as well as guerilla tactics in order to reveal the economic and military interests that drive technological development.

For the first years of its existence, BIT maintained its anonymity, as part of a strategy to draw attention to the anonymity of technical production. The deliberate reference to "bureau" reproduces and simultaneously parodies bureaucratic commercial structures. BIT uses this tactic in order to conceal, and even purposely mislead the public with respect to, what the Bureau of Inverse Technology actually is and does.

With simple modifications and technical adaptations, they employ existing technology, frequently including surveillance systems, toward new and often subversive purposes not intended by their corporate producers. "Bit Plane," for instance, is a remote-controlled model plane equipped with an espionage camera. During a flight through Silicon Valley, where any filming and photographing is strictly prohibited, the plane recorded an illegal espionage video. "Bit Rocket," by contrast, adapts commercially available hobby rockets to create wireless micro-surveillance systems, which can be used e.g. to assess the number of participants at a demonstration.

Besides a number of other appliances that facilitate and support activist practices, the Bureau of Inverse Technology's "product range" also includes economic indices such as the "despondency index": linking the suicide rate to the movements of the Dow Jones Index, it presents a cynical parallel to this stock market indicator. *EBS*

http://www.bureauit.org

Büro Bildwechsel (Sandy Kaltenborn/Pierre Maite)

Leben und arbeiten in Berlin / live and work in Berlin

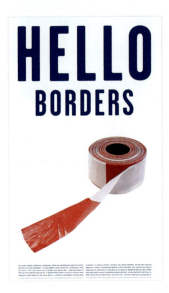 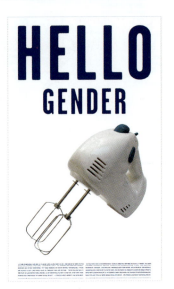

Diverse Plakate (2006-2008)

„Ichstreik. Prekarität, Arbeit und Alltag" – eine Losung, die zu ungehorsamem Verhalten ebenso aufruft wie darüber sinniert. Platziert war sie auf dem Plakat einer Serie, die das Büro Bildwechsel (image-shift) zum Mayday 2008, der Mobilisierung des so genannten Prekariats zum 1. Mai in enger Zusammenarbeit mit dem Maydaybündnis entworfen hatte.

    Das Büro Bildwechsel existiert nunmehr seit zehn Jahren. Kommunikations- und Grafik-Design stehen hier im Zeichen sozialer und politischer Kämpfe und Diskurse, sowohl politische Initiativen als auch soziale und kulturelle Institutionen gehören zu ihren AuftraggeberInnen. Kaltenborn und Maite entwickeln grafische Lösungen nicht nur zu bestimmten Anlässen wie Veranstaltungen, Festivals oder politischen Kampagnen. Auch Bücher, Plakate und Webseiten gehören zu ihren Arbeiten, die häufig in enger Zusammenarbeit mit ihren jeweiligen „KundInnen" entstehen. Sie verstehen ihre angewandte Kunst nicht als Dienstleistung, sondern als Teil einer kommunikativen Praxis. Gestaltung wird hier immer als ein gesellschaftliches Gestalten begriffen. Deren ambivalente Funktion wird immer schon mit reflektiert, mit der Adressangabe „Büro für Gestaltung und weitere Unwegbarkeiten" sprechen Bildwechsel/image-shift gleichsam sich selbst und die anderen an, ohne übertriebenes Vertrauen in gegenseitiges Verständnis. Als Zeichen des Bewusstseins gegenüber den eigenen Verwobenheiten, findet sich in einer Bildergalerie auf der Homepage neben der Werbung für den legalen Aufenthaltsstatus von Flüchtlingen auch ein buntes Kärtchen mit der Aufschrift „Trust me, I'm a Designer". JK

    http://www.image-shift.net
    Literatur: Sandy K. (2002): Just Posters, Stuttgart (Edition Schloß Solitude).

 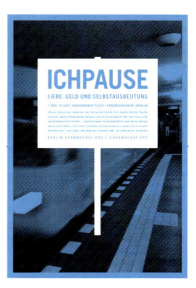

Various posters (2006-2008)

"Ichstreik. Prekarität, Arbeit und Alltag" ["Ego on Strike. Precarity, Work, and Everyday Life"]—a slogan that both calls for and muses about disobedient behavior. It was prominently displayed on a poster from a series designed by Büro Bildwechsel [image-shift] for Mayday 2008, the mobilization of the so-called precariat on May 1, in close collaboration with the Mayday coalition.

Büro Bildwechsel has now existed for ten years. Its work in communications and graphic design focuses on social and political struggles and discourses; its clients include both political initiatives and social and cultural institutions. Kaltenborn and Maite develop graphical solutions not only for specific occasions such as events, festivals, and political campaigns. Their work also includes books, posters, and web sites, which are often created in close collaboration with their respective "customers." They see their applied art not as a service but as part of a communicative practice, always emphasizing the socially constructive aspect of design and always already reflecting on its ambivalent function: calling themselves an "office for design and other inviabilities," Bildwechsel [image-shift] address, as it were, themselves and their others without unwarranted faith in mutual understanding. As a sign of their awareness of their own entanglements, the picture gallery on their homepage includes, besides an ad for the legalization of refugees, a colorful postcard inscribed "Trust me, I'm a Designer." *JK*

http://www.image-shift.net
Literature: Sandy K. (2002): Just Posters, Stuttgart (Edition Schloß Solitude)

Critical Art Ensemble

Germs of Deception (Bakterien der Täuschung), 2006

Critical Art Ensemble (CAE) ist ein Kollektiv von KünstlerInnen mit unterschiedlichen Schwerpunkten, deren Arbeit an der Schnittstelle zwischen Kunst, Technologie, radikaler Politik und kritischer Theorie angesiedelt ist. Es hat seit den 1980er Jahren maßgeblich zur Theoriebildung des elektronischen zivilen Ungehorsams beigetragen. In wegweisenden Publikationen wie „The Electronic Disturbance", „Civil Electronic Disobedience and Other Unpopular Ideas" und „Digital Resistance", die im Verlag Autonomedia erschienen sind und gleichzeitig auf der Website des CAE zum freien Download angeboten werden, haben sie wie niemand sonst die Bedingungen für zivilen Ungehorsam unter den veränderten Vorzeichen in einer neoliberalen, hochtechnologisierten Gesellschaft analysiert. Das Kollektiv bedient sich einer Reihe unterschiedlicher Medien wie z. B. Computergrafik, Webdesign, Film/Video, Fotografie, Texte, Bücher und Performances. Sie haben eine Vielzahl von Projekten durchgeführt, von denen einige im Museum, andere auf der Straße oder im Internet stattgefunden haben. In den letzten Jahren hat sich das Kollektiv, allen voran eines der Gründungsmitglieder, Steve Kurtz, Fragen der Biopolitik und -ethik zugewandt und in Aufsehen erregenden Arbeiten wie z. B. „The Marching Plague" Mythen der Biotechnologie im Hinblick auf biologische Kampfstoffe und Kriegsführung untersucht. Die Grundthese des CAE ist, dass die „Bereitschaft" zur biologischen Kriegsführung ein Euphemismus für die Entwicklung biologischer Kriegstechnologie und die zunehmende Militarisierung des öffentlichen Bereichs ist. Die wahre Bedrohung gehe demnach nicht von als Waffen eingesetzten Bakterien aus, sondern von den Institutionen, die von dieser Bewaffnung profitieren.

Steve Kurtz wurde wegen seiner Experimente mit harmlosen Bakterien, die für „The Marching Plague" benötigt wurden – die Gruppe hat ein britisches Militärexperiment aus den 1950er Jahren rekonstruiert – verhaftet und wegen Bioterrorismus angeklagt. Diese Anschuldigung hielt zwar nicht stand, aber Kurtz muss sich 2008 wegen Betrugs vor Gericht verantworten. Sein Verfahren ist zwar noch nicht abgeschlossen, aber derzeit zeichnet sich ein Freispruch ab. *EBS*
http://www.critical-art.net/

Germs of Deception (Bakterien der Täuschung), 2006

Critical Art Ensemble (CAE) is a collective formed by artists with a variety of interests whose works is located at the interface between art, technology, radical politics, and critical theory. Since the 1980s, it has made seminal contributions to the theory of electronic civil disobedience. In groundbreaking publications such as "The Electronic Disturbance", "Civil Electronic Disobedience and Other Unpopular Ideas", and "Digital Resistance", which have been published by Autonomedia and are also available for free download at CAE's web site, they have offered the most thorough analysis to date of the conditions of civil disobedience under the altered circumstances of a neo-liberal and highly technologically developed society. The collective uses a number of media including digital graphics, web design, film/video, photography, texts, books, and performance. They have carried out a great number of projects in a variety of locations including museums, the street, and the Internet. In recent years, the collective, led by one of its founding members, Steve Kurtz, has turned to questions of biopolitics and bioethics; in spectacular works such as "The Marching Plague," they have examined myths surrounding biotechnology with regard to biological warfare and warfare agents. CAE's fundamental claim is that the "preparedness" for biological warfare is a euphemism for the development of biological warfare technology and an increasing militarization of the public sphere. The true threat, they claim, is posed not by bacteria used as weapons but by the institutions that profit from the build-up of such arms.

Because of his experiments with harmless bacteria needed for "The Marching Plague"—the group reconstructed an experiment conducted by the British military in the 1950s—Steve Kurtz was arrested and charged with bioterrorism. The charge did not stand up in court, but in 2008, Kurtz will stand trial on fraud charges. While the criminal proceedings have not yet been concluded, he is cautiously optimistic that he will be acquitted. *EBS*

http://www.critical-art.net/

Coco Fusco

Lebt und arbeitet / lives and works in New York

„a/k/a Mrs. George Gilbert" (2004), Video

Coco Fusco setzt sich in Videos, Multimedia-Performances und zahlreichen Publikationen mit rassischer und sexueller Diskriminierung auseinander. In einer Reihe von Arbeiten hat sie sich mit der problematischen Situation an der Grenze zwischen Mexiko und den USA in Bezug auf illegale Einwanderung einerseits und die Ausbeutung billiger Arbeitskräfte andererseits beschäftigt. Zusammen mit Ricardo Dominguez, einem Mitbegründer des Electronic Disturbance Theater, hat sie ein Online-Spiel entwickelt, in dem man zwischen einer mexikanischen und einer US-amerikanischen Identität wählen und am „eigenen Leib" erfahren kann, wie unterschiedlich sich die Lebenssituationen den Menschen auf beiden Seiten der Grenze darstellen.

In dem teilweise fiktiven, teilweise auf historischem Dokumentationsmaterial basierenden Video „a/k/a Mrs. George Gilbert" (2004) setzt sich Fusco mit der Geschichte der afroamerikanischen Bürgerrechtlerin und Philosophin Angela Davis auseinander. Davis, damals Dozentin für Philosophie an der Universität von Kalifornien, wurde 1970 aufgrund ihrer Mitgliedschaft in der Black-Panther-Partei verhaftet. Darüber hinaus thematisiert die Arbeit die systematische Überwachung und Bespitzelung schwarzer Intellektueller und AktivistInnen in den 1960er und 1970er Jahren in den USA, die in der schwarzen Bürgerrechtsbewegung aktiv waren oder dessen verdächtigt wurden.

Coco Fusco ist die Autorin von "English is Broken Here" (The New Press, 1995) und "The Bodies That Were Not Ours and Other Writings" (Routledge/inIVA, 2001) und die Herausgeberin von "Corpus Delecti: Performance Art of the Americas" (Routledge, 1999) und "Only Skin Deep: Changing Visions of the American Self" (Abrams, 2003). *EBS*

http://www.thing.net/~cocofusco/

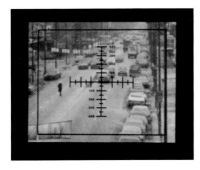

"a/k/a Mrs. George Gilbert" (2004), video

Coco Fusco's videos, multimedia performances, and numerous publications engage racial and sexual discrimination. In a number of works, she has examined the problematic situation at the Mexican-U.S. border with respect to illegal immigration on the one hand and the exploitation of cheap labor on the other hand. In collaboration with Ricardo Dominguez, a co-founder of the Electronic Disturbance Theater, she has developed an online game where players can choose between a Mexican and an American identity and gain a "visceral" experience of how different it feels to live on this and on that side of the border.

In her video "a/k/a Mrs. George Gilbert" (2004), which is part fiction and part based on historical documentary material, Fusco engages the life of the African-American civil rights activist and philosopher Angela Davis. Davis, then an assistant professor at the University of California, was arrested in 1970 because of her membership in the Black Panther Party. The work moreover addresses the systematic surveillance and wiretapping of African-American intellectuals and activists who were, or were suspected of, active in the African-American Civil Rights Movement in the U.S. during the 1960s and 1970s.

Coco Fusco is the author of "English is Broken Here" (The New Press, 1995) and "The Bodies That Were Not Ours and Other Writings" (Routledge/inIVA, 2001) and has edited "Corpus Delecti: Performance Art of the Americas" (Routledge, 1999) and "Only Skin Deep: Changing Visions of the American Self" (Abrams, 2003). *EBS*

http://www.thing.net/~cocofusco/

Andrea Geyer/Sharon Hayes

Andrea Geyer, * 1971 in Freiburg, lebt und arbeitet / lives and works in New York
Sharon Hayes, * 1970 in Baltimore, USA, lebt und arbeitet / lives and works in New York

Who are you with? Are you with a group? Why are you here? Who do you speak for? What do you stand for? Can you identify yourself? Where do you live? Have you lived there for more than 2 years? Where do you work? How much money do you make? Can I see your badge? Do you have documentation? Who do you represent? Are you authorized to make decisions? Who is the spokesperson for your group? How will I know who is who? You are authorized to speak on behalf of whom? Who do you report to? Do you have a partner? Why are you by yourself? Are you nervous? Why are you acting suspicious? What do you want? Do you have a permit? Why are you asking me these questions? Are you qualified? Where are your manners? Where are your values? Do you have a goal? And why are you here? Did you read the report? What do you believe in? What do you know? Why then did you stay? Do you know your rights? Are you prepared? Do you understand your responsibility? Are you taking responsibility? What are your duties? What are you trying to do? Are you taking a position? Can you take my position? Can you sit here? Are you a witness? Are you a victim? How are you organized? Are you a member of a party? What are you looking for? Who told you to say that? Don't you think I know my rights? What are your politics? Are you active? Who are you speaking to? Do you think your actions have consequences? Why don't you turn around? Are you speaking to me? What does it mean to express yourself? Whose interests are you speaking for when you talk? Were you told to represent those interests? Are you an investor? Are you clever? Are you proud? Do you prefer to be around like-minded people? Do you have friends? Do you agree with everyone? Do you talk or do you act? Do you follow others? Do you take the lead? Why are you upset? Are you complaining? Do you complain regularly? Who do you complain to? Are you considerate in your choices? Do you find it easy to be impartial? Would you call yourself a group? Do see yourself as one, two or more? Would you call yourself a crowd or an audience?

„In Times Like This Only Criminals Remain Silent" (2005), Posterprojekt

Andrea Geyer und Sharon Hayes thematisieren in ihrer gemeinsamen Arbeit die anscheinend zeitlose und ortsungebundene Protestform Demonstration. So wie die Konturen der Demonstrierenden auf der einen Seite dazu drängen, gefüllt zu werden, sind die Rückseiten der Poster mit dicht gedrängten Fragen beschrieben: Dabei werden ebenso grundsätzliche („Who do you speak for?") wie die Grenzen des Politischen überschreitende Fragen gestellt („Do I feel at home?").

    Die Erkundung der Räume des Politischen verbindet die Arbeiten beider Künstlerinnen ebenso wie ihre queer-feministische Perspektive.

    Sharon Hayes arbeitet an den Schnittstellen verschiedener Medien wie Video, Performance und Installation. Im Mittelpunkt ihrer künstlerischen Produktion stehen dabei individuelle und kollektive Kollektivierungsweisen, zu deren Untersuchung sie sich nicht nur originär künstlerischer, sondern auch akademischer Methoden bedient: Diese schließen anthropologische Forschung ebenso ein wie linguistische Theorieproduktion.

    Andrea Geyer kombinierte in den verschiedenen Teilen ihrer Arbeit „Spiral Lands" (2007/2008) Fotostrecken US-amerikanischer Landschaften mit fiktiven Reiseberichten und, im zweiten Teil, dem aufgeführten Vortrag eines Ethnologen. In Verknüpfung unterschiedlicher Techniken widmet sich Geyer der Wissensproduktion mittels künstlerischer Praktiken, den Wahrheitsdiskursen mittels bildnerischer Techniken, aber auch den Mechanismen der Sichtbarmachung und der ihnen zu Grunde liegenden sozialen Herrschaft.

    Beide Künstlerinnen haben an zahlreichen Ausstellungen in Nord- und Südamerika sowie West- und Osteuropa teilgenommen, u. a. in Kooperation mit David Thorne, Katya Sander und Ashley Hunt auch an der Documenta 12. *JK*

    http://www.andreageyer.info/
    http://www.shaze.info/

"In Times Like This Only Criminals Remain Silent" (2005), poster project

Andrea Geyer and Sharon Hayes's collaborative work examines the demonstration, a seemingly timeless and ubiquitous form of protest. Just as the demonstrator's silhouettes on front side of the posters urgently demand to be filled in, they are densely inscribed on the back with questions, raising fundamental issues ("Who do you speak for?") as well as questions that transcend the bounds of the political ("Do I feel it at home?")

The works of both artists share an exploration of the spaces of the political as well as a queer-feminist perspective.

Sharon Hayes works on the interfaces between different media, including video, performance, and installation. At the center of her artistic production stand individual and collective ways of collectivization; in her investigation of the latter, she employs not only originary artistic but also academic methods, including anthropological research as well as linguistic theoretical production.

The various parts of Andrea Geyer's work "Spiral Lands" (2007/2008) combined photo series on American landscapes with fictional travelogues and, in the second part, the quotation of an ethnological lecture. Fusing a variety of techniques, Geyer examines the production of knowledge by means of artistic practices, the discourses of truth by means of pictorial techniques, but also the mechanisms by which visibility is produced and the social domination that underlies them.

Both artists have participated in numerous exhibitions in North and South America as well as Western and Eastern Europe, including Documenta 12 (in collaboration with David Thorne, Katya Sander, and Ashley Hunt). *JK*

http://www.andreageyer.info/
http://www.shaze.info/

h.arta

Anca Gyemant, * 1977 in Oradea, Rumänien.
Rodica Tache, * 1977 in Piteflti, Rumänien.
Maria Crista, * 1976, Timifloara, Rumänien.

„NATO Meeting (d'après Ion Grigorescu)" (2008), Performance

Während des NATO-Gipfels, der vom 2. bis 4. April 2008 in Bukarest stattfand, liefen die drei Künstlerinnen durch die anlässlich des Treffens von Elend und Devianz gesäuberte Stadt. Ausgestattet waren sie mit Anti-NATO-Merchandise: Sprüche auf Tragetaschen und T-Shirts ließen keinerlei Zweifel an ihrer antimilitaristischen Haltung. Auf den Fotos, die sie bei dieser Tour durch die rumänische Hauptstadt gegenseitig von sich machten, sind wie zufällig Polizisten in zivil zu sehen. Die Alltäglichkeit der Überwachung wird in Rumänien eigentlich mit dem kommunistischen Regime assoziiert: Der Künstler Ion Grigorescu hatte 1975 auf einer von der Partei organisierten, „spontanen Versammlung" die sich wie zufällig am Rande aufhaltenden Geheimpolizisten fotografiert. Über diese kunsthistorische Bezugnahme thematisieren die Künstlerinnen zugleich gegenwärtige Kontroll- und Überwachungsmechanismen in westlich-kapitalistischen Demokratien.

Wie in dieser Performance haben h.arta in ihrer Arbeit bereits auf verschiedenen Ebenen künstlerische und aktivistische Interventionen miteinander verknüpft. Der öffentliche Raum war dabei ebenso Gegenstand ihrer Auseinandersetzung wie die Institutionen der Kunstausbildung.
JK

http://hartagroup.blogspot.com/
Literatur: H. ARTA (2008): AGENDA 2008. Köln 2007
(Verlag der Buchhandlung Walther König).

Rumänische Künstlerinnengruppe, gegründet 2001, in Timifloara und Bukarest.
Romanian women artist's group, founded in 2001, in Timifloara and Bucharest.

"NATO Meeting (d'après Ion Grigorescu)" (2008), performance

During the NATO summit held in Bucharest on April 2-4, 2008, the three artists walked through the city, which had for the occasion of this meeting been cleansed of misery and deviancy. They were equipped with anti-NATO merchandise: slogans on bags and T-shirts left no room for doubt about their antimilitarist attitude. The photographs they took of each other during this tour of the Romanian capital show plainclothes policemen standing nearby as though by chance. That surveillance should be an everyday phenomenon is something Romanians would associate with the communist regime: in 1975, the artist Ion Grigorescu had photographed the secret policemen standing, as though randomly, on the margins of a "spontaneous" assembly organized by the Party. Through this art-historical reference, the artists simultaneously address contemporary mechanisms of control and surveillance in Western capitalist democracies.

As in this performance, h.arta's work has fused artistic and activist strategies of intervention on a variety of levels. They have engaged the issue of public space as well as the institutions of arts education. *JK*

http://hartagroup.blogspot.com/
Literature: H. ARTA (2008): AGENDA 2008. Cologne 2007
(Verlag der Buchhandlung Walther König).

Christopher LaMarca

*1975, New York, USA – lebt und arbeitet / lives and works in Brooklyn/New York, USA

„Forest Defenders" (2003), Fotoserie

Vom Sommer 2003 an dokumentierte der US-amerikanische Fotojournalist Christopher LaMarca den Kampf von UmweltaktivistInnen für die Erhaltung der Wälder im Siskiyou National Forest. Die im Süden des US-Bundesstaates Oregon gelegenen Waldgebiete gehören zu den ältesten der USA. Im März 2005 wurden Teile des Biotops zur Abholzung freigegeben. Mit der Entscheidung der Regierung Bush, auch in bisher unzugänglichen, straßenlosen Wäldern Rodungen vorzunehmen, wird die Schaffung eines Präzedenzfalls befürchtet, dessen Folge der sichere Untergang jedes geschützten Waldgebiets in den USA wäre. Mit einer Vielzahl gewaltfreier Aktionen setzten sich die Gruppen von AktivistInnen dieser Abholzung entgegen.

LaMarcas Fotos sind mit dem Pathos des Kampfes spielende, Emotionen evozierende Darstellungen und parteiische Dokumentationen. Sie entwickeln eine eigene Ästhetik des Widerstands, mit der eine Form klassischen Zivilen Ungehorsam gleichermaßen bezeugt wie unterstützt wird.

Für seine Arbeit über die ÖkoaktivistInnen wurde er 2006 mit dem NPPA Best of Photojournalism (2. Platz für Environmental Picture Story) und PDN 30 Emerging Photographers ausgezeichnet. *JK*

http://www.christopherlamarca.com/
Literatur: Christopher LaMarca (2008): Forest Defenders. The Confrontational American Landscape, New York (PowerHouseBooks).

"Forest Defenders," (2003), photo series

Since the summer of 2003, the American photojournalist Christopher LaMarca has documented the struggle of environmental activists to preserve the woodlands of Siskiyou National Forest. The forest, located in southern Oregon, is among the oldest in the United States. In March 2005, parts of this biotope were opened up for logging. Activists fear that the decision of the Bush government to let logging proceed also in woodlands that had been inaccessible to vehicles creates a precedent whose consequence will be the assured demise of every last protected woodland in the US. Groups of activists oppose logging here with a great variety of non-violent actions.

LaMarca's photographs, which play with the pathos of battle, are emotional representations and create a partisan documentation. They develop a unique aesthetic of resistance that both attests to and supports a form of classical civil disobedience.

His work on the conservation activists was awarded the 2006 NPPA Best of Photojournalism prize (2nd place for Environmental Picture Story) and the PDN 30 Emerging Photographers. *JK*

http://www.christopherlamarca.com/
Literature: Christopher LaMarca (2008): Forest Defenders. The Confrontational American Landscape, New York (PowerHouseBooks).

fran meana

Lebt und arbeitet / lives and works in Barcelona

„Landschaft für Überwachungskameras" (2007), Performance und Installation

Die Auseinandersetzung, die der junge Künstler fran meana mit der Überwachung im städtischen Raum betreibt, ist eine poetische: fran meana hält verschiedene, auf Stöcken angebrachte Miniaturlandschaften vor Überwachungskameras, erst in dieser Performance tritt die bewegend-unbewegte Landschaft an die Stelle der hektischen Großstadt. In dieser Idylle passiert nichts, es gibt, so meana, also auch nichts zu überwachen. Stattdessen wird die Überwachungskamera, die die Landschaft aufzeichnet, zu einem Werkzeug der Landschaftsmalerei. Damit beansprucht fran meanas Arbeit nicht weniger als die temporäre Auflösung der binären Beziehung zwischen den AgentInnen der Ordnung und denjenigen, die sie mittels kritischer Strategien angreifen. Das Stillstellen der Überwachung ist zugleich ein momentanes Durchlöchern des Kontrollsystems. *JK*

"Landschaft für Überwachungskameras" ["Landscape for Surveillance Cameras"] (2007), performance and installation

The young artist fran meana's engagement with the surveillance of urban space is a poetic one: he holds a variety of miniature landscapes, mounted on sticks, in front of surveillance cameras; only by virtue of this performance does the movingly motionless scenery supplant the bustling metropolis. Nothing happens in this idyll; and so there is, thus meana, also nothing to monitor. Instead, the surveillance camera, recording the scenery, becomes an instrument of landscape painting. fran meana's work thus claims nothing less than to have temporarily dissolved the binary relationship between the agents of order and those who attack them using strategies of critique. To bring surveillance to a standstill is at the same time also to punch a momentary hole into the system of control. JK

Mujeres Creando

gegründet / founded in 1992, aktiv / active in La Paz, Bolivien / Bolivia 1992

Diverse Performances (1996-2005), Video

Gegen die fortdauernden Effekte der Militärdiktatur von Hugo Banzer – Diktator Boliviens 1971-1978 und erneut Präsident des Landes 1997-2002 – gingen die Mujeres Creando verschiedentlich auf die Straße: In einer Performance fließt ziemlich viel Blut über einen Platz, symbolisch das Blut der Verschwundenen und Gefolterten, bis die Akteurin in einer mit dramatischer Musik unterlegten Szene von der Polizei abgeführt wird. Die höhnischen Kommentare des Publikums nehmen die Mujeres Creando immer schon selbst vorweg, zu ihrem Standardensemble gehört die inszenierte Bürgerin, die sich mokiert.

    Das feministische Kollektiv betreibt ein kulturelles Zentrum namens „Virgen de los Deseos" („Jungfrau der Wünsche") in La Paz und hat verschiedene Performances und Filme gemacht, die alle im bolivianischen Fernsehen liefen. (Im deutschsprachigen Raum waren sie bisher nur in der feministischen Sendung an.schläge TV auf dem Wiener Community-Sender Okto zu sehen.) „Wir machen Politik und keine Kunst", schreiben die Mujeres Creando in einem ihrer vielen Texte, „und unser Raum für die Konstruktion von Gedanken und Kommunikation ist die Straße." Im öffentlichen Raum platzieren sie immer wieder Graffitis mit feministischen Sprüchen in bunten Lettern. Einer dieser an die Mauern von La Paz gemalten Slogans lautet: „Ungehorsam, deinetwegen bin ich glücklich". *JK*

    www.mujerescreando.com
    Literatur: Galindo, Maria (2005): Öffentlichkeiten der Mujeres Creando. Wir besetzen das Fernsehen genauso wie die Straße, in: Gerald Raunig und Ulf Wuggenig (Hg.): Publicum. Theorien der Öffentlichkeit, Wien (Verlag Turia + Kant), S. 204-211.

Various performances (1996-2005), video

Mujeres Creando took to the streets in a variety of ways against the lasting effects of the military dictatorship of Hugo Banzer, the Bolivian dictator from 1971 to 1978 and again its president between 1997 and 2002: during one performance, quite a lot of blood is flowing across a square, in symbolic terms the blood of the victims of forced disappearances and torture, until the activist, in a dramatic scene accompanied by background music, is led away by police. Mujeres Creando always anticipate and preempt the scornful remarks from their audiences; the mocking bourgeois woman is part of their standard ensemble.

    The feminist collective operates a cultural center called "Virgen de los Deseos" ["Virgin of desires"] in La Paz and has produced a number of performances and films, all of which were broadcast on Bolivian television. (In the German-speaking countries, they have so far been presented only on the feminist show an.schläge TV on the Viennese community station Okto.) "We are making politics, not art," Mujeres Creando write in one of their numerous texts, "and the space where we construct ideas and communications is the street." Time and again, they place graffiti containing feminist catchphrases in public space. One of these slogans painted on the walls of La Paz reads: "Disobedience, it is because of you that I am happy." *JK*

    www.mujerescreando.com
    Literature: Maria Galindo (2005): Öffentlichkeiten der Mujeres Creando. Wir besetzen das Fernsehen genauso wie die Straße, in: Gerald Raunig and Ulf Wuggenig (eds.): Publicum. Theorien der Öffentlichkeit, Wien (Verlag Turia + Kant), pp. 204-211.

Oliver Ressler / Dario Azzellini

* 1970, Knittelfeld, Österreich, lebt und arbeitet / lives and works in Wien / Vienna
* 1967, lebt und arbeitet in Berlin und Lateinamerika / lives and works in Berlin and Latin America

„Disobbedienti" (2002), Video

Die Bewegung der Disobbedienti (die Ungehorsamen) ging im Zuge der globalisierungskritischen Proteste gegen den G8-Gipfel in Genua 2001 aus den Tute Bianche hervor. Seit 1994 hatten die Tute Bianche ihre Körper, mit weißen Overalls bekleidet und mit Schaumstoff, Gummireifen, Helmen und gebastelten Schilden geschützt, als Waffe des zivilen Ungehorsams in die sozialen Kämpfe geworfen: Tute Bianche wie Disobbedienti engagierten sich in den Kämpfen gegen prekäre Arbeitsbedingungen, gegen Abschiebegefängnisse oder für den zapatistischen Aufstand in Chiapas/Mexiko. Als Disobbedienti gab die Bewegung ihre identifizierbare Form auf und ging in die Mulittude über. Oliver Ressler und Dario Azzellini porträtieren diese Bewegung, die Geschichte ihrer Entstehung, ihre politisch-theoretischen Grundlagen und ihre Aktionsformen anhand von Gesprächen mit sieben Beteiligten.

Das in Kooperation mit dem Politikwissenschaftler Dario Azzellini entstandene Video steht im Kontext einer ganzen Reihe von gesellschaftspolitischen Arbeiten Resslers. Neben der Auseinandersetzung mit Alternativen zum kapitalistischen Lebens- und Wirtschaftsmodell, die in seiner ständig erweiterten Videoinstallation „Alternative Economics, Alternative Societies" zum Ausdruck kommt, widmet sich Ressler verschiedenen sozialen Kämpfen: Antirassistische Initiativen sind dabei ebenso Thema wie die sozialen und politischen Milieus, die den „Bolivarianischen Prozess" in Venezuela tragen („Venezuela von unten", mit Dario Azzellini, 2004).

Seine schnörkellose Bildsprache richtet sich gegen die Undurchschaubarkeit der herrschenden Ordnung. Sie stellt hin und wieder aber auch die Selbstgewissheit(en) der AktivistInnen in Frage: Eine aktuelle Video-Arbeit, die gemeinsam mit Zanny Begg 2007 in Heiligendamm entstanden ist, heißt schlicht: „What would it mean to win?" *JK*

http://www.ressler.at/
http://www.azzellini.net

"Disobbedienti" (2002), video

The movement of the Disobbedienti (the disobedient ones) emerged from the Tute Bianche with the anti-globalization protests held in Genoa in 2001 during the G8 summit. Since 1994, the Tute Bianche had thrown their bodies, dressed in white overalls and protected with foam padding, rubber tires, helmets, and self-fashioned shields, into social struggles as weapons of civil disobedience: both the Tute Bianche and the Disobbedienti engaged in the battles against precarious working conditions, against deportation prisons, or for the Zapatista uprising in Chiapas (Mexico). Under the title of Disobbedienti, the movement gave up its identifiable form and transformed itself into the Multitude. Oliver Ressler and Dario Azzellini present a portrait of this movement, the history of its emergence, its political and theoretical foundations, and its forms of action through conversations with seven participants.

The video, made in collaboration with the political scientist Dario Azzellini, is part of an entire series of socio-political works by Ressler. Beyond his engagement with alternatives to the model of life and economic activity presented by capitalism, expressed in his continually expanded video installation "Alternative Economics, Alternative Societies," Ressler addresses various social struggles, portraying subjects as diverse as anti-racist initiatives and the social and political milieus that support the "Bolivarian process" in Venezuela ("Venezuela von unten" ["Venezuela from below"], with Dario Azzellini, 2004).

His unembellished pictorial language is directed against the obscurity of the prevalent order; occasionally, it also calls the self-confidence of activists and their certainties in question: one video work made in collaboration with Zanny Begg at Heiligendamm in 2007 is entitled simply "What would it mean to win?" *JK*

http://www.ressler.at/
http://www.azzellini.net

Allan Sekula
*1951 Erie, Pennsylvania/USA, lebt / lives in Los Angeles

„Waiting for Tear Gas" (1999/2000), Dia-Serie

Für seine Dia-Serie zu den globalisierungskritischen Protesten in Seattle 1999 begab sich Allan Sekula direkt ins Geschehen: „Die Arbeitsidee war, mich, wenn es sein musste, vom Morgengrauen bis drei Uhr nachts mit dem Strom des Protests zu bewegen – und die Flauten, das Warten und das Geschehen am Rand der Ereignisse aufzunehmen. Die Faustregel für diese Form des Anti-Fotojournalismus: kein Blitz, kein Zoomteleobjektiv, keine Gasmaske, kein Autofokus, kein Presseausweis und kein Druck, auf Teufel-komm-raus das eine definitive Bild dramatischer Gewalt einzufangen." Die teilnehmende Beobachtung ist aber nur eines von unzähligen Mitteln, die der Fotograf und Fototheoretiker seit den frühen 1970er Jahren in seiner Arbeit anwendet. In verschiedenen Serien und Foto-Text-Installationen hat sich Sekula sozialen und politischen Themen – vom kulturellen Ausschluss durch Bildungsinstitutionen bis zur Neoliberalisierung des Welthandels am Beispiel der internationalen Schifffahrt – gewidmet. Als Theoretiker hatte er bereits Ende der 1970er Jahre gegen dokumentarischen Funktionalismus und die Ästhetisierung des Sozialen für eine „Neuerfindung des Dokumentarischen" plädiert. Verschiedene Formen der praktischen Umsetzung dieser Erfindungsarbeit waren u. a. bei der Documenta 11 (2002), der Documenta 12 (2007) und wichtigen internationalen Einzelausstellungen zu sehen. *JK*

Literatur: Breitwieser, Sabine (Hg.) (2003): Allan Sekula. Performance under Working Conditions, Wien (Generali Foundation) und Köln (Verlag der Buchhandlung Walther König).

"Waiting for Tear Gas," (1999/2000), slide series

For his slide series on the anti-globalization protests held in Seattle in 1999, Allan Sekula joined the fray: "I worked with the idea that I would move with the flow of protest, if need be from dawn to three am—and record the lulls, the waiting, and what was going on on the fringe of events. The rule of thumb for this form of anti-photojournalism: no flash, no zoom telephoto lens, no gas mask, no autofocus, no press ID and no pressure to capture, devil-may-care, the one definitive picture of dramatic violence." Yet participating observation is only one of a great number of instruments Sekula, a photographer and photo theorist, has used in his work since the early 1970s. In various series and installations combining photographs and text, he has engaged social and political issues—from the cultural exclusionary effects of educational institutions to the neoliberal makeover of global trade on the example of international shipping. As a theorist, he argued as early as the late 1970s against documentary functionalism and the aestheticization of the social, and for a "reinvention of the documentary." Practical realizations of this work of invention in various forms were on view at Documenta 11 (2002), Documenta 12 (2007), and important international solo shows. *JK*

> Literature: Sabine Breitwieser (ed.) (2003): Allan Sekula. Performance under Working Conditions, Vienna (Generali Foundation) and Cologne (Verlag der Buchhandlung Walther König).

Surveillance Camera Players NYC

Surveillance Camera Players, diverse Performances, Videos

Die Kritik der modernen Kontrollgesellschaft in Form ihres Überwachungsapparates steht im Zentrum der Performances, Kartographien und Schriften der Surveillance Camera Players. Das 1996 in New York gegründete Kollektiv sieht in der öffentlichen Videoüberwachung einen Verstoß gegen die Verfassung der USA und gegen das Recht auf Privatsphäre. Die systematische Installation von hochtechnologisierten Überwachungskamerasystemen in New York, die Mitte der 1990er Jahre unter dem damaligen Bürgermeister Rudolph Giuliani vorangetrieben wurde, veranlasste die Surveillance Camera Players lange vor dem 11. September 2001 zu spektakulären Aktionen und Performances. In den ersten Jahren (1996-1999) adaptierte die politisch motivierte Gruppe an der Schnittstelle von Kunst, Theater, Performance und politischem Aktivismus bekannte Theaterstücke, Romanvorlagen sowie Performances und schrieb eigene Drehbücher. Mittels Texttafeln und Requisiten inszenierten sie diese Stücke vor Überwachungskameras in U-Bahn-Stationen und auf öffentlichen Plätzen und Straßen für das Personal in den Überwachungszentralen sowie PassantInnen. Sie zielen damit auf die Dekonstruktion des Mythos ab, Überwachung würde nur der Sicherheit und dem Schutz der Bevölkerung dienen. Wichtige Referenzen stellen u. a. die Situationistische Internationale, Antonin Artauds Theater der Grausamkeit und Michel Foucault dar. In Zusammenarbeit mit den New Yorker Surveillance Camera Players wurden weltweit zahlreiche weitere Surveillance Camera Players-Gruppen gegründet. *EBS*

http://www.notbored.org/the-scp.html

Surveillance Camera Players, various performances, videos

A critique of the modern society of control and, more specifically, its surveillance apparatus stands at the center of the performances, cartographies, and writings produced by the Surveillance Camera Players. This collective, founded in New York in 1996, considers public video surveillance a violation of the U.S. Constitution and an infringement of privacy rights. Long before September 11, 2001, the drive toward the systematic installation of technologically sophisticated surveillance camera systems in mid-1990s New York under then mayor Rudolph Giuliani prompted the Surveillance Camera Players to stage spectacular actions and performances. During its initial years (1996-1999), the politically motivated group, located at the interface between art, theater, performance, and political activism, adapted well-known plays, novels, and performances, as well as writing their own scripts. Using title cards and props, they staged these pieces in front of surveillance cameras in subway stations and in public spaces and streets for surveillance command center staff and passersby. They thus aim to deconstruct the myth that surveillance serves exclusively to safeguard and protect the population. Important points of reference include the Situationist International, Antonin Artaud's Theater of Cruelty, and Michel Foucault. In cooperation with New York's Surveillance Camera Players, numerous such groups have been founded all over the world. *EBS*

http://www.notbored.org/the-scp.html

Nasan Tur

* 1974 in Offenbach, lebt und arbeitet / lives and works in Berlin

„Backpacks", 2006, Installation

Eine Gruppe von Rucksäcken ist in einem Raum platziert. Aber es sind keine herkömmlichen Reiseutensilien, die hier zum Transport bereit liegen. Nasan Tur hat verschiedene Varianten von Ausrüstungen zusammengestellt, die AktivistInnen und andere Teilnehmer von Demonstrationen für ihr Tun verwenden können.

Die BetrachterInnen sind aufgefordert, sich die je nach Anlass adäquaten Rucksäcke auszuborgen. Damit greift Nasan Tur nicht nur das Klischee vom „Krawalltourismus" auf. Er verbindet zudem seine Installation to go mit einem aktivierenden Moment. Die Performance, die erwartet wird, muss selbst gemacht werden.

Nasan Tur arbeitet mit verschiedenen technischen Mitteln. Formale wie politische Anliegen entbehren dabei selten einer ironischen Note: ob sich ein Protagonist Purzelbäume schlagend durch eine belebte Innenstadtstraße bewegt oder der Künstler einen Balkon samt Mikro und Boxen zur Verfügung stellt, damit jede/r, der/die will, endlich mal „allen" sagen kann, was er oder sie immer schon mal sagen wollte. *JK*

http://www.nasantur.com

"Backpacks," 2006, installation

A group of backpacks has been placed in a room. But these are no ordinary traveler's utensils that sit here awaiting transportation. Nasan Tur has assembled diverse variants of an equipment set to be used during demonstrations by activists and other participants.

The viewer is invited to borrow a backpack adequate to a particular occasion. Nasan Tur thus not only takes up the stereotypical notion of the "riot tourist." He also lends a momentum of activation to his installation to go. The viewer must create the performance that is expected here.

Nasan Tur uses a variety of technical means. Both in formal and in political terms, these endeavors are rarely without a tinge of irony: now a protagonist turns somersaults through a crowded street in a city center, now Tur offers a balcony equipped with a mike and speakers so that anyone who wants can finally tell "the whole world" what he or she has always wanted to say. *JK*

http://www.nasantur.com

Videogruppe Bürgerinitiative Umweltschutz Lüchow-Dannenberg

„G – Das Gorlebengefühl" (2005), Video

Die Bürgerinitiative Umweltschutz Lüchow-Dannenberg ist eine der ältesten und bekanntesten Initiativen gegen die Atomkraft im deutschsprachigen Raum. Im Wendland, dem ehemaligen deutsch-deutschen Grenzland nordöstlich von Hannover, mobilisiert sie unter großer Beteiligung der örtlichen Bevölkerung seit drei Jahrzehnten gegen das geplante Atommüll-Endlager in Gorleben. Die Castor-Transporte in das dort bestehende Zwischenlager sind in den vergangenen Jahren immer wieder zu Brennpunkten sozialer Bewegungen gegen die Atompolitik geworden und haben Gorleben zu einem Ort massenhaften zivilen Ungehorsams gemacht.

Der Film der Videogruppe basiert auf einer Aktion von knapp 50 lokalen KünstlerInnen, die 2004 je eine rote Kiste zum Thema „Gorlebengefühl" gestaltet haben. Sechs dieser Kisten stehen am Anfang mehrerer Filmcollagen, die die Videogruppe aus Amateurmaterial zusammengestellt hat, das während verschiedener Anti-AKW-Proteste aufgenommen wurde. Dabei entstanden ist ein vielschichtiges Porträt eines Landstriches im Widerstand. JK

http://www.bi-luechow-dannenberg.de/

Citizen's Initiative for Environmental Protection Lüchow-Dannenberg, Video Section

"G – Das Gorlebengefühl" ["G — The Gorleben Feeling"] (2005), video

The Citizen's Initiative for Environmental Protection Lüchow-Dannenberg is one of the oldest and most well-known initiatives against nuclear power in the German-speaking countries. In the Wendland, an area located northeast of Hannover near the former inner-German border, it has been attracting much participation from local residents to its agitation against the Gorleben nuclear waste permanent storage facility, which has been in the planning stages for three decades. The Castor nuclear waste transports to the temporary storage facility at the same location have for years been a focal point of social movements' repeated actions against the government's nuclear policy and made Gorleben a site of mass civil disobedience.

    The film made by the video section is based on an action by close to 50 local artists, each of whom designed a red box on the theme of "The Gorleben Feeling" in 2004. Six of these boxes form the beginning of a number of film collages the video group composed from amateur stock shot during various anti-nuclear power protests. The result is a many-layered portrait of an area offering resistance. *JK*

    http://www.bi-luechow-dannenberg.de/

Christoph Wachter/Mathias Jud

Leben und arbeiten / live and work in Berlin

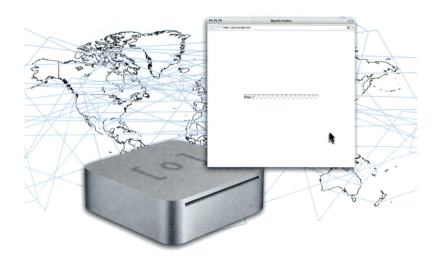

„Picidae" (2007)

Das Schweizer Künstlerduo Christoph Wachter und Mathias Jud setzt sich in seinen Arbeiten der letzten Jahre mit der Wahrnehmung im elektronischen Raum auseinander. Sie machen das Internet zu ihrem Untersuchungsgegenstand und gleichzeitig zum Mittel ihrer Untersuchung. Im Zentrum ihrer Kritik stehen der Mythos vom World Wide Web als Freiraum und die Vorstellung vom Internet als einer globalen Kommunikationsform, die allen Menschen den gleichen Blick auf die Welt ermöglicht. Dem setzen Wachter/Jud entgegen, dass unser Umgang mit dem Internet einerseits von Projektionen und Vorstellungen davon, was man sehen kann, und andererseits von regionalen, kulturellen, religiösen und politischen Rahmenbedingungen sowie von wirtschaftlichen und militärischen Interessen geprägt ist.

Mit Arbeiten wie „Zone*Interdite" und „Picidae" versuchen sie auf diese verborgenen (Macht-)Strukturen, die mittels Internetprovider, Browser, Firewalls und Filterprogrammen das Internet kontrollieren, aufmerksam zu machen.

Das recherchebasierte Projekt „Zone*Interdite" zum Beispiel machte sichtbar, was nicht sichtbar sein sollte: militärische Sperrgebiete (www.zone-interdite.org). International Aufsehen erregten Wachter/Jud, als sie beim Sichten und Vergleichen von Bildmaterial den Beweis für die vermutete, aber unbestätigte Existenz des geheim gehaltenen Gefängnisses Bagram in der Nähe von Kabul erbringen konnten. Ihr jüngstes Projekt „Picidae" (lateinisch für Specht) basiert auf einem Server und einer Software, die Textdateien in Bilddateien umwandelt und auf diese Weise die Internetzensur zu umgehen vermag. In China, einem der weltweit meistzensurierten Länder, haben sie die Funktion des Picidae-Servers erfolgreich getestet. Sie konnten ohne weiteres nach brisanten Wörtern wie „Tiananmen" suchen, was in China ansonsten undenkbar ist. *EBS*

http://www.pricidae

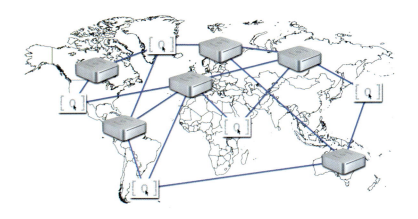

"Picidae" (2007)

In recent years, the works of the Swiss artists' duo Christoph Wachter and Mathias Jud have engaged the question of perception in electronic space. The Internet becomes here both the object of examination and its instrument. Their critique focuses on the myth of the World Wide Web as an uncontrolled space and the notion that the Internet is a global form of communication that enables all human beings to adopt the same perspective on the world. Wachter and Jud counter these illusions with an emphasis on how our use of the Internet is shaped by projections and ideas about what one can see on the one hand, and by regional, cultural, religious, and political conditions and by economic and military interests on the other hand.

In works such as "Zone*Interdite" and "Picidae," they aim to draw attention to these concealed structures (of power) which control the Internet through service providers, browsers, firewalls, and filtering software.

The research-based project "Zone*Interdite," for instance, rendered visible what was not meant to be visible: military prohibited areas (www.zone-inderdite.org). Wachter and Jud caused an international stir when, reviewing and comparing image material, they were able to produce evidence for the existence of a prison at Bagram near Kabul, which had been suspected but not confirmed. Their most recent project, "Picidae" (the Latin word for a woodpecker), is based on a server and a software that converts text into image files, which allows information to circumvent Internet censorship. They have successfully tested the function of their Picidae server in China, one of the world's most heavily censored countries. They were able to run searches for explosive terms such as "Tiananmen," something that is otherwise inconceivable in China.
EBS

http://www.pricidae

AutorInnen / Authors

Inke Arns ist Kuratorin, Autorin und Künstlerische Leiterin des Hartware MedienKunstVereins in Dortmund. / Inke Arns is a curator, author and artistic director of Hartware MedienKunstVerein in Dortmund.

John Holloway ist Politikwissenschaftler und lehrt an der Universität Puebla/Mexiko. / John Holloway is apolitical scientist and professor at the University of Puebla/Mexico.

Jens Kastner ist Soziologe, Kunsthistoriker und Wissenschaftlicher Mitarbeiter am Institut für Kunst- und Kulturtheorie der Akademie der bildenden Künste Wien. / Jens Kastner is a sociologist, art historian and research associate at the Institute for Art and Cultural Theory at the Academy of Fine Arts Vienna.

Ulrike Laubenthal ist gewaltfreie Aktivistin und arbeitet in der Sichelschmiede, Werkstatt für Friedensarbeit in der Kyritz-Ruppiner Heide. / Ulrike Laubenthal is a non-violent activist and works at Sichelschmiede, workshop for peace work in the Kyritz-Ruppiner Heide/Germany.

Lou Marin ist Autor, Übersetzer, Aktivist und Mitherausgeber der gewaltfrei-anarchistischen Monatszeitschrift graswurzelrevolution. Er lebt in Marseille. / Lou Marin is a translator, author, activist and co-editor of the non-violent and anarchist monthly magazine graswurzelrevolution. He lives in Marseille.

Andrea Pabst ist Doktorandin an der Fakultät für Sozial- und Verhaltenswissenschaften der Universität Tübingen und lebt in Berlin. / Andrea Pabst is a doctoral candidate at the faculty of social and behavioural sciences at the University of Tübingen and lives in Berlin.

Gerald Raunig ist Philosoph und Kunsttheoretiker und arbeitet am European Institute for Progressive Cultural Policies (eipcp) in Wien. / Gerald Raunig is a philosopher and cultural theorist and works at the European Institute for Progressive Cultural Policies (eipcp) in Vienna.

Elisabeth Bettina Spörr ist Kunsthistorikerin und Kuratorin und arbeitet in der Secession, Wien. / Elisabeth Bettina Spörr is an art historian, curator and works at the Secession, Vienna.

Maureen M. Eggers, Grada Kilomba, Peggy Piesche, Susan Arndt (Hg.):
Mythen, Masken und Subjekte
Kritische Weißseinsforschung in Deutschland

ISBN 3-89771-440-X | 544 S. | 24 EUR [D]

Für den hiesigen Kontext einzigartig geht dieser Band auf die kritische Auseinandersetzung mit der Kategorie Weißsein aus einer Schwarzen Perspektive als konzeptionellem Schwerpunkt ein und würdigt damit den enormen und durchaus nachhaltigen Einfluss Schwarzer Menschen und People of Color in Wissenschaft und Kunst, die bereits seit geraumer Zeit mit einem hegemonialkritischen Fokus im Diskurs um Ethnisierung und Rassifizierung arbeiten.

Kien Nghi Ha, Nicola Lauré al-Samarai, Sheila Mysorekar (Hg.)
re/visionen
Postkoloniale Perspektiven von People of Color auf Rassismus, Kulturpolitik und Widerstand in Deutschland

ISBN 978-3-89771-458-8 | 456 S. | 24 EUR [D]

Im vorliegenden Band werden erstmals kritische Stimmen ausnahmslos von People of Color zusammen gebracht – Schwarze Deutsche, Roma und Menschen mit außereuropäischen Flucht- und Migrationshintergründen. Ihre widerständige Wissensproduktion und ihr politischer Erfahrungsaustausch bringen alternative Diskussionen hervor. Sie setzen sich mit Rassismus, Islamophobie und ausgrenzenden Migrations- und Integrationsregimes auseinander und diskutieren Fragen von individuellem und kollektivem Widerstand, antirassistischer Kulturpolitik und postkolonialen Denkansätzen.

jour fixe initiative berlin (Hg.)
Kunstwerk und Kritik

268 Seiten | 16 EUR [D] | ISBN 3-89771-421-3

Es macht den grundsätzlich widersprüchlichen Charakter von Kunst aus, zwar aus der gesellschaftlichen Totalität entstanden zu sein, jedoch in der ästhetischen Erfahrung einen Raum zu eröffnen, der über diese hinausweist. An diese Tatsache knüpft sich bis heute die Hoffnung, dass ästhetische Erfahrung, indem sie die Alltagserfahrung der Individuen revolutioniert, auch zu einer Position führt, von der aus eine Kritik der Gesellschaft formulierbar wird.

www.unrast-verlag.de